D1075138

ECONOMIC ANALYSIS BEFORE ADAM SMITH

By the same author
NON-RICARDIAN POLITICAL ECONOMY

ECONOMIC ANALYSIS BEFORE ADAM SMITH

Hesiod to Lessius

Barry Gordon

University of Newcastle, New South Wales

BARNES & NOBLE
BOOKS

10 East 53d St. New York 10022
(a division of Harper & Row Publishers, Inc.)

© Barry Gordon 1975

All rights reserved. No part of this publication may be
reproduced or transmitted, in any form or by any means,
without permission.

First published 1975 by
THE MACMILLAN PRESS LTD

Published in the U.S.A. 1975 by
HARPER & ROW PUBLISHERS, INC.
BARNES & NOBLE IMPORT DIVISION

ISBN 0-06-492497-1

Printed in Great Britain

HB
75
.G67
1975b

To my mother, Lillian May Gordon

1/31/77 Kub.

LIBRARY
ALMA COLLEGE
ALMA, MICHIGAN

Contents

Contents

Preface

The roots of modern economic analysis extend much further back in time than a good many contemporary students of economics are led to realise. Even some of the most widely-read, general treatments of the history of economic thought create an impression that meaningful starting points can be set in the era of European mercantilism, or with the advent of the Physiocratic school, or even later in the eighteenth century. One purpose of this book is to correct such false notions. More positively, the book aims at putting the modern student in a better position to appreciate the *how* and *why* of the scope and content of current economics. Ideas, personalities and events of antiquity, the middle ages and the Renaissance continue to reach out and condition that scope and content. Awareness of such conditioning is an important ingredient in the process by which a developing economist may graduate from subservience to, towards command of, his discipline as it is understood by his contemporaries.

'By History of Economic Analysis,' wrote Joseph Schumpeter, 'I mean the history of the intellectual efforts that men have made in order to understand economic phenomena or, which comes to the same thing, the history of the analytical or scientific aspects of economic thought.'[1] The relevant efforts involve attempts at penetrating the meaning of economic phenomena taken together as one aspect of human existence in society, and attempts at explaining particular features of that group of phenomena. Hence, the present study focuses on shifting appreciations of the nature and significance of economic life, as well as on examinations of such issues as determination of commodity prices, the functions of money, or the bases of interest payment.

[1] Joseph A. Schumpeter, *History of Economic Analysis* (N.Y., Oxford University Press, 1959) p. 3.

Consideration of the general question of the status of economic activity as an aspect of existence seems particularly relevant at present, given the myopia and narrowness of much economic enquiry in recent decades. These defects have worried a number of the members of the profession in latter years, among them Paul Samuelson, who states:

> . . . it is possible to argue that American economists — and Western economists generally — far from being too divided among a number of competing schools, today present a united front that reflects too little basic disagreement on fundamentals. Today, surveying leading graduate schools in America, one finds them competing for the same men, teaching the same basic economic doctrines and methods. Although there are one, two, or three exceptions to this, even they are moving toward the common pattern — and one might have expected, in a great Nation, countless exceptions to any one pattern.'[2]

Since this book deals with conflicting assessments of economic life, and hence, divergent conceptions of the appropriate direction and scope of economics as a form of social enquiry, it may be of especial interest to those who, like Professor Samuelson, are disturbed by the fact of conformity.

Throughout the text, leading ideas of some major figures in the history of economic thought are cited to provide perspective on the reasoning of earlier thinkers. Chief among those figures is Adam Smith. Among the reasons for employing Smith as the most prominent benchmark are: his widespread subsequent influence; the likelihood of the reader having some acquaintance with his thought; and, the key role he played in the emergence of economics in the modern sense. There is more than a grain of truth in Sir Alexander Gray's statement that, 'Before Adam Smith there had been much economic discussion; with him we reach the stage of discussing economics.'[3]

[2] P. A. Samuelson, *Collected Scientific Papers*, ed. Joseph E. Stiglitz, Vol. 2 (Cambridge, Mass., M.I.T. Press, 1965) p. 1652.
[3] Alexander Gray, *The Development of Economic Doctrine* (1931; London, Longmans, 1959), p. 123.

The book does not attempt to encompass the entire range of analytical endeavour in economics before Adam Smith. Notable omissions are the contributions of the Reformers, the natural law theorists, mercantilists of many persuasions, and the Physiocrats. Given the current state of historical writing in the English language concerning economics, a student is able to gain an introduction to the thought of writers from these groups much more readily than he can begin to appreciate the economic reasoning of the authors dealt with in this volume. It seemed most useful, at this stage, to concentrate on areas of relative neglect.

Considerable space is devoted in the text to translation of key passages from the works of prominent writers discussed. Location and translation of such passages, particularly in the case of the scholastics, has been no easy task, and it could not have been accomplished without reliance on the published research of a number of scholars. The work of certain American historians of ideas has been particularly valuable. Special mention is due original investigations by John W. Baldwin, Bernard W. Dempsey, John T. Noonan, and Raymond de Roover. The writer is also indebted directly to translations so generously undertaken by Michael Bailey, S. J., of St Ignatius College, Enfield, Middlesex.

For permission to reproduce copyright material the publishers and I are grateful to the Clarendon Press (extracts from Herbert Danby's translation of *The Mishna* (1973) and from *The Roman Law of Sale* (1945) by F. De Zulueta) and the University of Pennsylvania Press (extracts from Robert Burke's translation of *Treatise on the Power and Utility of Moneys* (1930) by Gabriel Biel).

Mr J. S. Poole, Associate Librarian, Heythrop College, University of London, was very helpful with assistance in obtaining works by scholastic authors. Mrs Elaine Sheehan, Graduate Assistant, University of Newcastle, typed the bulk of the manuscript with her customary despatch and efficiency. Throughout the entire project, my wife has sacrificed much of her own research time to act as an attentive and stimulating critic.

University of Newcastle,   Barry Gordon
New South Wales

. . . the master economist must possess a rare combination of gifts. He must reach a high standard in several different directions and must combine talents not often found together. He must be mathematician, historian, statesman, philosopher — in some degree. He must understand symbols and speak in words. He must contemplate the particular in terms of the general, and touch the abstract and concrete in the same flight of thought. He must study the present in the light of the past for the purpose of the future. No part of man's nature or his institutions must lie entirely outside his regard. He must be purposeful and disinterested in a simultaneous mood; as aloof and incorruptible as an artist, yet sometimes as near the earth as a politician.

J. M. Keynes

1 Before Plato

The birth of economic analysis in the West was the result of a union of two elements in Hellenic thought. One of these was ability to reason about social relationships in a generalised or abstract form. The second was reflection on living in a sophisticated economic environment created during an upsurge of export-led growth. Presiding over the union was a profound humanism, limited in scope to exclude aliens and slaves, but associated with genuine concern for the welfare of those who could be regarded as fellows.

The earliest reference points for charting the emergence of economic thought are found about 700 B.C. At that time, an entirely oral tradition of discourse and education began to give way in Greek culture to written communication. The first significant steps were transfers to manuscript of the poems of Homer and Hesiod. These had been composed in the ninth and eighth centuries, and were the mainstays for instruction on morals, history and social order in the Hellenic world. Later, a new literary form was devised for the education of the populace. This was pioneered in fifth-century Athens by the dramatists Aeschylus, Sophocles and Euripides. Their plays, like the earlier poems, provide some insights into the state of economic enquiry at the time.

As early as the sixth century B.C., there is evidence of a trend towards a scientific approach to the understanding of social issues. An important influence was the work of Pythagoras of Samos. Born about 580 B.C. he had established by the end of the century a brotherhood of thinkers who pooled their possessions and sought purification of the spirit in preparation for eternal life. Social and political problems of the day were also of concern to them, and in these matters they emphasised the new technique of reasoning by means of numbers. This development of the possibilities of pure mathematics was a major stimulus to the achievement of a

1

new degree of abstraction and conceptualisation in social thought. Another contribution to the same movement was begun in Miletus, an Ionian coastal town, to the east of Athens. Literary remains of the period suggest that Thales was the pioneer here, and he was followed by Anaximander and Anaximenes.

The new mode of reasoning, free from the narrative framework demanded by epic poetry or drama, is found in the fragments which remain of the writings of Democritus of Abdera. A resident of Athens in the second half of the fifth century, he generalises on aspects of economic behaviour. At the same time, in the same city, the organisers of the first European system of higher education appear to have included economics in their teaching. These first professional instructors in economics were the Sophists. Protagoras, Hippias, Gorgias and Thrasymachus are some of the Sophists who taught at this period. Unfortunately, only sketchy evidence concerning their ideas is available, and the bulk of this is merely the report of their critics, the Philosophers.

Underlying the emergence of economics at Athens is the transformation of that city from a minor centre of purely local significance to the focal point of the richest and most powerful state of Europe by the middle of the fifth century B.C. A process of economic growth was set in motion during the sixth century, and this gave rise to a cluster of innovations unparalleled until the Europe of the late middle ages. Concentration of the cluster in the one centre resulted in the establishment of a complex web of new economic relationships which threatened social and political upheaval. Those who were concerned with the fate of their society were obliged to explore a new world of fluctuating trade and financial arrangements. The structure of the economy of Periclean Athens and the tensions which its complexity created are decisive elements shaping the course of economic thought.

Hesiod and the economics of self-sufficiency
For the earliest stirrings of economic analysis it is necessary to look back to the period before the economic ascendancy of Athens and the surrounding region of Attica. The stirrings are

evident in the poetry of Hesiod, composed about the middle of the eighth century B.C. His picture of an economy is in marked contrast to the one with which Athenians were to become familiar. Notably, the poet has only a faint grasp of the mechanisms of economic growth. Yet in his *Works and Days*, he gives an exposition of 'the economic problem' as it appears to be understood by many writers of economics textbooks today. In fact, there are strong affinities between Hesiod's account of the matter and that provided by Lord Robbings in his influential, *An Essay on the Nature and Significance of Economic Science* (1932).

Hesiod was a Boeotian, a resident, as he tells us, 'of Ascra, a sorry place near Helicon; bad in winter, hard in summer, never good'. His world is that of the small-scale subsistence farm, isolated from market involvements, and striving to maintain self-sufficiency. Production and consumption are geared to the workings of an autonomous household in the fashion which pertained throughout the Greek dark ages after the fall of Mycenae in 1175 B.C. and the Dorian invasion of the Peloponnese. The poetry reflects existing tensions between peasant farmers and the land-owning aristocracy which was paramount in Boeotia, as well as in nearby Attica. Hesiod calls for the establishment of a code of social justice to protect the weak against the arbitrary use of power by the economically advantaged.

In his poem, Hesiod, like Homer, is not speaking primarily as an artist or entertainer. Rather he is adopting the role of educator, passing on traditional wisdom concerning the organisation of law, both public and private. Unlike Homer he is very ready to break out of the story line of his verses to give explicit rules for conduct, and to generalise from the materials at hand. This tendency to abstract, a new literary phenomenon, looks forward to the achievements of the Philosophers and their immediate predecessors over two hundred years later. It also yields the first essay into economic analysis. Hesiod is intent on the solution of a particular problem; how can one explain the existence of an obligation to work? With remarkably few interruptions, he pursues the analysis of the central issue.

The *Works and Days* is designed for recitation with musical accompaniment. Its 828 verses are broken up into small groups suited to the requirements of solo vocal presentation. Rather than a continuous logical development appropriate to an academic treatise on the nature of work, different groups of verses take up individual aspects of the central theme in a pattern appropriate to song. Of these groups, those comprising the first 383 verses are of greatest interest, since they contain a well-conceived treatment of the problems of scarcity, choice, and allocation of resources at a micro-economic level. The solution of these problems is seen as crucial for the achievement of human well-being.

Hesiod begins by outlining the economic problem, stressing its universal urgency and explaining its origins. Human existence, he believes, is dominated by the desire to achieve ends which are summarised as the attainment of 'ease and peace' such as existed in the Golden Age. However, these aspirations, inevitably, are not realised in full. The present age is far from golden, and 'men never rest from labour and sorrow by day and from perishing by night.'[1] To explain this contradiction Hesiod introduces the notion of scarcity of resources. 'The gods', he claims, 'keep hidden from men the means of life.' This is the central phenomenon which requires explanation, and accounts are provided as to how the limitation of means has arisen. Two specific answers are given both of which are akin to the Eden story which Lord Robbins employs as an illustrative reference in his modern discussion.[2] One of these is the myth of Pandora's Box. The other is the theory of a regression of the human creations of the gods through five races of mortals.

The poet then turns to the behaviour which continuing scarcity necessitates. Certain choices are to be made, and labour, time and materials need to be allocated efficiently. In the first place, he excludes the choice of unjust methods of solving the ends-means contradiction. He invokes the wrath

[1] This and subsequent quotations from Hesiod are drawn from the translation by H. G. Evelyn-White, *The Homeric Hymns and the Homerica* (London, Heinemann, 1954).
[2] 'We have been turned out of Paradise. We have neither eternal life nor unlimited means of gratification.' Lionel Robbins, *An Essay on the Nature and Significance of Economic Science* (London, Macmillan, 1952) p. 15.

of the gods as well as demonstrating the worldly wisdom of the just course. Excluding injustice then, the problem is only to be overcome by a vigorous application of labour and capital. 'If your heart within you desires wealth,' he writes, 'work with work upon work.'

The particular set of allocation questions which is given special attention is choice between work and leisure. Hesiod believes that there is an innate desire for the god-like state of leisure, but in his analysis he isolates three main factors which induce men to choose work. The first of these is basic material need. The second is that of social disapproval, and the third, associated inducement, is the desire to emulate the consumption habits of those in one's immediate social grouping. Further, he observes that emulation leads to the development of the spirit of competition in work, which he calls 'good conflict'. In his opinion, 'This conflict is wholesome for men, and potter is angry with potter, and craftsman with craftsman, and beggar is jealous of beggar, and minstrel of minstrel.' For Hesiod then, as for Adam Smith, competition is a fundamental force working to relieve the scarcity problem.

These general issues settled, Hesiod takes up the particular problems involved in ordering the life of a small isolated farm as an efficient production unit, in the light of existing technology. This is a logical step, but it leads discussion away from questions of general analytical interest into the cataloguing of techniques. However, this section of the manuscript is prefaced by a series of general observations, one of which constitutes a further important insight relevant to his exposition of scarcity and allocation.

Although he has been emphasising the urgency of the economic problem, he now indicates that it is not a problem without limits. One limit is of course abundance. The other is extreme dearth. Here, when he sets out general instructions on how best to use the stock of goods available over time, Hesiod affirms that rational allocative activity is not relevant in extremes of either poverty or plenty. 'Take your fill when the cask is first opened, but midways be sparing,' he advises, 'it is poor saving when you come to the dregs.' It is 'midways' then that questions of apportioning the stock are of importance. Economic behaviour in the sense of allocative activity, and economic science as the study of such behaviour, become significant in the situations where wants and the means of satisfying those wants are not too disproportionate.

This outline of the economic problem by Hesiod is undertaken against the backdrop of an agricultural economy conceived in terms of relatively stable states of consumption and production. Clearly, the poet is not familiar with a process of cumulative growth, and his invocation of the myth of regression of the human creations of the gods could be taken to suggest that he is pessimistic concerning future possibilities. Such an inference is incorrect however, as the regression to which he refers is not continuous. Each race of mortals is a distinct creation, and the history of the existing human species need not be seen as regress when considered in isolation from cosmic history. In fact, men as they are, are in a better position than their ancestors. According to Hesiod, when the race was first conceived by the gods it was formed to exist without even rudimentary technical aids. A decisive break came when the hero Prometheus (Forethought) stole fire and passed it on to man. From this point development was a possibility.

Hesiod's programme for growth is embryonic, but it embraces two of the fundamental features of Adam Smith's scheme. The first, is the establishment of order and harmony in society. This is achieved through adherence to the rule of law, and respect in the community for the requirements of justice. The second, we have seen, is hard work spurred on by a competitive struggle. Here, the poet looks to the celebrated Greek passion for contest, and the fame accruing to the victor, to push men towards a better standard of material well-being.

Beyond these prescriptions he does not venture. His contemporary frame of reference does not permit him to consider technological change, financial innovation, or industrial specialisation as growth factors. Further, he does not perceive that there may be a certain incompatibility between the 'good conflict' he recommends and the maintenance of justice in society. Some three hundred and fifty years later, the philosophers Plato and Aristotle reviewing the intervening events of Greek history were to decide that social justice could not be assured in communities pursuing economic growth in a regime of vigorous competition.

Solon and sixth-century Athens

Early in the sixth century B.C., Athens was set on a path of commercial development through a series of reforms introduced by the poet and merchant Solon. In the face of serious internal conflict between land-owning aristocrats and small-scale farmers, he was appointed chief magistrate for the city-state in 594 B.C. As prescribed by Hesiod, he first used his wide-ranging powers to establish a measure of peace and justice in community relations. A form of democracy based on voting power and entry into public office by way of wealth qualification was set up. Land was redistributed, enslavement for failure to repay debt was abolished, and a partial moratorium was declared on existing loan obligations. Loans on personal security were forbidden.

Other legal innovations were undertaken with a direct eye on encouragement of commercial enterprise. Among these was the bestowal of legal personality on business partnerships. Also, to exploit the local silver mines at Laureion, a type of joint stock company was formed. Athens began to mint and issue its own silver coinage in imitation of the practice begun about a century earlier in Ionian towns such as Phocaea, Miletus and Ephesus. In addition, the state fostered a movement into specialised agriculture with particular emphasis on olive oil production. An expansion of the merchant fleet began, and this eventually gave Athens a dominant role in the trade of the Aegean. Apart from these specific measures, the political constitution itself, which equated an individual's political influence with the differential between his own wealth and that of others, served to channel the citizens' passion for contest into economic endeavour.

A surviving fragment of Solon's own poetry indicates that foreign trade was seen as the leading edge of an expansionary movement. In a list of six worthy occupations, sea commerce is given first place ahead of agriculture, manufactures, teaching, prophecy and medicine.[3] This emphasis on trade, monetisation of the economy, and the alliance of political with economic power suggests that it is appropriate to apply the term 'mercantilist' to Solon's programme. The future of Athens was being shaped in accordance with policies akin to those adopted by the nation-states of Europe in the late sixteenth and early seventeenth centuries A.D. As in the European case over two thousand years later, these policies led quickly to attempts at colonisation, the formation of wider political alliances, and other familiar trappings of a vigorous economic imperialism.

Solon himself was a sober judge of the process he had set in train. He recognised the dependence of his new, diversified economy on advances in applied technology. The traditional regard, as is shown by Hesiod, for the agriculturalist who 'cleaves the fruitful earth' is supplemented by respect for one who, 'skilled in the works of Athena and Hephaistos, master of many crafts, brings together a livelihood with his hands.'

The new emphasis was reflected in Solon's policy of encouragement of skilled tradesmen to migrate to Athens, and in provision for organised technical training of local artisans. He also saw that it was no once-over change that had been effected in society, but rather, a cumulative movement. 'To wealth men have set themselves no clear bounds,' he writes, 'for those of us who now have most substance but redouble our zeal for more.' Like Plato and Aristotle in later years, Solon fears that a growth process tends to slip out of control and result in political disaster. 'But the men of the city themselves, hearkening to the call of wealth, are minded by their folly to destroy a mighty city . . . For they know not how to check their greed or to order the good-cheer that they have, in quiet enjoyment of the feast.'

Solon was right. After his term as chief magistrate, Athens was rent by internal faction fights. In these disputes, the new working class of the city found a leader in the landowner Peisistratus, who had achieved local renown in a war with

---

[3] The relevant passage together with other fragments from Solon may be found in, M. L. W. Laistner, *Greek Economics* (London and Toronto, Dent, 1923) pp. 1–3.

nearby Megara for possession of the island of Salamis. With support from the assembly of citizens he seized the reins of government in 560 B.C. His rule as a Tyrant was bitterly contested in its early stages, but by 546 B.C. he was in full command. During his term of effective exercise of power to 527 B.C., the rate of economic expansion of Athens was further accelerated along mercantilist lines.

Under Peisistratus, Athens established colonies in Thrace to the north. At home, a second programme of land reform was undertaken in the city's surrounding rural province of Attica. Trade expanded into new areas. Fine pottery from the Athenian suburb of Kerameikos found its way throughout the Aegean and even further afield. More utilitarian pottery ware was used to transport cargoes of olive oil and wine in the holds of Athenian ships. Returning vessels brought grain, since Athens had by this long departed from older ideas of economic self-sufficiency. Imports of wheat were crucial to the survival of the urban work force. Timber for ship-building was another strategic commodity which it was necessary to import. A fleet of warships was constructed to protect merchant shipping, colonial enclaves, and major trading centres. Public expenditures were increased to improve civic amenities and to sponsor religious and artistic activities.

The resulting changes in the manner and quality of life in Athens and associated centres of the Aegean region are accompanied by new insights in the literature coming down to us from the latter part of the sixth century. Of particular interest in the sphere of economics is evidence of a growing realisation that the level of technology is a variable, subject to human control. This realisation is found, for example, in the writings of Xenophanes (c. 565–470 B.C.), a wandering scholar-artist from the Ionian town of Colophon. Xenophanes is a critic of the popular mythology of the region concerning the existence of a set of Olympian gods. He affirms that there is only one true God whose life should not be confused with the activities of humans. Technical change, for instance, is predominantly a matter of human agency. 'Men did not originally receive from gods a demonstration of all matters,' he observes, 'it is by research carried out in the course of time that they come to improve their invention.'[4] Innovations are treated as discrete historical events. Anaximander (c. 550 B.C.) discusses the invention of the alphabet, while Xenophanes claims that the Lydians were the first to employ coined money.

The second to last decade of the sixth century was marked by a renewal of civil strife in Athens on the death of Peisistratus. Law and order were not restored until the constitutional reforms of Cleisthenes who became Archon in 508 B.C. The new constitution redefined the meaning of citizenship, breaking up divisions based on old tribal brotherhoods, and introducing territorial bases for representative government. A genuine transfer of power was effected in favour of the Assembly, the legislative body of which all citizens could be members. A fresh political equilibrium was attained and this re-established a basis for economic growth to continue in the directions mapped out at the commencement of the century.

Dramatists and Sophists in Periclean Athens

External events over the next thirty years did not allow economic growth to follow a steady course. However, through an effective military response to the pressure of those events, the republic was brought to the apogee of its ascent to economic pre-eminence.

The closing years of the sixth century and the first two decades of the fifth were marked by a buildup of Persian power in the eastern Aegean. Athens and the other states in the West felt an increasing threat to their trading interests and political autonomy. After clashes with the Persians on land and at sea, the Athenians decided in 484 B.C. to use a windfall gain of wealth from the discovery of a new silver lode in their Laureion mines to finance construction of a fleet of warships. This decision was a major turning point in the democracy's history.

The crisis came in 480 B.C. with a massive Persian land attack. The invasion was met by an alliance of most of the

---

[4] The translation is by Eric A. Havelock, *The Liberal Temper in Greek Politics* (London, Cape, 1957) p. 105. The passage is attributed to Xenophanes by Stobaeus.

Greek city-states, but at first the invaders had the upper hand. After conquering northern Greece, they occupied Attica and burnt Athens which had been evacuated. However, the tide was turned by a crushing Athenian naval victory in the narrow waters between Athens and the island of Salamis. This was followed up by a Spartan land victory at Plataea, and the Persian forces were driven out of Europe. The Athenians pressed home their advantage by the organisation of a naval confederacy to liberate Iona and destroy the sea power of the Persians in the Aegean. With Athens as leader, the confederacy included most of the maritime states of the Aegean. Islands of the eastern Mediterranean, Byzantium, cities on the Asia Minor coast and in Thrace came under Athenian sway. Through military success, Athens had acquired a trading empire of considerable dimensions. The only Greek state to rival Athenian power, Sparta, was oriented to agriculture and uninterested in trade.

For the next fifty years Athens controlled the confederacy, drew tribute from its allies, and renewed on a greater scale the economic imperialism which the reforms of Solon and the administration of Peisistratus had fostered. During this period, the politics of the city were dominated by the figure of Pericles from about 461 B.C. until his death in 430 B.C. a year of plague. Under Pericles, Athens was transformed into a commercial centre with a complex of economic activities that was to remain unsurpassed until post-Renaissance Europe. Almost all the phenomena associated with modern market economies were present: commercial agriculture, manufacturing, business consortiums, monopoly trading. Commodity speculation was a feature of the exchange markets in the Agora and the port of Piraeus, and this speculation was unhampered by government legislation or gentlemen's agreements as to rules of the game. Banking companies were formed and exercised a powerful influence. Their main business was money changing, since a wide variety of coinage was brought into the city by foreign trade. Nevertheless, they also received deposits, made payments for clients, undertook debt recovery, issued letters of credit, and invested in business ventures.

The upsurge of commercial activity was resisted to some

extent by sections of the old Athenian landed aristocracy.
They clung to agriculture in the traditional manner, and
devoted their energies to the extensive round of civic
administrative duties with which the democratic constitution
encouraged involvement. However, this conservative element
was more than balanced by the employment of skilled slaves
as managers, and by an influx of aliens who could not own
land, but who played leading roles in trade, industry and
banking. Pericles, himself a landowner, organised his own
estates according to the principles of commercial logic. For
example, he confounded the conservatives by selling the
produce of his own land and purchasing food in the market.
Through such innovation, the regime of tradition, routine,
and chance which had governed the economics of the
individual household was restricted. At the level of 'the
household writ large', the community of the city-state, the
same regime gave way to the logic of market development.

The Greek historian of this period, Herodotus of Hali-
carnassus (c. 484–425 B.C.), who came to live in Athens,
recounts something of the economic practices in the nations
with whom the Athenians had opportunities for trade. His
observations underline the novelty associated with the
direction in which the Athenian economy was tending. For
example, the very existence of marketplaces such as that in
Athens is seen as having no parallel at all in Persian practice.
Again, Greek esteem for the trader and the craftsman is
contrasted with attitudes prevailing among the Thracians,
Scythians, Persians and Lydians. In drawing such contrasts,
however, Herodotus does not take the opportunity to explain
their significance in terms of any theoretical analysis of the
forces underlying economic growth.[5] Surprisingly enough,
greater analytical insight on this matter is displayed by the
Athenian dramatists of the period.

At the height of its power, the state of Athens proper
encompassed about 1000 square miles. Estimates of the
numbers of citizens in Athens vary, but there were at least

---

[5] For an account of Herodotus' observations on economic customs, see J. J.
Spengler, 'Herodotus on the Subject Matter of Economics', *The Scientific
Monthly*, Vol. 81 (Dec 1955) pp. 276–85. In Professor Spengler's estimate,
'Herodotus had no notion of an economic system.' (p. 284).

20,000. The dependent population of Attica was in the order of 250,000 plus resident aliens and slaves accounting for an additional 100,000. Living standards were generally well above a mere subsistence level, although average life expectancy could not have been much more than twenty-nine years. In enjoyment of the new standards, Athenians showed a marked propensity to take out their gains in the form of increased leisure rather than increased material possessions, and literature and learning flourished as never before in the cosmopolitan atmosphere of the trading capital.

Surviving examples of the literature of fifth century Athens show an enhanced appreciation of the economics of a growth based on increasing mastery of a variety of technical and social skills. Such economics is not merely a matter of social justice allied to hard work facilitated by the Promethean technology of fire, as it was for Hesiod. Thus, Aeschylus in his *Prometheus Bound*, written in 450 B.C., celebrates the 'triumph of scientific mind', and catalogues the material achievements of which his audience were heirs. These include the improvement of transportation both by land and sea, the growth of medicine as a science, increasing literacy, and the utilisation of mineral resources.[6]

Again, Sophocles (495–405 B.C.) in his *Antigone* writes of the 'self-taught arts, the total resource of man'. He goes on to list those technical advances which have flowed from 'the skill of the technical hand which is an intellectual thing that guides man on his journey'. The rise of the city-state itself is associated by Sophocles with this enhanced command of the arts, as is the extended acceptance of law and order. To the lists of the attributes of a programme of economic development, the later dramatist Euripides (d. 406 B.C.) adds the exploitation of differing resource patterns by foreign trade. In the *Suppliants*, Euripides extols the desirability 'mutually to supply by cross exchange the earth's deficiencies'. Elsewhere, the same author generalises on this principle of the international division of labour to extend it to all activities. 'Each has his special excellence,' he writes, 'one

[6] A study of the treatment of growth in the texts of Aeschylus, Sophocles and Euripides may be found in E. A. Havelock, op. cit., Ch. 3.

ought to place a man where he can do most good.'[7]
Organisation for specialised effort has replaced individual
self-sufficiency as the ideal.

Concern for the best form of organisation for effort is also
present in the writings of the scholar from Abdera, Democritus (c. 460–c. 370 B.C.). The empirical basis for his
observations is likely to have been the contrast between the
individualism given rein in the Athenian economy and the
communal organisation in the rival city-state of Sparta. In his
opinion, a society organised in terms of private ownership of
resources will enjoy economic superiority over one where
communal ownership prevails. The possibility of private
ownership lends the stronger incentive for productive activity. He states that 'Toil is sweeter than idleness when men
gain what they toil for or know that they will use it.'
Privately owned resources are likely to be handled with
greater diligence than those which are public, since 'income
from communally held property gives less pleasure, and the
expenditure less pain.' Not only the contrast between the
static agriculturalism of Sparta and the trading bustle of
Athens, but also the difference between private frugality and
public opulence in the latter city seems to underlie these
remarks. Democritus is the first in a long line of thinkers to
argue the superior efficiency achieved by a division of
resources. His views are echoed a little later by Aristotle, and
eventually become central in the writings of the medieval
schoolmen. Organisation of economic activity in terms of
division of resources and division of labour is a major feature
of the message of Greek social thought.

No systematic treatise by Democritus survives. Yet a
variety of short political and social observations on his part,
like the above, have been transmitted by other authors. These
are important as indicators of the extent to which economic
analysis had flowered by this stage. They betray considerable
involvement in debate on the problems of organisation for
efficiency in the business of the city-state as a whole and in
the operation of the basic unit of economic life at the time,
the household. Among the fragments of analytical interest to

[7] *Rhesus*, 107 and 626.

an economist are those relating to the theory of value. Democritus' approach to value determination is utilitarian and subjectivist. Moral values may be objective, but not those of economic life. 'The same thing is good and true for all men,' he affirms, 'but the pleasant differs from one and another.' Again, men generally value a present commodity more highly than the same future commodity since, 'the good on hand is superior to the one still to come.' Further, he suggests, the utility ascribed to commodities diminishes if they are consumed in abundance. 'The most pleasant things,' he observes, 'become most unpleasant if moderation does not prevail.'[8]

Another scholar from Abdera, the sophist Protagoras, some of whose views are recorded in the Platonic dialogue which bears his name, also seems to have been involved in economic enquiry. This involvement stemmed from his vocation as a teacher in higher education. Athens in the Periclean era had become Europe's first university centre. The size of the city, its cosmopolitan populace, and the disposition of its citizens to use the fruits of economic growth to procure increased leisure rather than commodities had permitted a new upsurge in systematic education. Sophists like Protagoras, many of whom were not Athenians by birth, were the men of science or learning who taught professionally.

Although their activities came under attack from Socrates and his disciples, the Sophists were a potent force in the intellectual life of Athens between about 450 and 350 B.C. Their methods of instruction superseded the old poetic tradition of education, stressing the analytical and technical rather than the artistic. Economics was part of the curriculum.

In Plato's *Protagoras*, the sophist is asked by Socrates to explain the content of his teaching. He replies that his instruction is aimed at enabling the pupil to reach correct decisions with respect to efficient management of households and administration of the affairs of the city. Protagoras'

[8] The quotations from Democritus are derived from Cyril Bailey, *The Greek Atomists and Epicurus* (London, Oxford University Press, Clarendon Press, 1928) pp. 186–212.

answer is a clear indication that his students were obliged to study the application of both micro- and macro-economic principles. At that time, despite the growth in complexity of the Athenian economy, the household continued as the main unit of economic activity. This was true not only in agriculture, but also in the manufacturing and financial sectors. The household was not just an organisation of consumers, and the word 'economy' itself designated household management. When the Greeks thought of such management they had in mind a wide range of micro-economic considerations. Further, by direct analogy between the conduct of household affairs and those of the state, the science of household management could be applied to the solution of macro-economic problems.

The manner in which economics was taught by the Sophists has a strong affinity with the approach which has come to be dominant in the twentieth century. In fact, their approach is much closer to that of the majority of modern professional economists than are those adopted by Plato, Aristotle, and the scholastics. For the Sophists, economics is a technology. Its techniques can be taught and mastered without reference to the desirability or lack of desirability attached to the ends or purposes which the technique can be made to serve. The discipline can be applied, for example, to increase the affluence of a particular household or a particular state. However, the question as to whether the form of affluence envisaged is worth acquiring is not a question with which economics is concerned. This same technological outlook is evident in the way in which the Sophists taught the discipline of rhetoric. Students were equipped with a box of rhetorical tools to argue the merits of any case in law without regard to the issue of whether they believed that case to be a just one.

Evidence concerning the specific economic doctrines of these first 'modern' economists is sketchy. It is highly probable that some of their analyses are incorporated in the writings of Plato and Aristotle, but the philosophers did not acknowledge any debt to the economics of their intellectual opponents, so the degree of incorporation is difficult to judge. Where the philosophers are critical of Sophistic doctrine, it stands out in greater relief. From Aristotle's attack in his *Politics* on the discipline of wealth-making *chrematistike*, it appears that Sophistic economics had a strong mercantilist bias. As in Europe in the seventeenth and eighteenth centuries, great stress was placed on monetisation of the economy and the accumulation of precious metals. These processes were seen as central to a growth path for an economy in which military conquest, the acquisition of colonies, and the expansion of trade were inextricably linked. All we know of the history of Periclean Athens points to the fact that Sophistic economics had its rationale as a technology which could be usefully employed in the service of an aggressive economic imperialism. When, centuries later, Adam Smith described the mercantilism of his age as 'the interested sophistry of merchants and manufacturers', his use of the term 'sophistry' conveyed an historical truth of which even he might not have been aware. Smith's negative reaction to 'the mercantile system' is anticipated by Plato and Aristotle in their opposition to the Sophists, although their reaction took economics along a rather different path from that explored by the Scottish philosopher.

Given that Sophistic economics was mercantilist in outlook, there is one surviving Greek treatise which might be cited as an example of the work of the school. The manuscript in question is *Ways and Means to Increase the Revenues of Athens*. As the title suggests, it is an exercise in applied economics, and concerned with an issue, financial viability of central government, which predominates in mercantilist literature. Written about the middle of the fourth century B.C. by a contemporary of Plato, it remained the only essay to be devoted exclusively to this particular topic for well over 1500 years.

There are two objections, at least, to a citation of this work as Sophistic. One problem is its date of composition which is generally set at about 355 B.C. By that time, the influence of the Sophists on Athenian thought may not have been particularly strong. Again, there is the existence of a long tradition which ascribes authorship of the treatise to an adherent of the Socratics, Xenophon (430–354 B.C.). Against both these objections must be set the profoundly un-Socratic nature of the essay's policy proposals. The claim that the work is part of a Socratic legacy is difficult to sustain when it is considered alongside Plato's and Aristotle's approach to economic issues.

The central problem for the author of *Ways and Means* is how Athens might prosper without taking tribute from its allies. For many years the city had covered the balance of payments deficits by a levy on the allies protected by the Athenian fleet. This tribute was an important part of the public revenues of Athens during its years of leadership of the League, other sources of income being provided by taxes on foreigners resident in Athens and on imported goods. In the absence of the levy, the writer proposes a programme of mercantile development which is akin to those put forward by the pamphleteers and economic publicists of Europe many centuries later.

Among the policies suggested is that of increasing the population of the city by the admission of aliens and their families who will be liable to the payment of poll tax. Again, greater recognition should be given to the services performed by the merchant class. 'It would be a sound and proper course', the author states, 'to bestow free seats at the festivals on merchants and ship-owners as a mark of distinction.'[9] Through such recognition, more merchants will be attracted to Athens, the volume of trade increased, and public revenue from customs duties enhanced. In general, by using legislative means, the merchants' pursuit of profit and prestige can be chanelled to serve the interests of the government. 'To effect such increase in our revenues,' it is observed, 'no previous outlay is required but only liberal-minded legislation and supervision.'

These standard mercantilist proposals of population expansion, social mobility for the merchant, and state intervention to manipulate the search for private gain are supplemented by suggestions for state investment in improvement of commercial infrastructure. State housing for mariners, construction of warehousing and retail facilities, and even a

---

[9] This passage and the others quoted below are taken from the translation of *Ways and Means to Increase the Revenues of Athens* in M. L. W. Laistner, op. cit., pp. 10–27.

state-owned mercantile fleet to be 'hired out on security like other contracts given by the state' are seen as desirable. Above all, there should be reorganisation of the working of the local silver mines. At the present time, it is affirmed, the mines are underworked because operations are in the hands of individuals who lack the necessary risk-capital for research and development. New ore bodies can only be discovered and exploited by state intervention. To this end, the government should purchase about 10,000 slaves, brand them with the state stamp, and hire them out for mining purposes. If private contractors are unwilling to employ the necessary workforce, a state mining company should be formed to spread the loss and gain from unsuccessful and successful strikes across the Athenian citizenry as a whole.

In the chapters of this policy document there are few observations of genuine analytical interest. However, near the opening of the fourth chapter where the question of silver mining is taken up, the author distinguishes the case of a constant or increasing returns industry from one of diminishing returns. Agriculture is an example of the latter, and silver mining of the former. He writes:

> For in truth, when a few persons mine and explore, the wealth that is brought to light is also small, when many are engaged, the ore is seen to be many times more prolific. Consequently this is the only commercial enterprise that I know where no one feels envious towards those who try to carry out new developments. Again, the landowners could all tell you how many teams and how many labourers are required for their estates. If anyone employs hands in excess of requirements, it is reckoned as a loss. But in the silver mines all the employers say that they are short of workers, for here the case is different to that in other industries.

The distinction between silver mining and agriculture has been achieved here by the assumption of a fixed supply of agricultural land, but no such limitation exists on veins of ore. The case in which ore deposits are a known quantity is not considered. The only limitation on silver production is lack of risk-capital. Public and private investment is best

directed where returns are constant or increasing, despite the
risk of occasional loss of capital consumed by exploratory
work.

The author then turns immediately to counter the argument that returns to silver mining can be diminished by
over-supply of the product. He argues that there is no
limitation to the demand for silver. It is not subject, as are
other commodities, to any principle of diminishing utility.
'In truth, when a man has acquired sufficient furniture for his
house,' he writes, 'he does not purchase any more; but so far
no one has acquired so much silver than he no longer requires
more. If some have a superabundance, they take as much
pleasure in burying the superfluous portion as if they used it.'
He adds that in both peace and war, in plenty and in famine,
a city will require silver. The purpose for which it is used may
change, but the demand remains.

While drawing this contrast between silver mining and
other industries, the writer enters into some discussion of the
phenomenon of market disequilibrium. He fails to state the
point at which equilibrium is established but he isolates
mobility of labour and capital as the means whereby
equilibrium is restored. He states that, 'When there are too
many coppersmiths and copper articles become cheap, they
go bankrupt; similarly with iron founders. And when corn
and wine are plentiful and these commodities are cheap,
agriculture ceases to be profitable and many abandon
working on the land and turn to wholesale and retail trade
and to money lending.'

This insight on markets, along with the discussion of
production and investment decisions, bring the author of
Ways and Means to Increase the Revenues of Athens to the
beginnings of an involvement in a range of analytical issues
that was ignored by the Socratic school. It provides a very
different basis for future development of economic theory
from that suggested by the teaching of Plato and Aristotle.

2 The Socratic Conception of Economics

The direction in which the Sophists led economics was not to be pursued again with vigour until the latter part of the sixteenth century A.D. Plato and Aristotle reacted against the mercantilist tendencies of their intellectual opponents, and this reaction was to prove decisive. Further, they refused to treat economics as a technology. Consideration of the relative desirability of alternate goals of economic action was at the core of their conception of the discipline. In this chapter, we examine both the philosophers' rejection of the growth of wealth of the nation as the object of economic enquiry, and then, the type of science of choice amongst ends which they sought to promote as the appropriate form of study. First, however, it is necessary to appreciate the coincidence of historical events and intellectual currents which produced such a radical change of direction in the progress of economics.

Decline of the city-state

The last quarter of the fifth century B.C. saw a beginning to the decline of the city-state in Athens and elsewhere as a major form of political and economic organisation. Warfare between the Greek city-states broke out in 431 B.C. when the dominant position of Athens was contested by an alliance of the city-states of the Peloponnese and Boeotia formed under the leadership of Sparta. In the following year, plague struck Athens, and Pericles was one of the many who died. The war continued on until 404 B.C. when the Spartans defeated Athens and installed a puppet government known as 'the thirty tyrants', Their reign of terror was short-lived, and the democracy was restored in 403 B.C.

Further weakening of the social and political fabric of Greece continued on through the early years of the next century. Serious conflict was renewed between Athens, Sparta, and other Greek states between 395 and 387 B.C., and some resolution was achieved only by recourse to Persian intervention. Yet the decisive blow to the framework of the Hellenic world was not to come from the former antagonist, Persia, but from the northern kingdom of Macedonia. There, Philip II gained the throne in 360 B.C. and adopted an expansionist policy which led to conquest of the Aegean coastal regions, of Thrace, and later, defeat of the Athenians in 338 B.C. His son Alexander, who became king on the assassination of Philip in 336 B.C., went on to excel his father. The conquest of Asia Minor, Phonecia, Palestine, Egypt, Tyre and an expedition to the frontiers of India were completed before his death at Babylon in 323 B.C. By the conclusion of these exploits a new social order had been created. The autonomy of the Greek city-states was one of the casualties, and economic decline accompanied the loss of political independence.

The Socratic philosophers were witnesses of the disintegration of the political, military, and economic strength of Periclean Athens. Socrates (470–399 B.C.), the son of a stonemason, twice fought in the ranks of Athenian soldiery and endured the reign of the Thirty Tyrants after the defeat by Sparta. He was then condemned to death by his fellow citizens. His aristocratic disciple Plato (428–347 B.C.) experienced the Spartan triumph, the execution of his master by the restored Athenian democracy, the withering away of Athens' former empire, and, in his last years, the growing Macedonian threat in the north. Plato's pupil Aristotle (384–322 B.C.) watched the final acts as first Philip, and then Alexander, whom Aristotle had tutored, completed the destruction of the old order.

It is not surprising then, to find that the economics of the Socratics is not a technology of an age of growth and development. Rather it is the product of an age of anxiety, part of an attempt to work towards establishment of a social order that might ensure a reasonable quality of life for individuals, despite a political environment threatening chaos.

Economic analysis in the hands of the philosophers is not a tool to be developed for use in the pursuit of transitory national strength such as the Athenian proved to be. Instead, it is an intellectual activity required for an understanding of the nature of a just society and the application of that understanding to the preservation of a certain quality of life.

Plato and Aristotle

Plato was born in 427 B.C., the son of a noble Athenian family which was intimately involved in the day-to-day political life of the city. A deep concern with contemporary political events was to continue throughout Plato's career, but, after contact early in life with the questing intellect of Socrates, he was led into the wider field of speculative enquiry. In a series of writings, cast in the form of discussions or dialogues, he established a new mode of conceptual discourse. The reasoning is characterised by the maintenance of a level of abstraction unmatched by earlier literature. His thought extends through many areas including political theory and sociology, and a minor feature of his work in these latter fields is analysis of certain economic phenomena. This analysis is found mainly in his *Republic*, written about 381 B.C., and in the *Laws* which remained incomplete on his death in 347 B.C.[1]

When Plato was twenty-three years old the Spartans established the reign of the thirty tyrants in Athens, and this event and its aftermath were to have important consequences for his thought. In the era of the restored democracy which followed, near relatives and friends of Plato were accused of treachery to the Athenian cause, and, above all, his teacher Socrates was condemned to death. It was evident to Plato that society in general, and democratic society in particular, could offer no guarantee of the maintenance of social justice without extensive and radical reform. This view provides the essential backdrop to his social theories and approach to economics.

[1] An English translation of the works of Plato in ten volumes has been published by The Loeb Classical Library (London, Heinemann; N.Y., Putnam, 1917–29). Also, in the series is a translation by Paul Shorey of *The Republic*, 2 vols (London and N.Y., 1930–5). Notable earlier translations are by Benjamin Jowett, *The Dialogues of Plato*, 5 vols, 3rd ed. (Oxford, 1892).

During his lifetime, he made at least three unsuccessful attempts to encourage the establishment of what he envisaged as a superior form of social organisation in the state of Syracuse. In 387 B.C. he set up a school at Academia on the outskirts of Athens to bring young men to a realisation of the meaning of a just way of life for the individual and the city. The orientation of the Academy was not merely towards teaching and disinterested research. The institute also functioned as a 'think-tank' offering programmes of social policy to meet contemporary needs. Like Plato himself, numbers of his students set out to create new political regimes. At least nine of them managed to establish themselves as tyrants of city-states within the orbit of the Hellenic world.

Aristotle's social thinking also was developed in close proximity to the cut and thrust of contemporary politics. Many of his writings, like the dialogues of Plato, are aimed at a reconstruction of the existing social order which will salvage what he sees as valuable in the disintegrating structure of Greek civilisation. These writings range even more widely than those of Plato, extending into biology as well as physics, and into aesthetics as well as psychology and the various branches of philosophy. Economic analysis is undertaken as part of the investigation of moral and political issues. Hence, the bulk, but not all, of Aristotle's economics is located in passages of the *Nicomachean Ethics* and the *Politics*.[2]

Although his family was Ionian in origin, Aristotle was born in 384 B.C. at the Macedonian coastal town of Stagira. When seventeen he entered Plato's Academy at Athens and studied there for twenty years until Plato's death is 347 B.C. Leaving the Academy, he moved east across the Aegean to lecture in Lesbos and other centres, but returned later to Macedonia. Here, he joined the court of Philip at Pella and tutored the young Alexander who was destined to achieve immensely greater political power than any of Plato's students. After Alexander's accession to the throne, Aristotle

---

[2] A complete English edition of the works of Aristotle in twelve volumes was published under the direction of W. D. Ross (Oxford, Clarendon, 1908—52). The works are also available in seventeen volumes of the Loeb Classical Library (Cambridge, Mass., Harvard, 1926—65). Ernest Barker's translation of the *Politics* has appeared in paperback (Oxford University Press, 1958).

left for Athens and established a school in the Lyceum about
335 B.C. At the Lyceum, he offered a wide lecture programme, and it is these courses which have come down to us
in written form, from either his own hand or as edited by
students. His teaching there was brought to a halt in 323 B.C.
when, on Alexander's death, Athenians felt free to give vent
to their resentment of the Macedonians. Accused of impiety,
Aristotle was forced to leave for Chalcis where he died in the
following year. The school he had founded remained,
however, as a centre for dissemination of his teachings for the
next 850 years. Only in 529 A.D. it was closed by order of
the Emperor Justinian.

Foundations of Socratic economics

It had been a fundamental principle of Socrates that the
proper study of mankind is Man himself. Reflection on the
nature of the ultimate Good for Man is the overriding goal of
human speculation. Both Plato and Aristotle remained true
to this outlook. The dominant concern for both was the
question, 'what is the good life?', and they equated 'the
good' with 'the happy'.

This same question has exercised outstanding intellects in
all ages, yet it has not always led them into the realms of
economic analysis. It produced this result in the case of the
Socratics, however, because to them the question had
meaning only in social terms. They did not reason about men
as if they were isolated individuals, but rather as members of
communities. Men, they observed, are not found in isolation.
They are grouped in households and states, and any
exploration of the nature of the good life must focus on
living in those contexts. That living has inevitable economic
dimensions as part of its social orientation.

In Plato's *Republic*, it is economic necessity which obliges
men to live together in a city-state, although in the *Laws* the
origin of the state is ascribed to the institution of the family.
Aristotle sees the family as the basic unit of society, but men
form wider associations in response to objective need and
subjective promptings. The objective factor is lack of
self-sufficiency of the isolated individual. The subjective
element is a natural instinct for living in community. For

Aristotle, the very nature of man is such that he must dwell in society. Man is a being designed to live and function best in a *polis*, a city-state of the moderate dimensions common in Greece at that time. 'The polis belongs to the class of things that exist by nature,' he writes, 'man is by nature an animal intended to live in a polis.'[3] Aristotle has little respect for the isolated type of existence which Hesiod described.

This unswerving focus on the idea of the good life as attainable through full participation of the individual in the communal interchanges of a moderately-sized society led Plato and Aristotle into examination of economic questions. One set of issues was bound up with the manner in which social life in the household and state comes into being. A second set was associated with ethical problems involved in the just ordering of social interchange. Justice, according to Aristotle, 'is the bond of men in states', and its absence in economic matters contributes to a disintegration of the communal structure necessary for the full development of the individual.

The philosophers' investigations of social evolution and ethics yield not only a distinctive approach to economic enquiry, but also a number of significant generalisations relating to particular aspects of that enquiry. From the discussion of the formation of community life arise observations on the role of specialisation in economic activity, the functions of money, and the organisation of property. Out of the concern with justice comes an essay into the theory of value and consideration of the phenomenon of interest payment.

In dealing with these particular issues still of concern to modern economists, the philosophers constantly referred them to a broader framework than is usually chosen as the setting for similar discussions today. Aristotle, like Plato before him, did not conceive of the economy as a group of relationships which could be considered meaningfully apart from the other forms of interaction which characterise social life. Thus, as Karl Polanyi has observed,

---

[3] *Politics*, trans. E. Barker, 1253a.

whenever Aristotle touched on a question of the economy he aimed at developing its relationship to society as a whole. The frame of reference was the community as such which exists at different levels within all functioning human groups. In terms, then, of our modern speech Aristotle's approach to human affairs was sociological. In mapping out a field of study he would relate all questions of institutional origin and function to the totality of society. Community self-sufficiency and justice were the focal concepts.[4]

Given this sociological emphasis economics did not emerge as an autonomous discipline related to a distinct department of human activity. Both Plato and Aristotle would see the modern claim to autonomy for economics as most inhibiting for the progress of social enquiry. Economic analyses can only be conducted properly as aspects of a much broader study than that for which most modern economists seem content to settle.

Specialisation and the rejection of growth

The philosophers' steps in economic analysis are not motivated by any desire to stimulate a process of economic development. Plato's and Aristotle's economics is not the economics of growth. Their approach is guided by a belief in the desirability of establishing a relatively stationary state of economic activity at a level which ensures the maintenance of a moderate standard of material well-being for the citizenry. In this respect, their outlook recalls that of the philosopher-economist John Stuart Mill in the nineteenth century. Middle-class intellectuals of affluent societies of the twentieth century who inveigh against growth could also .claim some kinship with them.

A reader of Plato's *Republic* might contest the view that the author was an advocate of the stationary state. At the opening of the second book of that work, the writer pays particular attention to elements of a growth process. Plato

---

[4] K. Polanyi, 'Aristotle Discovers the Economy', in K. Polanyi, C. M. Arensberg, and H. W. Pearson (eds), *Trade and Market in the Early Empires* (Free Press, N.Y., 1957) p. 79.

argues that, historically, men have been obliged to come together in order to satisfy their material needs. In the course of social evolution, households are increasingly linked by exchanges which help promote the emergence of the city-state. A key feature of the movement into state organisation is the benefit derived from the scope given for extensions of the division of labour.

Concerning the division of labour, Plato affirms that a greater social product of better quality and involving less work-effort will result from a system where persons are allowed to specialise in those productive activities for which they are naturally suited. Yet the beneficial impact on growth of output is not the reason for Plato's interest in this agent of development. He advocates division of labour to the extent that the quality of an individual's life is improved by his being able to perform that function for which he is best fitted by his natural endowments. Impact of the division on the growth of national product is, at best, a secondary consideration.

Plato is opposed to the extension of the division of labour by international specialisation of productive activity as advocated by Euripides or Adam Smith. For the state as a whole, self-sufficiency is the goal. Where international trading activities loom large, as in Athens, the social fabric is likely to be continually torn by internal disruptions and the importation of foreign manners and customs. Mutual dependence of citizen on citizen because of specialisation is welcome in the interests of social solidarity, but a dependence of one state on another is an invitation to social unrest.

Plato also does not advocate a stimulation of growth through a division of productive processes into segments, each segment being repeatedly performed by the one man. In this respect too, there is a marked difference between Plato's and Adam Smith's treatments of the division of labour. Like Smith, Plato was concerned about the dehumanisation and alienation that might accompany such fractionalisation of tasks. In his dialogue, the *Apology* (21–3), Plato warns that all specialists, whether industrial workers or managers, are forced into a narrow mould by exclusive concentration on one line of activity. Aristotle believed that this narrowing was likely to be most severe in the case of manual workers.

Adam Smith remained optimistic in the face of this danger and looked to an expansion of educational facilities to mitigate the evils involved.[5] Both of the earlier professional educators were no means as sanguine as Smith, and were less willing to face up to the problems posed by a dynamic economy. They believed the price of growth to be too high if it was to involve anything other than division of labour in a restricted sense.

Plato and Aristotle are interested in economic growth only as a prelude to the achievement of a certain modest standard of material well-being. That standard is one which provides the opportunity for maximisation of quality of life as they understand it. Neither philosopher is an advocate of poverty as a way of life. Plato, for example, sees it as a threat to social stability, a prime source of revolution. Aristotle associates poverty with degradation for the individual. The poor man loses the ability to direct his own activities, becoming subject to the directions of an employer. But, given the elimination of poverty, they are prepared to choke off further economic growth for the sake of imposing their conception of the good life on future generations. In this respect, their intellectual elitism foreshadows that of a proportion of modern writers who view growth as a threat.

The philosophers' stand against growth is supported by views which are evident also in the modern debate on the issue. Plato's opposition, for example, is linked with fears for the maintenance of the position of the ruling class in his projected city-state, if that state should experience an expansion of population. In his *Laws*, population increase is seen as one of the major threats to the continuance of the necessary degree of order and hierarchical control in society. This same fear is present today in the alarm concerning a 'world population explosion'.

Aristotle is critical of Plato's position on population policy. Support for his own opposition to growth does not come from that direction, but rather from a particular attitude to man in relation to natural forces. The role of man is seen as one of adjustment to, or at the most, harmonisation

[5] On this aspect of Smith's thought see W. J. Samuels, *The Classical Theory of Economic Policy* (Cleveland, 1966) p. 67, and E. G. West, *Education and the State* (London, 1965) p. 118.

of, those forces. His role is not one of mastering and re-shaping natural processes in a fashion which a deliberate attempt at economic expansion requires. Aristotle's emphasis is on sound management of what is given man by nature, rather than entrepreneurship and innovations which transform it. This emphasis has had a new lease of life in Western thinking over recent years. As S. T. Lowry has commented, '. . . modern thought, has at the popular level at least, apparently kept the feeling that nature is a self-contained process that should be adjusted to rather than used as an adjunct of human values.'[6]

Aristotle's view of the man-nature relationship gives rise to a doctrine of the supremacy of agricultural pursuits in any socioeconomic order. Farm management is seen as a most commendable vocation. Here, man is working along with 'natural' processes in an intimate fashion not open to those in secondary industry. More remote than even secondary production is the disreputable business of retailing. Specialised retail distributors are given a place in his city-state by Plato on the grounds that they fulfil a useful function, namely, 'they equalise our needs and possessions.'[7] Aristotle is far less sympathetic and wishes to eliminate the activity altogether. This lack of sympathy is bound up with Aristotle's opposition, not only to economic growth, but also to a society in which goods are exchanged by means of free market transfers subject to the vagaries of supply-demand mechanisms. His discussions of money and of exchange justice, which are treated in the next chapter, reveal the extent of his antipathy. Retail trading is a potentially subversive occupation.

One further dimension to the philosophers' neglect of positive analysis of the mechanisms of future growth has no strong counterpart in modern Western thought. This dimension is provided by what Oswald Spengler has called the 'plastic ideal of being'. He writes,

The word that stands in the classical vocabulary where 'personality' stands in our own is 'persona' — namely, role

[6] S. T. Lowry, 'The Classical Greek Theory of Natural Resource Economics', *Land Economics*, XLI, No. 3 (Aug 1965) p. 208.
[7] *Laws*, XI, 918.

or mask. In late Greek or Roman speech it means 'the public aspect and mien' of man, which for classical man is tantamount to the essence and kernel of him. . . . What is indicated is not the personality (that is, an unfolding of inward possibilities in active striving) but a permanent and self-contained posture strictly adapted to the so-to-say plastic ideal of being . . . it always amounts to the well-ordered group of tangible and publicly evident traits, defined for other men rather than specific to one's self. A man was the object and not the subject of outward life.[8]

The plastic ideal of being is inimical to a favourable evaluation of the innovatory activity which is central to economic development. Only in cases where innovation is forced on a community in response to pressures which threaten to destroy it is the innovator recognised as praiseworthy. This antagonism arises because the ideal encourages the individual to estimate his own worth by reference to the public image he creates through the exercise of a public office or role. He is not encouraged to assess himself by reference to a private, internal calculus of loss and gain in the manner in which that abstraction, 'economic man', is assumed to operate.

Discouragement of reference to a private calculus was a feature of Athenian culture. As Alvin Gouldner has observed, for the citizens of Athens

A validation of the self based upon pecuniary success is limited in effectiveness inasmuch as such activities, if not viewed with contempt, are frequently dubious and of low repute and considered of little account in comparison with performance in a public role. To a great extent, then, a man's self-image and sense of worth are shaped by his political-public involvements, and the Greeks, far more than we, tend to conceive of themselves in terms of these roles. The self is invested more heavily in the public roles; . . .[9]

On occasions, the public role may require the individual to promote innovation. Thus, a Solon may introduce reforms in

[8] O. Spengler, *The Decline of the West*, Vol. I (London, Allen and Unwin, 1954) pp. 316—17.
[9] A. W. Gouldner, *Enter Plato* (London, Routledge and Kegan Paul, 1967) p. 110.

the face of internal conflict in the state, or a Themistocles may urge public investment in naval power as a response to the menace of Persia. However, if a society is ruled by justice and has internal peace, and if it is strong enough to deal with any external threat to its autonomy, a satisfactory self-image for the individual does not require him to innovate in any significant manner. Quite the reverse. His energies, in this situation, ought to be devoted to maintenance of the social *status quo*. Under these circumstances, to promote change — and hence social disturbance — for the sake of private ends is to tarnish one's public standing and, hence, one's estimate of self-worth. The promotion of change is a matter for alien merchants, foreign bankers, and slave-managers, and their activities need to be watched closely as potential sources of subversion of the existing order.

Plato and Aristotle shared this negative attitude to innovation and development, partly because they were influenced by the ideal of being which was at its root. In Plato's approach to the concept of personality, for example, '... his assumptions seem to be, first, that the psyche reflects and is influenced by group structures, role needs, and modes of social interaction (such as strife and conversation) and, second, that the psychic states may be viewed on the model of the qualities of the group.'[10] Aristotle's Man, who by his very nature is meant for life in a *polis*, is a similar creature. True, the state exists for him, not he for the sake of the state. But the latter is his natural habitat. As Aristotle writes, 'The state comes into existence for the sake of a good life. And therefore, if the earlier forms of society are natural, so is the state, for it is the end of them, and the nature of a thing is its end. For what each thing is when fully developed, we call its nature.'[11] Man finds his fulfilment by the performance of roles dictated by the status of citizenship.

The philosophers' exclusion of analysis of future possibilities for economic growth from the realm of serious scholarship was to be the accepted practice for social thinkers in Europe for many centuries. One reason, perhaps, was the

[10] Op. cit., p. 250.
[11] Aristotle, *Politics*, trans. B. Jowett, 1252b.

continuing influence of the plastic ideal of being. Further, at the level of economic practice, this same ideal may have continued to lock in by a congruence of pressures, those individuals who possessed capacity for enterpreneurship. Planned innovation for personal gain, which was not simply a reaction to exogenous forces such as warfare or famine, was discouraged by public disapproval and private shame. There was positive disincentive, for example, against translating the mechanical inventions made in Greece into new technologies of production which might result in alteration of existing social frameworks. Although this source of disincentive was eliminated eventually in Europe through the evolution of new concepts of personality, it may continue to be effective in regions of the world which have remained in that customary historical condition of society which today is termed 'underdeveloped'.

Economics as a science of ends

The possibility that maintenance of a positive rate of economic growth is necessary to sustain an adequate scope for individual choice in role-playing or for social choice in such matters as population policy or management of the natural environment, does not seem to have been considered by either Plato or Aristotle. Such scope is ensured by achieving and holding a given level of material well-being. This belief is associated with an approach to the question of quality of life which emphasises the static aspects of the issue. Little attention is given to the variable features of the good life, which features may alter in the course of economic and social evolution. Both philosophers reason in terms of a system of natural law which, in essentials, is taken to be independent of temporal change and of location. Of Aristotle, for example, Werner Jaeger has written: 'The human world of state and society and mind appears to him not caught in the incalculable mobility of irrecapturable historical destiny, ... but as founded fast in the unalterable permanence of forms that, while they change within certain limits, remain identical in essence and purpose.'[1][2]

[1][2] Werner Jaeger, *Aristotle, Fundamentals of the History of his Development* (Oxford, Clarendon Press, 1934) p. 389.

Further, because the nature of the good life is their chief concern, when they come to consider the economics of the stationary state, the problem of scarcity is seen as mainly a question of selecting ends. The allocation of scarce means under conditions of economic stability, the issue which had been central in Hesiod's conception of economics, is pushed to the margin of their schema. The outlook is crystallised in Plato's statement, in *Laws* (V.736), that 'poverty results from increase of man's desires, not from diminution of his property.' Aristotle gives a detailed exposition of the conception involved.

For Aristotle, economics is concerned chiefly with the ordering of human purpose and function within the two dominant economic institutions of his day — the household and the state. There are no important distinctions to be made here between the two institutions. He accepts Plato's view, expressed in the *Statesman* (259), that small states are like large households and that 'politics' and 'economics' are terms which are freely interchangeable. Economics then, is an exercise in government or management, and the primary responsibility of the manager is choice of goals to be pursued. The economic problem is primarily a problem of selection among competing ends. The studies of an economist are related mainly to the establishment of priorities with respect to aims, rather than the ordering of means to achieve a set of aims which should be taken by him as given. The difficulties imposed by scarcity can be solved as readily by readjustment of human attitudes and ends, as by reallocation or multiplication of available means.

In his *Politics*, Aristotle writes that 'household management attends more to men than to the acquisition of inanimate things, and to human excellence more than to the excellence of property which we call wealth.'[13] He distinguishes between *oikonomike* (economics) and *chrematistike* (wealth-making, or, the science of supply). 'The art of household management', he affirms, 'is not identical with the art of getting wealth, for the one uses the material which the other provides.'[14] His approach here is akin to that expressed

[13] Aristotle, op. cit., 1259b.
[14] Op. cit., 1256a.

in the following statement from the German sociologist Max Weber: 'Economic action is primarily oriented to the problem of choosing the end to which a thing shall be applied; technology, to the problem, given the end, of choosing the appropriate means.'[15]

In Aristotle's view, economics is not the competing technology it has tended to become in the hands of many of its twentieth-century practitioners. Much of the engineering-style literature which pervades modern professional journals and monographs in the field would seem pointless to him. This pointlessness stems, given his perspective, from the dissociation of that literature from explicit consideration of what he takes to be the central question of human thought and action, the nature of the happy life.

Quality of life, according to Aristotle, depends mainly on the ends to which acquired possessions are put. The multiplication or the more efficient allocation of possessions comprise necessary but not sufficient elements in the solution of difficulties imposed by scarcity. In his opinion, 'A good man may make the best even of poverty and disease, and the other ills of life; but he can only attain happiness, under the opposite conditions . . . This makes men fancy that external goods are the cause of happiness, yet we might as well say that a brilliant performance on the lyre was to be attributed to the instrument and not to the skill of the performer.'[16]

It is pointless then to investigate means of increasing the community's command over the use of resources while dissociating the investigator from analytical involvement in the question of how that enhanced command might result in a genuine improvement of quality of life for the community. The investigator cannot rest in a vague generalisation such as 'ends are various' or claim that his evaluation of ends must be derived from sources outside the discipline of economics, if his work is to be meaningful for Aristotle. Modern social scientists have been criticised in these terms by the American, Norton E. Long. He writes that many of these scientists

[15] M. Weber, *The Theory of Social and Economic Organisation* (Glencoe, Free Press, 1947) p. 162.
[16] Aristotle, op. cit., 1332a.

... are in the unhappy position of seeming to believe that
reason and evidence have persuasive roles in scientific
inquiry but are somehow either absent, or radically
different in their efficacy in evaluation. Since it is through
evaluation that we determine what is important, it comes
perilously close to saying of the important we have
nothing important to say ... For social scientists concerned with human affairs, the evaluatory impasse has
meant a serious lack of direction and entrapment in an
outmoded view of science as a descriptive enterprise
uninformed by human purpose.'[17]

With Aristotle, evaluation of purpose is the primary task of
economic enquiry.

The acquisition of means

Despite this emphasis on selection of ends, the provision of
means is not excluded entirely by Aristotle. It has a
subordinate role to play in economic thought and activity.
He allows that 'Of the art of acquisition then, there is one
kind which by nature is a part of the management of a
household, in so far as the art of household management
must either find ready to hand, or itself provide, such things
necessary to life, and useful for the community of the family
or state, as can be stored.'[18] This acquisitive activity which is
subordinate to rational selection of ends, is to be
differentiated from acquisition which is irrational and uneconomic in Aristotle's view. The latter involves the heedless
accumulation of phoney wealth, usually in the form of
money. Unchecked by sober assessment of the purposes of
acquisitive activity, men are led into the uneconomic pursuit
of accumulation for its own sake. Men dissipate their energies
in the absurd and sub-human process of money-making as an
end in itself.

At this point in his *Politics*, the eighth chapter of the first
book, Aristotle is making a distinction that was also to be
used for analytical purposes by Karl Marx. There is one

[17] N. E. Long, introduction to E. J. Meehan, *Value Judgement and Social Science*
(1969), pp. v-vi.
[18] Aristotle, op. cit., 1256b.

process in which money is exchanged for commodities in order to obtain money (M–C–M'), and another in which money is merely a middle term facilitating the exchange of one bundle of commodities for another (C–M–C'). The latter is economic activity, and a subsidiary part of the discipline of economics is concerned with it, according to Aristotle. The former is uneconomic and not worth serious study. Hence the accumulation of capital, particularly in the form of money, is designated by Aristotle as uneconomic to the extent that, to use Marx's phrase, 'the accumulation of money capital is an end in itself.'

Aristotle's condemnation of wealth-making betrays his lack of sympathy with the Athenian capitalists by reason of a feature of their psychology that was to be portrayed clearly by Karl Marx. 'Use values', Marx wrote, 'must therefore never be looked on as the real aim of the capitalist, neither must the profit on any single transaction. The restless, never-ending process of profit-making alone is what he aims at.'[19] This divorce of accumulation from use-value makes the former irrational and uneconomic for Aristotle. The only rational type of accumulation is that conducted with a clear understanding of the personal and communal consumption ends the accumulated commodies are meant to serve. 'Riches', he states, 'may be defined as a number of instruments to be used in a household or in a state.'[20] The needs of the *polis* or of an individual household can be established, he believes, in a reasonably objective fashion, given the circumstances pertaining in any one community. Therefore, there is a definable limit to the 'number of instruments' which will ensure fulfilment of those needs. It can also be remarked that this failure of Aristotle to see any useful purpose in accumulation or acquisition that is not related directly to consumption is quite consistent with his own and Plato's focus on quality of life in a stationary state. The rationale of encouraging such a form of acquisitive activity in a community is the promotion of economic growth which they regard as damaging.

[19] K. Marx, *Capital*, Vol. I (London, Allen and Unwin, 1938) p. 130.
[20] Aristotle, op. cit, 1256b.

Through the stress on the primacy of use-values in economic reasoning, Aristotle sought to guard against an analytical error that was to be the source of considerable confusion in later thought. This error was the failure to distinguish between accumulated capital and the services to be derived from that capital. A clear distinction between the two did not emerge in modern Economics until the publication of Leon Walras' *Elements of Pure Economics* (1874–7). Walras described the distinction as the 'key to the whole of pure economics' and as essential for any valid theory of price determination. Aristotle's conception of economics, embracing the demarkation of economic and uneconomic acquisitive activity, also emphasised this distinction as a key feature of the discipline. Accumulated capital is of economic significance only where it is yielding services that ultimately serve consumption needs of men. If no such services are present, as in the case of acquisition of money capital for its own sake, the accumulation is meaningless. This point is illustrated in the *Politics* by reference to the Midas story with which his readers were quite familiar:

> Originating in the use of coin the art of getting wealth is generally thought to be chiefly concerned with it and to be the art which produces riches and wealth, having to consider how they may be accumulated. Indeed riches is assumed by many to be only a quantity of coin, . . . But how can that be wealth of which a man may have a great abundance and yet perish with hunger, like Midas in the fable, whose insatiable prayer turned everything that was set before him into gold?[21]

Elsewhere in the *Politics*, Aristotle indicates that capital is not obliged to yield a direct service to the consumer to have economic significance. He draws a distinction between capital whose services are direct — 'possessions' or 'instruments of action' — and capital providing use-value indirectly — 'instruments of production'.[22] Acquisition of capital of both varieities is part of household management. It is noteworthy, however, that nowhere is there any clear

[21] Op. cit., 1257b.
[22] Op. cit., 1254a.

perception that accumulated capital yields a meaningful service to its possessor by satisfying, through its very possession, the owner's need for liquidity. This failure on Aristotle's part is most inhibiting for his theory of money. It has serious consequences also for the subsequent development of monetary theory. However, the lack of perception at this point is consistent with his adherence to a conception of human personality which stressed public role-playing rather than the existence of a private, internal calculus of loss and gain.

Xenophon and other Socratic contributions

There is a small number of other writings in the Socratic mould which touch on issues raised in this chapter. Some of these are by Xenophon (430–354 B.C.), while others come from unknown hands. Xenophon, a contemporary of Plato, was an Athenian landed aristocrat who, while on military service, was elected general of an army of Greek mercenaries stranded in Mesopotamia. He led them home successfully, but was later exiled from Athens and retired to farm on a small scale near Olympia. Here, in retirement, he wrote the bulk of his works.

Xenophon's *Economist* is an orthodox Socratic treatise on estate and house management. It is cast in the form of a dialogue between Socrates and Ischomachus, an aristocratic Athenian farmer. The conversation of the two ranges over a variety of practical topics including the training of wives and servants, the physical arrangement of household possessions, and the daily round of the head of the house. Discussion of domestic detail is interspersed with generalisations which embody the same stress on the choice among ends as the central concern of economics as is present in the writings of Plato and Aristotle.

For example in the dialogue (II, 3), Socrates claims that he has solved the difficulties imposed by scarcity in a much more efficient fashion than one, Critobulus, who is much more affluent in terms of possessions than Socrates. The superiority of Socrates' solution resides in the fact that his ends are better adjusted to his personal means than is Critobulus' style of living to the resources available to him.

An anonymous work, the *Eryxias*, also takes up the question of resource availability in relation to the happy life. Once again, the judicious ordering of ends is claimed to be a far more significant activity in terms of the scarcity problem than is multiplication and allocation of means. Those who are rich in goods can be miserable, if their desires are not well adjusted to the means available for their satisfaction.

A second feature of Xenophon's *Economist* is its adherence to the same vision of the role of man, in relation to natural forces as was evident with Aristotle. Man adjusts to or harmonises those forces rather than re-shaping or transforming them. With respect to human activity aimed at the production of commodities, for example, it cannot be said that man creates something that can be termed 'new'. Instead, in such activity man is 'arranging the relevant natural elements so as to form a more desirable, but naturally inherent result, for example a chord rather than a discord.'[23] He is harmonising natural elements, not changing their essential properties by virtue of his agency.

This understanding of productive activity is linked to a type of agricultural fundamentalism which looks forward to the doctrines of some of the Roman writers and of the French Physiocrats of the eighteenth century. Primary industry, according to Xenophon (V, 17), is the key source of all wealth: 'It has been nobly said that husbandry is the mother and nurse of the other arts. For when husbandry flourishes all the other arts are in good fettle; but whenever the land is compelled to lie waste the other arts of landsmen and mariners alike well-nigh perish.' Human economic activity whether in production or distribution, is most meaningful in the case of agricultural production, where men are merely the managers of what are natural processes. The agricultural case is the exemplar for all other forms of economic endeavour.

This premier rating for agriculture is emphasised in an anonymous work, the *Oeconomica*, which used to be attributed to Aristotle but is now considered to be a contribution of a disciple. It consists of two short chapters in

---

[23] S. T. Lowry, op. cit., p. 204.

which the superiority of a life connected with farming is a major theme. Farming is the most morally commendable form of employment, since it is bound up with the eminently 'natural' task of deriving a living directly from the soil. Again, it is a just occupation in which one can prosper without disadvantaging one's fellow man. Prosperity gained through trade, in contrast, is like the fruits gathered from war and conquest. Success in trade and war must always be at the expense of some other party. This latter sentiment may help explain Aristotle's condemnation of retail trading. It also exhibits an affiliation with mercantilist doctrine in which international trade, at least, is seen often as a type of warfare. This doctrine found no definitive counter-argument until the emergence of the theory of comparative advantage in the nineteenth century.

A third notable element in the economic thought of Xenophon is his treatment of the division of labour. He penetrates the economics of the phenomenon to a greater degree than does Plato. The matter is considered in the second chapter of the eighth book of a work, the *Cyropaedia*, which was written about 362 B.C., some twenty years after Plato's *Republic*. Here, Xenophon writes:

> But in great cities, because there is a large demand for each article, a single craft is enough for a living, or sometimes, indeed, no more than a single branch of a craft; — we find one man making men's boats only; and another, women's only; and another, cobbling or cutting out merely, for a livelihood; one man lives by cutting out garments, another by fitting together the pieces. The smaller the work the greater the skill in the craftsman.

In this passage there is recognition of the link between fractionalisation of production functions and greater quality or quantity of output. Also, it is seen that the extent to which the division of labour can be taken, is a variable dependent on the size of the market. Great cities, Xenophon observes, afford the opportunity for extensions which smaller units do not offer. These insights bring the Socratic analysis of the division of labour much closer to that of Adam Smith than a reading of Plato only would suggest.

3 Four Issues in Socratic Economic Analysis

The philosophers did not leave a legacy which merely recommended a manner of approach to economic issues. Their concern with the origins of social life and the maintenance of just relationships within it gave rise to a series of insights on particular problems in economics. Apart from those noted above in connection with their conception of economics, these insights included influential analyses touching on the theories of money and interest, the question of communal versus private ownership of resources, and the theory of value. The contributions of Aristotle in these areas are of special significance for the future development of economic thought in Europe. It is quite impossible to chart the course of that development without an appreciation of the positions he took and the ways in which those positions were interpreted. As one modern scholar has observed, 'Aristotle's influence on medieval city economy exerted through Thomas Aquinas was as great as later that of Adam Smith and David Ricardo on nineteenth century world economy.'[1]

Opinion is divided sharply on whether or not Aristotle's widespread influence was something which economists should welcome in retrospect. For one writer, Aristotle is 'the first analytical economist', and it is he 'who laid the foundations of science and who first posed the economic problems with which all later thinkers have been concerned.'[2] For another, Aristotelian economic theory 'was to exert an influence both far-reaching and disastrous over

---

[1] K. Polanyi, 'Aristotle Discovers the Economy', in Karl Polanyi, Conrad M. Arensberg and Harry W. Pearson (eds), *Trade and Market in the Early Empires* N.Y., Free Press 1957) p. 65.
[2] E. Roll, *A History of Economic Thought* (London, Faber, 1961) p. 31.

historians and theologians of succeeding centuries.' This second writer sees Aristotle's 'primitivism and ruralism' as dead weights which inhibited the thinkers of Rome and the middle ages, such that tendencies to genuine economic analysis were thwarted. In particular, Aristotle was an arch-enemy of economics, since he was equipped with 'a mind that never really understood what currency was' and turned his back on any 'prospect of indefinite increase of real wealth'.[3] That such a difference of opinion should exist is explained to a great extent by the combination of bold analytical initiatives and sometimes puzzling failures encountered in the analyses considered in this chapter.

The nature and functions of money

In the *Republic*, Plato recognises that the presence of a division of labour in society gives rise to the need for exchanges of commodities amongst its citizens. The process of exchange will be facilitated by the introduction of 'a currency to serve as a token for purposes of exchange'. The end or purpose of money then is its action as a medium of exchange, and for this function a mere symbol or token can suffice.[4] The material of which money is composed is of little or no account.

Here, Plato is adopting a theory of money which can be called 'non-metallist'. Money, to function effectively as money, need not consist of a material that has a value independent of its role as money. Community contract or state fiat establishes the status of something as the medium of exchange. There is no necessary 'commodity' dimension to that medium because of its substance. That Plato was consistent in his non-metallism is illustrated by a passage from the *Laws*, his last written work. In this passage he advocates a type of policy that was an anathema to orthodox monetary theorists of eighteenth- and nineteenth-century Europe. He proposes a divorce between international trading currency and the internal circulating medium of the city-state. The latter, he believes, should be devoid of intrinsic,

[3] The foregoing criticisms are those of E. A. Havelock, *The Liberal Temper in Greek Politics* (London, Cape, 1957) pp. 359–64.
[4] *Republic*, 371B. See also *Laws*, 742, A. B.; 918B.

material value. Plato writes:

> For these reasons we say our people should possess
> coined money which is legal tender among themselves but
> valueless elsewhere. As regards the universal Hellenic·
> coinage — for the sake of expeditions and foreign visits, as
> well as embassies or any other missions necessary for the
> State, if there be need to send someone abroad — for such
> objects as these it is necessary that the State should always
> possess Hellenic money. If a private citizen ever finds
> himself obliged to go abroad he may do so, after first
> getting leave from the magistrates; and should he come
> home with any surplus of foreign money, he shall deposit
> it with the State and take for it an equivalent in home
> coinage . . . [5]

This system of currency control, so familiar in twentieth-
century practice, is not proposed out of any concern with
economic policy issues. Rather, as in the case of his advocacy
of a division of labour, it is based on moral considerations.
He is not concerned, for example, with balance of payments
equilibrium or with the appropriate volume of internal
money circulation. Instead, through this system, he is hoping
to curb any excessive involvement by the citizens of the state
in money making or in the pursuit of vulgarising occupations.
Here, as elsewhere, the moral quality of life is the decisive
issue. He also has his eye on the maintenance of general social
equilibrium, as against mere economic stability. Social
equilbrium can be disturbed by too much regard for private
monetary gain in the community.

Aristotle follows Plato's emphases in his own discussion of
money in the fifth book of his *Nicomachean Ethics*. The tone
of the discussion is non-metallist, and money's significance is
attributed to its function as the medium of exchange.
However, Aristotle expands considerably on his teacher's
remarks. In this fifth book, Aristotle investigates the problem
of justice in commodity exchange, and the role of money is
considered in that context. For the exchange of commodities, he argues, it is necessary to make unlike commodities

[5] *Laws*, trans. R. G. Bury, (Harvard University Press, 1952) Bk. V, 742.

comparable. It was to achieve this end that money was invented. Money acts as a type of middle term, measuring all things, and indicating their greater or lesser value, e.g. just how many shoes are equal to a house or a certain quantity of food. He continues,

> All goods must therefore be measured by some one thing, as we said before. Now this unit is in truth demand, which holds all things together (for if men did not need one another's goods at all, or did not need them equally, there would be either no exchange or not the same exchange); but money has become by convention a sort of representative of demand; and this is why it has the name 'money' [i.e., currency] — because it exists not by nature but by law [current law] as it is in our power to change it and make it useless.[6]

Money is what it is, for Aristotle, because it has conventional acceptance for the performance of certain functions. Money is not what it is because of any intrinsic or 'natural' properties it may possess. As with Plato, it is a creature of the law. To Plato's description of the function of money as a medium of exchange, Aristotle adds its role as a unit of account, a measuring rod. Then, in a later passage he distinguishes a third function of money, viz., as a medium for deferment of consumption. Aristotle writes: 'And for the future exchange — that if we do not need a thing now we shall have it ever we do need it — money is as it were our surety; for it must be possible for us to get what we want by bringing the money.'[7]

The philosopher goes on immediately at this point to recognise that this third function of money gives rise to a problem, a difficulty connected with the introduction of the dimension of time into the operation of a network of social exchanges of commodities. The service to society which money offers by facilitating deferment of consumption opens up the possibility of social disequilibrium arising out of fluctuations in the purchasing power of money. The unit of currency today may be worth more or less in terms of goods

[6] *Ethics*, 1133a.
[7] Op. cit., 1133b.

than it will be in the future, yet the continuance of a viable exchange system requires the maintenance of equity and comparability of purchasing power over time. Aristotle states the problem as follows:

> Now the same thing happens to money itself as to goods — it is not always worth the same; yet it tends to be steadier. This is why all goods must have a price set on them; for then there will always be exchange, and if so, association of man with man. Money, then, acting as a measure makes goods commensurate and equates them; for neither would there have been association if there were not exchange, nor exchange if there were not equality, nor equality if there were not commensurability.[8]

The above passage also indicates Aristotle's policy for countering this threat to social equilibrium. 'All goods' he states, 'must have a price set on them.' Viability of a domestic system of commodity trade in a monetised economy requires statutory fixation of money prices. Aristotle fears the disruptive consequences of a regime of *laissez faire* marketing as much as those stemming from a process of economic growth. His entire examination of exchange justice betrays this fear. He is at one with that section of the aristocracy in Athens who look with distaste and apprehension at the trend to wider free-market intrusions into the more traditional pattern of trade and exchange. Throughout the discussion of justice in exchange, in which these observations on money occur, Aristotle is not considering how prices are formed by the operation of supply-demand mechanisms in markets. Instead, he is putting forward criteria for statutory price fixation in a stable economy.[9] In fact, in a full reading of Aristotle on exchange justice, he emerges as an advocate of a comprehensive policy of income and price stability. Of course, his advocacy is based on slightly different grounds from those of modern economists who advocate the same course. Aristotle's grounds are much more

---

[8] Loc. cit.
[9] Cf. K. Polanyi, op. cit, pp. 83—91. This aspect of Aristotle's thought is also discussed in the later section of this chapter on value theory.

like those of the modern politicians who choose to accept the advocacy of the economists involved.

When he returns to the subject of money in the ninth chapter of the first book of his *Politics*, Aristotle considers it not in the context of exchange justice, but rather in relation to the form of acquisitive activity which he condemns as uneconomic. This activity, we saw in Chapter 2, is the drive to accumulate private monetary capital without reflection on the use-values such accumulation might serve. The origins of this drive are bound up with the historical widening of boundaries to trade and exchange, and the invention of money.

According to Aristotle's account, barter systems are established as formerly isolated, self-sufficient households begin to trade. Then, as the scope of trade widens, money is introduced. He writes:

> When the inhabitants of one country became more dependent on those of another, and they imported what they needed, and exported what they had too much of, money necessarily came into use. For the various necessaries of life are not easily carried about, and hence men agreed to employ in their dealings with each other something which was intrinsically useful and easily applicable to the purposes of life, for example iron, silver and the like. Of this the value was at first measured simply by size and weight, but in process of time they put a stamp upon it to save the trouble of weighing and to mark the value.[10]

This passage retains the view of the *Ethics* that the dominant end of money is to serve as a medium of exchange. However, it represents an unusual departure by Aristotle into an aspect of the economics of development (admittedly, only in retrospect), and it suggests a 'natural' as well as a conventional basis for the existence of money. This natural basis is not in production but in trade where 'the various necessaries of life are not easily carried about.' Further, he

[10] Aristotle, *Politics*, 1257a.

observes that historically, money has consisted of materials that are useful apart from their employment as money.

In later eras of economic thought when, from the fourteenth century onwards, certain monetary theorists wished to argue that money must consist of a material that has a value independent of its role as money, this piece of Aristotelian pseudo-history was invoked frequently in support of the case. A remarkably durable segment of Aristotle's economics, it was repeated by Adam Smith, by orthodox writers on money in the nineteenth century, and lives on in school textbooks to this day. Because of this passage, Aristotle is often portrayed as the founder of the school of theoretical metallism, the school which dominated monetary analysis from the age of the mercantilists until the middle decades of the twentieth century. Yet, this portrait is based on a misunderstanding of his position, and on a too ready acceptance of the use made of Aristotle by writers who were out to promote such policies as maximisation of a national inflow of precious metals or rejection of currency debasement as a tool of public financing or employment creation.

Plato, and Aristotle in the *Ethics*, are both non-metallists, as we have seen. For them there is no necessary connection between the functions of money and the material of which it is made. Conventional acceptance and/or state ruling gives a currency its status. In the *Politics*, Aristotle adds one further requirement, the material must be 'easily carried about'. Thereafter, it is a matter of history, not functional necessity, that precious metals were employed. Where state ruling is not effective, both Plato and Aristotle seem to suggest that conventional acceptance may require the use of precious metals. This is the case in international trade, the type of trade which Aristotle is considering when he mentions metal content and which Plato recognises may require his state in the *Laws* to hold metallic coinage in a public treasury. However, in domestic exchange, where local statute can be decisive, neither Plato nor Aristotle have any doubt that an effective currency system can be established by means of tokens which have no value apart from their function as 'representatives of demand'.

The payment of interest

Plato, in a manner typical of the moralists of antiquity, expresses general opposition to the practice of interest payment on loans. In his case, the opposition is based on the belief that the existence of obligations to pay interest is a major threat to the maintenance of peace and social solidarity in a state. Athenians of his day had such sobering examples of local history as the civil strife early in the sixth century B.C. to remind them of how the very existence of the state could be threatened by escalation of internal debt repayment premiums. On that particular occasion, only the reforms of Solon involving debt remission and a ban on loans on personal security, saved the state.

In the *Laws*, Plato goes as far as suggesting that repayment of voluntary extensions of credit should not be enforceable at law. He states, '. . . they shall exchange money for goods, and goods for money, neither party giving credit to the other; and he who gives credit must be satisfied, whether he obtains his money or not, for in such exchanges he will not be protected by law.'[11] However, the case is somewhat different where involuntary extensions of credit are concerned. He allows that where a supplier has not been paid when he has met a customer's order correctly, then, after a time, the supplier may oblige the customer to pay interest in addition to the original amount due.[12] This exception which he makes to the prohibition of interest-taking in the case of delay in payment was to become crucial in later centuries of economic thought. Out of this very exception was to flow the scholastic analysis of damages incurred in lending, and eventually, an investigation of interest-taking which took the scholastics to the heart of certain basic theoretical issues in economics. Again, the distinction between voluntary and involuntary grants of credit is a quite fundamental element in scholastic thinking and served to shape the course of their enquiry into the economics of lending.

Aristotle is sweeping in his condemnation of professional

[11] Plato, *Laws*, trans. B. Jowett, 850. See also 915.
[12] Op. cit., 921

money-lending. However, this condemnation unlike Plato's is
characterised by an attempt to link his opposition to
interest-taking with the theory of money. This step is taken
in the context of his discussion of economic and uneconomic
acquisitive activity. Money-lending as a form of business is
regarded as falling within the second category. It is a
commercial pursuit uninformed by reflection on the ends of
economic life. Merchants and bankers are prone to lose a
grasp of the real meaning of wealth, and this is even more
likely to occur in the case of money lenders. The latters'
vocation, in fact, is not even connected with commodity
exchange, and it involves a distortion of the true function of
money. 'The trade of the petty usurer is hated most,' states
Aristotle, 'and with most reason: it makes a profit from
currency itself, instead of making it from the process which
currency was meant to serve. Currency came into existence
merely as a means of exchange; usury tries to make it
increase.'[13]

These words of Aristotle resound throughout later economic discussion. His linking of the condemnation of
interest-taking with the theory of money had far-reaching
consequences. Money, on this view, has a fixed, natural end.
That end is to facilitate exchange. To use it for another
purpose is unnatural, and hence immoral. Commodities,
according to Aristotle, can be used for consumption or for
exchange, but this duality is not present in the case of
money. Given the one, fixed end, interest-taking implies
unnatural use of money, a distortion of its character as a
social institution.

In his *Ethics*, Aristotle had allowed that there are two
subsidiary functions of money which flow from its use as the
medium of exchange. One of these is its function as a unit of
account, the other is as a medium for deferment of
consumption or security for future exchanges. To modern
economists this second function might suggest that there is a
basis for interest-taking in Aristotle's monetary theory. It
suggests that a money balance held by an individual confers
on him a certain service, the satisfaction of knowing now that

[13] Aristotle, op. cit., 1258b.

certain future expenditure requirements can be met. To deprive oneself of that satisfaction by lending the money concerned warrants compensation by way of receipt of interest. Yet this idea escaped Aristotle and it did not enter into economic analysis until very much later in the writings of the Belgian scholastic Leonard Lessius at the outset of the seventeenth century. One reason for Aristotle's failure of perception here may be his adherence to a plastic idea of being, as noted above in Chapter 2. Whatever the reason, it was a failure that had serious results for the future progress of economics.

It is also significant that the philosopher does not consider money as capital, the employment of which in productive activity gives rise to a legitimate return. His distaste for accumulation, his rejection of growth, and sharp distinction between money and commodities combined to block this as a possible line of reasoning on interest. The idea of interest payment as a legitimate transfer payment out of the profits accruing from the productive enterprise was not to emerge as a prominent feature of European economic thought until after the Reformation.

One persistent fallacy concerning Aristotle's position is that it is based on the notion that money is 'barren metal'. It is sometimes claimed that he argued that because metal cannot breed, any return on money over and above the principal loaned could be due in no way to that principal. However, this is not the case. It is clear that the condemnation of interest-taking by Aristotle turns on a supposed distortion of the social function of money. The argument by way of genetic analogy is not his. In fact it appears to have had its origin in fourteenth-century Europe during a popular intellectual vogue when lesser lights felt obliged to claim the authority of *the* philosopher even for points which were misrepresentations of him or questionable inferences from his works.[14] It was about this time too, that the practice began of invoking Aristotle in support of the doctrine of monetary metallism which he had not expounded.

---

[14] E. Cannan, W. P. Ross, J. Bonar, P. H. Wicksteed, 'Who said "Barren Metal"?', *Economica*, No. 5 (June 1922) pp. 105–11.

The signal contribution of Aristotle on interest was to link discussion of the morality of its payment to analysis of the functions of money. Because his appreciation of those functions had limitations he failed to find an economic basis for interest. Above all, he failed to ask the question why, in the absence of fraud or force, the rate of interest was not zero. Greek legal codes at the time did not generally prohibit interest entirely, although regulation of maximum rates was not uncommon. A positive rate of interest was a social phenomenon requiring explanation in his day, but no explanation emerged and the cost in terms of the future progress of economic analysis was a high one.

Communal versus private ownership

An important issue on which Plato and Aristotle disagreed was the position of the ruling class of an ideal city state with respect to ownership of property. In the *Republic*, Plato's elite, the intellectuals and the military, are to hold property and women, as well as rear children, in common. By these means he hopes to minimise disputes within the group and to detach it from debilitating involvement in the accumulation of personal wealth. Communal ownership is put forward as an ideal again in his later work, the *Laws*. However, here, as a practical approximation of the ideal, he proposes that a series of limits be set on the amount and type of property the citizen can hold as his own. One example of such restrictions, we have seen above, is the retention of any private foreign currency earnings by the central state authorities.

Aristotle, in contrast, advocates private ownership for his ruling class, although most of the other inhabitants of his state will possess little or nothing that is exclusively their own. Plato's type of communism is criticised on a variety of grounds, one of which is a supposed lack of economic incentive when resources are pooled. In a fashion that recalls the reasoning of Democritus, he argues that better use will be made of available resources under a system where private possession is the rule. 'That which is common to the greatest number has the least care betowed upon it,' he contends in the *Politics*, 'Everyone thinks chiefly of his own, hardly at all of the common interest; and only when he is himself concerned as an individual.'[15] A division of resources, like a division of labour, makes for greater efficiency in the community.

This particular argument concerning the division of resources plays a minor role only in Aristotle's rejection of a communal form of social and economic organisation. Yet it is an argument that was to be very significant for the development of economic thought in Europe. In the hands of St Thomas Aquinas and his successors, this line of reasoning, backed by the authority of Aristotle, provides a major rationale for their acceptance of a free market economy as a framework for economic analysis. It becomes a basic ground on which communistic aspects of living in early Christian communities are held to be inapplicable to the wider society of medieval Europe.

The theory of value

The nature of Aristotle's contribution to value theory is a topic that has given rise to considerable controversy. Commentators, both old and new, are quite divided on the question of the philosopher's true position on the matter. Passages from his works have been cited in support of widely conflicting approaches to value determination, and some writers have gone so far as to suggest that on this issue he has nothing to offer by way of meaningful analysis. Even if this latter were true, it would be still necessary to consider Aristotle as a contributor, since he has exercised a profound influence on later writers who are recognised as significant figures in this fundamental area of economic enquiry.

Much of the continuing controversy is due to the oblique fashion in which Aristotle approached the topic of value, when compared with modern and even medieval approaches to the same issue. For example, in the key passages on exchange of commodities in his *Nicomachean Ethics* he is discussing a type of 'international' trade rather than domestic exchange. Further, he is reasoning in terms of a concept of social as against market equilibrium, and he is employing a mathematical model which is not clearly articulated. In

[15] Aristotle's attack on Plato's communism is set out in detail in the second book of the *Politics*.

addition, he locates exchange transactions within a category of justice which is given no distinct title. There is little wonder that his true position has been the subject of deep division amongst his readers. Nevertheless, in its oblique manner, Aristotle's performance in this area was seminal.

Given the difficulties involved in appreciating Aristotle's work relating to value, it is useful to highlight some of its more prominent features at the outset. First, that work must be considered in relation to his distinctions between various types of justice. Second, it can be seen to embody a strand of thought which seems to commit him to a utility theory of value. Third, there is another strand which has suggested to many that Aristotle's was a labour theory of value. Fourth, he combines these strands in a model of pricing which appears to be based, although most obscurely, on Pythagorean mathematics. Fifth, his schema of commodity exchange is not one in which many potential buyers of a particular commodity face a number of potential sellers of the same commodity. He is dealing with a case in which two agents, who are simultaneously both buyer and seller, exchange two commodities. His aim is to establish what the terms of trade should be when two independent and autonomous households exchange their surplus produce. He is analysing the conditions of inter-household trade and reaches conclusions which are analogous to those of later pioneer theorists on international trade. Unlike modern economists, he is not concerned with the process of price formation in localised markets.

Types of justice
The most important statements relating to value are located in the fifth book of Aristotle's *Nicomachean Ethics* (1129a–33b), where he is discussing the nature of justice and its application in the matter of exchange transactions. Exchange of goods in society is seen by Aristotle as a matter of the persons involved contributing to the material well-being of the community of which they are members. It is a practice which is justified in so far as one householder transfers his surplus produce to another and receives a different type of produce in return, thereby ensuring that the means of

maintaining an adequate standard of living is available to all citizens and their dependants.

This practice of mutual support is viewed as 'natural'. It is distinguished from the business of professional commodity traders whose activities are condemned as a form of 'unnatural' exploitation of human need that is linked to that type of acquisitive behaviour which is divorced from an appreciation of use-values. Aristotle believes that inter-household trade is amenable to regulation by the canons of justice. He is not prepared to accept that justice can prevail, and hence a satisfactory condition of society maintained, where exchange of goods is given over to the wheeling and dealing of commercial marketing. Adam Smith's invisible hand which guides self-seeking traders to produce a socially beneficial result out of their collective activity remained invisible when Aristotle considered the markets of his day. The 'good conflict' of which Hesiod spoke was not seen by Aristotle to be relevant to market phenomena.

The type of justice applicable to inter-household trade is that which conforms to the formula of 'reciprocal pro-portion'. Aristotle did not give this form of justice a distinct title, although it plays a distinct role in his classifactory schema of justice. In that schema, universal justice, which involves the praiseworthy behaviour of good men in general, is distinguished from particular justice where dealings are motivated by 'the pleasure that arises from gain'. Such gain may relate to honours, or money, or personal security. One type of particular justice is distributive, and refers to the way in which honours or wealth should be dealt out in any community. Here, the apportioning of gain is in accord with the unequal contributions or variations of status which exist in the community concerned. In the community of a business partnership, for example, 'the distribution is made from the common funds according to the same ratio which the funds put into the business by the partners bear to one another.'[16]

A second type of particular justice is corrective, and this is concerned with restoring equality between parties to 'contracts' of either a voluntary or involuntary nature. Here, the

---

[16] *Ethics*, trans. W. D. Ross, 1131b. In this type of justice unequal persons are dealt with in accordance with the degrees of inequality existing between them.

persons involved are regarded as equal for purposes of the law. In an involuntary situation such as theft or assault for example, the damages to the aggrieved party to the 'contract' must be awarded without reference to his social status. Similarly, in the case of voluntary contracts, such as sale and purchase or money loans, the object initially transferred between the parties must be balanced by a subsequent transfer of its exact equivalent in money terms or by a return of the same quantity and quality of object.

Neither distributive nor corrective justice by itself fits the two-commodity case of inter-household exchange. As Aristotle writes, 'Now "reciprocity" fits neither distributive nor rectificatory justice . . . But in associations for exchange this sort of justice does hold men together — reciprocity in accordance with a proportion and not on the basis of precisely equal returns.'[17] In this case, two objects of different types are being transfered, and the exchange is made by persons who are not equals. The heads of respective households are men of differing status who possess skills of greater and lesser worth and thus make more and less meaningful contributions to the life of the city-state community. The maintenance of justice, on which the survival of any community depends, requires that the terms of trade established take account of the unequal standing of the trading parties. It also requires attention to the inequality of the two objects exchanged. Objects will differ in accord with their respective abilities to satisfy human need.

The emphasis on the relevance of the unequal standing of the persons exchanging is expressed clearly in Aristotle's attempt at an explanation of the workings of 'reciprocity in accordance with a proportion'. He writes:

> Now proportionate return is secured by cross-conjunction. Let *A* be a builder, *B* a shoemaker, *C* a house, *D* a shoe. The builder then must get from the shoemaker the latter's work, and must himself give him in return, his own. If then, first there is proportionate equality of goods, and then reciprocal action takes place, the result we mention will be effected. If not, the bargain is not equal,

[17] Op. cit., 1132b.

and does not hold; for there is nothing to prevent the work of one being better than that of the other; they must therefore be equated ... For it is not two doctors that associate for exchange, but a doctor and a farmer, or in general people who are different and unequal; but these must be equated ... The number of shoes exchanged for a house must therefore correspond to the ratio of builder to shoemaker. For if this be not so, there will be no exchange and no intercourse.[18]

At this point in his argument, Aristotle introduces the factor of satisfaction of human need as also relevant to the establishment of just terms of trade. He continues:

This proportion will not be effected unless the goods are somehow equal. All goods must therefore be measured by some one thing ... Now this unit is in truth demand [i.e., need] which holds all things together (for if men did not need one another's goods at all, or did not need them equally, there would be either no exchange or not the same exchange)...[19]

Both need and inequality of persons must be taken into account if exchanges are to be effected in an orderly manner compatible with continuity of existing social and economic relationships. If these two factors are not present, the pattern of exchange breaks down into a chaos of exploitation and social unrest. Just as Adam Smith's 'laws' of market logic required a stable social framework within which to operate, so Aristotle's 'laws' of inter-household relationship require the establishment of peace and order. Further, in Aristotle's case, failure to operate in terms of those 'laws' will be a source of revolution and overthrow of the existing order. His 'laws' are the laws of social equilibrium.

The utility strand

Human need must be present for exchange to occur, and that need measures all goods. Such a statement by Aristotle has led many commentators to infer that his was a utility theory

[18] Op. cit., 1133a.
[19] Loc. cit.

of value. The exchange value of any article depends on its use-value or ability to satisfy want or need. This inference finds support from other passages in Aristotle's works, and by bringing them together, a coherent utility-based position on value can be constructed.

The use-value of an article or service, according to Aristotle, derives from its being productive of an individual person's good. He writes: 'Thus (e.g.) the relation of the pleasant to pleasure is like that of the useful to the good; for in each case the one produces the other. If therefore pleasure be a kind of 'good,' then also the pleasant will be a kind of 'useful;' for clearly it may be taken to be productive of good, seeing that pleasure is good.'[20] Further, Aristotle appears to attach a purely subjective status to use-value, stating that, '. . . the useful is not permanent but is always changing,' and illustrating this statement by instances of sudden shifts in human desires and motives.[21] Like Democritus, he observes that, at some point, the use-value of any one article will begin to decline as the quantity of the article possessed increases: '. . . external goods have a limit, like any other instrument, and all things useful are of such a nature that where there is too much of them, they must either do harm, or at any rate be of no use to their possessors . . .'[22] Aristotle is also aware that the use-value of an article can be enhanced by the opportunity to consume it in a conspicuous manner: 'Again, those things which we are seen to possess are better than those which we are not seen to possess, since the former have the air of reality. Hence wealth may be regarded as a greater good if its existence is known to others.'[23]

The demand for an article or service is seen by Aristotle to be a function of its use-value, and demand will vary as the range of use of the article is extensive or limited. In the course of a general discussion of 'desirability' he writes: 'Moreover, you should distinguish in how many senses "desirable" is used, and with a view to what ends, e.g. expediency or honour or pleasure. For what is useful for all

[20] Aristotle, *Topics*, 124a.
[21] *Ethics* 1156a.
[22] *Politics*, 1323b.
[23] *Rhetoric*, trans. W. Rhys Roberts, 1365b.

or most of them may be taken to be more desirable than what is not useful in like manner.'[24] It is by the expression of use value through demand that the exchange value of an article can be established. Demand, as we have seen above, is the unit by which goods are measured, and which 'holds all things together.'[25]

Aristotle adds that value will be influenced by scarcity or rarity. He states that 'what is rare is a greater good than what is plentiful. Thus gold is a better thing than iron, though less useful; it is harder to get, and therefore better worth the getting.'[26] By this introduction of rarity he is not suggesting that price is directly influenced by cost of production as well as utility. Rather, he is noting that where an individual acquires a rare article, the very rarity of the article is productive of good, e.g. social prestige, sense of pride, etc. Thus, the article possesses a greater utility. 'Good too', he writes, 'are things that are a man's very own, possessed by no one else, exceptional; for this increases the value put upon them.'[27] Elsewhere, he states: 'Another rule is that the more conspicuous good is more desirable than the less conspicuous, and the more difficult than the easier; for we appreciate better the possession of things that cannot be easily acquired.'[28]

The utility strand in Aristotle's reasoning embraces an important set of insights on the subject of value. These insights recur in the writings of the scholastics, and they comprise part of the extensive statement of marginal utility theory undertaken by Austrian economists in the latter part of the nineteenth century. Some historians of economic thought have claimed that Aristotle went even further in anticipation of the Austrians. These historians attribute the discovery of the importance of diminishing utility for value determination to Aristotle, as well as the idea that the value of productive factors can be derived by imputation from the market values of final products.

[24] *Topics*, 118b.
[25] *Ethics*, 1133a.
[26] *Rhetoric*, 1364a.
[27] Op. cit., 1363a.
[28] *Topics*, 117b.

However, such attributions are of rather doubtful validity.[29] It is true that Aristotle thought that utility would decline after a certain quantity of articles were possessed or consumed. But missing from Aristotle's reasoning, although it is present in the thought of the Austrians, is the vital concept of a schedule expressing a continuous functional relationship between marginal utility and quantity consumed. Again, on the question of imputation of value, it can be observed that Aristotle clearly distinguished final goods ('instruments of action') from productive factors ('instruments of production').[30] He also adhered to the general principle that the desirability of means to an end will vary with the desirability of that end.[31] It seems reasonable to infer then, that in the case of economic quantities, Aristotle may have held that the value of non-human productive agents is determined by the value of their product. But this must remain merely an inference, as nowhere does he apply the general principle concerning ends and means to the relationship of 'instruments of action' and 'instruments of production.'

The labour-cost strand
The foregoing reasoning suggests that Aristotle stands at the head of the tradition in economic thought which ascribes the existence of value in exchange to the influence of subjective assessment of utility as expressed through market demand.[32] However, many notable scholars have found in his work, not a utility, but a labour-cost theory of value. Among these scholars are Saint Thomas Aquinas, the distinguished modern classicist W. D. Ross, and the economist Joseph Schumpeter. According to their interpretations, Aristotle is contending that goods will exchange in such a ratio as will equate costs of production rather than the satisfactions experienced in the use of goods. Schumpeter, for example, writes that, '. . . Aris-

[29] Consult, J. J. Spengler, 'Aristotle on Economic Imputation and Related Matters', *The Southern Economic Journal,* XXI (Apr 1955) pp. 371–89.
[30] Aristotle, *Politics,* 1253b.
[31] See, e.g., *Topics,* 116b.
[32] On the continuing influence of Aristotle see Emil Kauder, *A History of Marginal Utility Theory* (Princeton, Princeton University Press, 1965) esp. pp. 15–29.

totle was groping for some labour-cost theory of price which he was unable to state explicitly.'[33] If that is the case, he was working towards a position enunciated eventually by the philosopher John Locke and adopted by Adam Smith.

The possibility of this line of interpretation of Aristotle was opened by his insistence that the unequal standing of the two trading parties must be recognised in setting the terms of trade in inter-household exchange. The nature of the inequality which he had in mind was not clearly specified, and many later readers took this to refer to a difference in costs of production incurred by persons involved. Thus, in his commentary on Aristotle's *Ethics*, Aquinas wrote: 'Justice will be served if as many shoes be given in exchange for a house or for food as the builder or the farmer exceeds the cobbler in labour and costs.'[34] St Thomas also added that 'The arts will be destroyed if the workman who has made some article does not receive for it another article similar in quantity and quality. One man's labour must be compared with another's if the exchange is to be just.'[35] In this latter comment, Aquinas is referring to a particularly obscure passage in Aristotle's discussion of exchange justice (*Ethics*, 1133a) which reads that the arts 'would have been destroyed if what the patient suffered had not been just what the agent did, and of the same amount and kind.' Like his teacher St Albert the Great, Aquinas believed this passage meant that unless the terms of trade covered costs of production, supplies would not be forthcoming. St Albert wrote, 'Equal amounts of labour and expenses must be exchanged for each other if each productive effort is to receive its equivalent. If the carpenter does not receive as much in quantity and quality as corresponds to his own effort then he will discontinue to produce beds; thus the profession of the carpenter will be destroyed . . .'[36]

A host of writers through to the present day have found the same meaning in Aristotle as did St Albert and St

---

[33] J. Schumpeter, *History of Economic Analysis* (New York, Oxford University Press, 1959) p. 61.
[34] *Commentarium in X. libros Ethicorum ad Nicomachum, Liber IV*, Lectio. 9.
[35] Op. cit., Lectio. 8.
[36] *Ethicorum lib. V, tract. II*, Cap. 7, number 28.

Thomas.[37] However, it is by no means clear that when the philosopher referred to the inequality of persons in the context of exchange he was indicating a difference in production costs. Just what Aristotle had in mind is a matter on which commentators who deny the presence of labour cost in Aristotle's thought are divided. Josef Soudek, for example, argues that for Aristotle 'skill is what creates inequality among people,' and that the different values of skills 'can be measured by the quantity of products of other skills for which (they) can be exchanged.'[38] On the other hand, Karl Polanyi contends that in Aristotle's view, 'Prices are justly set if they conform to the standing of the participants in the community, thereby strengthening the good will on which the community rests.'[39] Social standing in the type of 'status society' to which Aristotle referred was not determined in the market place as Soudek's analysis affirms. Inequality amongst men is a function of such non-economic factors as birth, political significance and religion. The relative worths of men and such skills as they might possess were determined by non-economic criteria, and a ranking of men in terms of those criteria had an autonomous impact on terms of trade. If, as Aristotle seems to suggest, variation in utility of goods offered in trade was also relevant, then two independent hierarchies of worth — that of utility and that of status — interacted to produce the effective exchange ratio in any particular instance of inter-household trading.

The formula of proportionate reciprocity

The way in which utility interacted with labour cost or labour skill or relative social status of parties to an exchange,

[37] For a critical survey of some of the relevant literature, see Josef Soudek, 'Aristotle's Theory of Exchange. An Inquiry into the Origin of Economic Analysis', *Proceedings of the American Philosophical Society*, Vol. 96, No. 1. (Feb 1952) pp 64—8.

[38] Op. cit., p. 60.

[39] K. Polanyi, op. cit., p. 80. Support for this view may be found in Aristotle's statement (*Ethics*, 1131a.) that 'all men agree that what is just in distribution must be according to merit in some sense'. Merit, for Aristotle, is not to be equated with degree of success in economic terms. It has a much broader frame of reference.

in order to produce just terms of trade is by no means clear in Aristotle's account. However, modern research suggests that the clue to their interaction is provided by appreciation of the influence of Pythagorean mathematics on Aristotle's distinctions between the workings of the different forms of particular justice.[40] The Pythagoreans had built a mysticism of numbers out of experiments in musical harmony, and Aristotle used their findings concerning mathematical relationships as tools of analysis shorn of any mystical content. Thus, underlying the operation of distributive justice is the idea of the geometric mean drawn from geometric proportion. In the case of corrective or rectificatory justice, the relevant mean is the arithmetic derived from arithmetic proportion.

It may be, that where commutative justice, the form of justice relevant to exchange between households, is concerned, the appropriate mean is the harmonic. The idea of harmonic proportion is attributed to a thinker influenced by Pythagoras, Archytas of Tarentum, who was a contemporary and friend of Plato. The mathematician Sir Thomas Heath quotes Archytas' *On Music* as follows:

> We have the arithmetic mean when, of three terms, the first exceeds the second by the same amount as the second exceeds the third; the geometric mean when the first is to the second as the second is to the third; the 'subcontrary' which we call the 'harmonic' when the three terms are such that, by whatever part of itself the first exceeds the second, the second exceeds the third by the same part of the third.[41]

The harmonic mean then, can be represented by the formula, $a - b/b - c = a/c$, where b is the harmonic mean between a and c. When Aristotle referred to reciprocal proportion he may have had the idea of harmonic proportion as developed

[40] The following remarks in this section of the chapter are based, in the main, on the findings of Josef Soudek, op. cit., and S. Todd Lowry, 'Aristotle's Mathematical Analysis of Exchange', *History of Political Economy*, Vol. 1., No. 1. (Spring 1969) pp. 44–66.

[41] Sir Thomas Heath, *A Manual of Greek Mathematics* (Oxford, Clarendon Press, 1931) p. 51.

by Archytas in mind. The interaction of persons and commodities in exchange should conform to a pattern suggested by such proportion.

Another clue to Aristotle's thought in applying proportionate reciprocity to establishment of just terms of trade is found in the writings of Euclid. The latter's *Elements* was derived from earlier Pythagorean treatises on geometry, and includes observations on proportionate reciprocity. According to Heath, Euclid affirms that 'Two magnitudes are said to be reciprocally proportional to two others when one of the first is to one of the other magnitudes as the remaining one of the last two is to the remaining one of the first.'[42] The formula of proportionate reciprocity can be written as $A/C: B/D::A/D:B/C$. On the basis of this formula, Josef Soudek claims Aristotle's analysis of exchange was intended to show that 'The ratio of exchange of two products is the reciprocal of the ratio of the utilities of what A gives away to what he receives, and conversely to what B gives away to what he receives.'[43] Soudek writes this finding as $A/C:A/D::C/D::B/D:B/C$, where C/D represents the ratio of exchange. In achieving this result, he interprets Aristotle's emphasis on inequality of persons as referring to differences in the purchasing power of their respective skills. As was seen above, such an interpretation is open to debate.

In line with Soudek's finding, S. T. Lowry is of the opinion that, for Aristotle, 'In determining fair shares in a barter arrangement between two parties, each desirous of the other's goods, the attraction is that A desires B's goods more than he desires his own, and *vice versa.* These four values make up the preconditions for trade if the respective viewpoints cross or overlap.'[44] Given these preconditions, Lowry adds, 'A formal dying pendulum-like mathematical formulation of the bargaining process within the confines of 'natural' justice and mutual benefit in trade also seems intrinsic in the extant material.'[45] Aristotle in his model of

---

[42] Sir Thomas Heath, *The Thirteen Books of Euclid's Elements*, Vol. II (Cambridge University Press, 1926) p. 189.
[43] J. Soudek, op. cit., p. 74.
[44] S. T. Lowry, op. cit., p. 51.
[45] Op. cit., p. 64.

exchange is establishing the constraints surrounding a process of price formation in which the price actually is the outcome of bargaining by the parties concerned or of arbitration which weighs the conflicting forces involved. Much of the obscurity surrounding the interaction of the determinants of terms of trade in Aristotle's model is due to the absence of adequate mathematical tools with which a bargaining or an arbitral process could be depicted.

Households versus market

In Chapter 2 it was seen that Aristotle's conception of economics as a science differed considerably from that of most modern economists. There is also a marked contrast between his understanding of what constitutes 'the economy' and the views which are prevalent today. This contrast helps account for the difficulties which modern readers experience in gaining a clear idea of his approach to pricing and, hence, the nature of his insights on the question of value.

In 1894, the French economist Leon Walras wrote, 'The whole world may be looked upon as a vast general market made up of diverse special markets, where social wealth is bought and sold. Our task is to discover the laws to which these purchases and sales tend to conform automatically.'[46] This vision of the economy as a series of inter-dependent markets operating according to the same set of basic 'laws' inherent in them, was something which informed the entire structure of neo-classical economic thought. It was anticipated to some extent by earlier thinkers, for example, the late sixteenth-century scholastic Leonard Lessius, but was obscured in the early part of the nineteenth century by the focus of the classical economists on relationships between three so-called 'classes' — the landlords, the capitalists, and the labourers. Only in the latter half of the nineteenth century did it come into its own. The vision was quite foreign to Aristotle's experience and philosophy.

For Aristotle, economic relationships are not market relationships in Walras' sense, but rather links within and

[46] L. Walras, *Elements of Pure Economics*, trans. W. Jaffe (Allen and Unwin, 1954) p. 84.

between households. There is no autonomous world of markets which cuts across household relationships. There are domestic or internal economic activities which concern the functioning of each independent household, and the public affairs of the macrocosm of the independent household, i.e. the city-state. In addition, there are external or 'foreign' activities embracing the relationships of one city-state with another, and the dealings of one household with another. When households exchange commodities, even if they are both located in the one state, it is a case of 'foreign' trade. This is the vision of economic structure which informs Aristotle's approach to pricing.

The philosopher's vision involves the existence of a sharp division between inter-household trade and local commodity marketing. It also implies that the latter is of little or no consequence, something that is not germane to the life of any society. Aristotle was able to adopt such views, since they correspond to much of the social practice of his time. Exchanges between worthy citizens of the community were not conducted by way of open-market operations, and permanent local markets were relatively rare institutions. Where these latter existed, they were often confined to the margin of a city's social framework. As Aristotle's fellow Socratic, Xenophon observes, 'The hucksters with their wares, their cries, and their vulgarities are excluded from this to another part of the city in order that their tumult may not intrude upon the orderly life of the cultured.'[47]

For Aristotle, as we have seen, 'the orderly life of the cultured' was a world apart from retailing and financial operations. When he examined the question of justice in exchange amongst his citizens, he had in mind a quite different set of relationships from those existing among the foreign merchants and alien bankers of a marketplace like the Athenian agora. The merchant and banking world of supply-demand and mechanisms was, at best, peripheral to a system of orderly interchanges between citizens. Aristotle's economy was firmly emplanted in this latter system.

[47] *Cyropaedia*, I, ii, 3.

The formation of price in open markets is not a phenomena which Aristotle explores in the interests of the analysis
of exchange justice. He does not investigate that equilibrium
mechanism which a neo-classical economist like Alfred
Marshall was able to depict by a graphical treatment in which
a horizontal axis represented total quantity of an individual
commodity and a vertical axis price per unit. Instead, his
attention is focussed on the case which Marshall chose to
treat graphically with the use of two axes, each of which
represented the total quantity of one of two commodities,
i.e. determination of the terms of trade in a situation where
two agents exchange two commodities.

The entire tone of Aristotle's discussion of exchange
suggests that he is dealing with a situation akin to international transactions. For example, when he is explaining the
role of need (demand) in inter-household exchange, he
illustrates that role by reference to inter-city trade. He
writes: 'That demand holds things together as a single unit is
shown by the fact that when men do not need one another,
i.e. when neither needs the other or one does not need the
other, they do not exchange, as we do when someone wants
what one has oneself, e.g. when people permit the export-
ation of corn in exchange for wine.'[48] This same illustration
is repeated in the *Politics* (1257a). Again, when the role of
money in exchange is dealt with, it is seen as something
which makes good 'the excess and the defect' when one
buyer/seller is offering less or demanding more in actual
commodity-value than the other. The 'balance of payments'
between the two households is brought into equilibrium by a
transfer of currency. 'Money', he states, 'becomes in a sense
an intermediate; for it measures all things, and therefore the
excess and the defect – how many shoes are equal to a house
or to a given amount of food.'[49]

If Aristotle's model of exchange is akin to that of the
two-country, two-commodity case in international trade
theory, the question arises as to the extent to which he

[48] *Ethics*, 1133b.
[49] Op. cit., 1133a.

anticipated the much later discussion of determination of the
terms of trade. Here, the pioneering work of John Stuart
Mill, which, in Alfred Marshall's reckoning,[50] 'called the
tune' for later developments, is an appropriate point of
reference. Mill's position has been summarised by Jacob
Viner as follows:

> Mill held that the equilibrium terms of trade must be
> within the upper and lower limits set by the ratios in the
> respective countries of the costs at which the two
> commodities could be produced at home, but that the
> exact location of the terms of trade would be determined
> by the demands of the two countries for each others'
> products in terms of their own products, or the 'reciprocal
> demands'. Equilibrium would be established at that ratio
> of exchange between the two commodities at which the
> quantities demanded by each country of the commodities
> which it imports from the other should be exactly
> sufficient to pay for one another, a rule which Mill labels
> the 'equation of international demand' or 'law of inter-
> national values'.[51]

Mill is dealing with the conditions of market equilibrium,
whereas Aristotle is dealing with the conditions of social
equilibrium, i.e. the just solution. However, once this
difference of focus is allowed for, their accounts of the
equilibrium terms of trade point to the operation of similar
forces. Mill's 'equation of international demand' is parallelled
by Aristotle's stress on the need for the exchange of
equivalencies between households as a condition of social
equilibrium.[52] Further, Mill's 'reciprocal demands' recall
Aristotle's isolation of relative demands or needs as key
elements in the working of 'proportionate reciprocity'.
Thirdly, the existence of definite upper and lower limits
within which the terms of trade are set is a feature of both
analyses. However, it is doubtful that Aristotle's limits,

[50] A. C. Pigou (ed.), *Memorials of Alfred Marshall* (1925) p. 451.
[51] J. Viner, *Studies in the Theory of International Trade* (London, Allen and
Unwin, 1955) p. 536.
[52] On the crucial role of exchange of equivalencies in archaic society where trade
and markets are distinct entities, see K. Polanyi, op. cit., pp. 87–91.

unlike Mill's, are merely a matter of costs of production, or that they even refer to economic cost at all. His households are not producing according to a commercial calculus. Rather, they aim at self-sufficiency as communities of consumers, while 'exporting' those surpluses with which their specialised activities as producers happen to leave them.

Aristotle's limits on determination of the terms of trade appear to be broad social determinants, bound up with inequalities of social status or acquired skills of the persons responsible for production and exchange. There is, in this respect, an attempt at a much greater degree of generalisation in the analysis of social exchange by Aristotle than Mill or any subsequent thinker has attempted through the medium of economic enquiry.[53] Aristotle is endeavouring to relate establishment of just terms of trade to that general framework of social realities which condition and mould the interactions of economic variables.

[53] Cf. George Dalton (ed.), *Primitive, Archaic and Modern Economics: Essays of Karl Polanyi* (N.Y., Doubleday, 1968) pp. 79–80, where it is claimed that Aristotle explored 'the problem of man's livelihood with a radicalism of which no later writer on the subject was capable — none has ever penetrated deeper into the material organisation of man's life.'

4 Biblical and Patristic Assessments of Economic Activity

The main schools of Greek philosophy to emerge in the post-Socratic period did not follow the lead of Plato and Aristotle into aspects of economic analysis. The Socratics, we have seen, undertook their analyses to help explain the formation of social life, and for the sake of developing criteria for the regulation of that life within the city-state. As the *polis* system began to crumble, they laboured to salvage and improve the traditional form of political framework. However, other philosophers, Cynics, Sceptics, Epicureans, and Stoics, accepted the demise of the old order, thereby losing the type of rationale for economic enquiry that had guided Plato and Aristotle.

Focus on man as a 'city-state animal' came to be replaced by concern with man as an isolated entity who might also be thought of as a member of a general brotherhood embracing the whole human race. Individualism and universalism replaced regionalism, and both of these new emphases ran counter to the view that modes of involvement in local community relationships were decisive for questions of human morality. Hence, economic activities bound up with those relationships ceased to have any direct interest for the newer moralists.

To an even greater extent than the Socratics, subsequent Greek philosophers regarded restriction and control of personal wants by the individual as the most rational means of solving scarcity issues. Diogenes the Cynic (412–323 B.C.), for example, adopted a life-style of extreme material simplicity. The hero Prometheus, he argued, was quite rightly punished by the gods for setting in train the innovatory processes upon which sophisticated living standards depended. Again, even limited acquisitive activity such as Aristotle allowed was economic, was rejected by Diogenes as a vain pursuit for those who wished to be truly free of the pressures arising from scarcity.

Epicurus (342—270 B.C.) and his followers, although they made minimisation of pain and maximisation of pleasure the goals of human existence, taught that these were best attained by diminution of desires. The Stoic philosophers too, aiming at freedom from emotional involvement in the fluctuating fortunes of the world, encouraged detachment from any great concern with the material conditions of living. Summarising the attitudes of these schools of philosophy, Bertrand Russell wrote:

> ... Aristotle is the last Greek philosopher who faces the world cheerfully; after him, all have, in one form or another, a philosophy of retreat. The world is bad; let us learn to be independent of it. External goods are precarious; they are the gift of fortune, not the reward of our own efforts.[1]

This retreatism served to reinforce the tendency to move away from economic analysis in the Socratic mould, as well as excluding analyses in the styles of Hesiod or the Sophists. However, at the same time, in Palestine there was current a long-standing tradition opposed to retreatism and to the notion that command of 'external goods' is merely the result of 'fortune' or the workings of blind fate. That tradition embodied a conception of economic activity unmatched by any we have considered thus far, and it was to prove to be extremely influential in determining the way in which European social thought evolved in later centuries.

The Old Testament

Long ago when the world with its inhabitants was not yet in existence, You conceived the thought, and commanded

---

[1] B. Russell, *A History of Western Philosophy* (London, Allen and Unwin, 1949) p. 255. On Cynicism and Stoicism consult also Ernest Barker, *From Alexander to Constantine*, (Oxford, Clarendon Press, 1956) Ch. 2.

with a word, and at once the works of creation stood before You. You said You would make for Your world man an administrator of Your works, that it might be known that he was not made for the sake of the world, but the world for his sake.[2]

The idea of economic activity as administration of goods and resources on behalf of the One God is a central feature of Jewish thought. This approach to economic life is found in the earliest books of the Bible and was taken over by the Gospel writers of the Christian era who characterised man's role as one of 'stewardship'. In the religion of Israel the people belonged entirely to God, and their time, their land, its produce, in fact everything they had were seen as being held in stewardship from him. Economic activity then, was an aspect of the exercise of their stewardship, and economic enquiry was a part of the investigation into the correct conduct of the office conferred on man. When, in the seventeenth century A.D. the English mercantilist Thomas Mun (1571–1641) protrayed the merchant as 'the steward of the kingdom's stock',[3] he was giving secularised expression to a fundamental tenet of both Jewish and Christian religious thought.

Significant contrasts between Jewish and Greek understandings of economic issues are provided especially by the oldest Jewish books, the five books of Moses, which began to assume definite written form in the ninth or eighth centuries B.C. These five books, 'the Pentateuch', consisting of Genesis, Exodus, Leviticus, Numbers, and Dueteronomy, reflect an essentially Oriental culture. Particularly, they reflect the long, cultural domination of Western Asia by the Babylonian Empire. The roots of the Pentateuch (or, 'Torah') extend back into the experiences of those nomads whom the Egyptians called 'Asiatics', which experiences were transmitted in oral form for many centuries before being set down in writing.

---

[2] *Syriac Baruch*, 14: 17.
[3] Thomas Mun, *England's Treasure by Foreign Trade* (1664; Oxford, Blackwell, 1959) p. 1.

The Pentateuch

The keynote of the Jewish understanding of economic life is established at the very outset of the book of Genesis. In the second chapter, work is portrayed as a pre-Fall function of man, a response to the design and command of the Lord, not a response to scarcity as the Hesiod—Robbins line of reasoning proposes. Before the Fall, and before any suggestion that man is under any pressure from an imbalance of ends and means, 'the Lord God took the man and put him in the garden of Eden to till it and keep it.' (Gen. 2:15).[4] The Economic Problem is, first and foremost, a problem in carrying through the Plan of the Creator, and that Plan involves man as the prime agent of growth and development: 'Be fruitful and multiply, and fill the earth and subdue it; and have dominion over the fish of the sea and over the birds of the air and over every living thing that moves upon the earth.' (Gen. 1:28).

In these passages, work is seen as a positive good, economic growth is enjoined, and man is made lord of created things. Man's likeness to God, it is suggested, is located primarily in man's lordship of created things, which are subordinate to him in a fashion analogous to his subordination to the Creator. The Socratic philosophers, we have seen, envisaged man as harmonising with, rather than dominating, nature. In addition, they despised work and looked on economic growth as an evil. There are profound differences then, between their understanding of the meaning of economic activity and the Jewish conception.

As the story of Genesis continues, man's fall from grace through disobedience does not alter his basic role as the Lord's administrator.[5] However, his task as the agent of growth and development now takes on painful aspects, since

[4] This passage and others below are from the English translation of the Old Testament known as the Revised Standard Version (1952). In this particular instance, the King James Version (1611) describes man as 'dressing and keeping' the garden, a phrase more in keeping with the general treatment of the progression of productive activity in the early chapters of Genesis.
[5] In the post-Fall story of Noah, for example, the Lord renews the command to 'be fruitful and multiply' and 'to bring forth abundantly on the earth and multiply in it.' Man's dominion over the rest of creation is reaffirmed. (Gen. 9:1—7).

the created world has fallen with man and has become less amenable to his command. The Lord tells Adam that

> cursed is the ground because of you; in toil you shall eat of it all the days of your life; thorns and thistles it shall bring forth to you; and you shall eat the plants of the field. In the sweat of your face you shall eat bread till you return to the ground . . . (Gen. 3:17–19).

There is also the suggestion here that man's standard of consumption is now linked to his productive activity in a way which did not pertain before the Fall. Now, he eats 'the plants of the field', whereas before he was able to 'freely eat of every tree of the garden', which garden was planted by the Lord who Himself 'made to grow every tree that is pleasant to the sight and good for food.' (Gen. 2:8–16). The choices concerning the way in which men develop the world are conditioned by their struggle for survival in the face of a Nature turned niggardly. Scarcity has entered, not to replace, but rather to restrict, growth as the focus of economic activity.

While scarcity is restrictive, it is depicted as accounting for innovatory movement. Adam's new-found difficulties lead him and his descendants into systematic pastoral and farming pursuits. Noah's extraordinary ingenuity is a response to the onset of natural disaster. Again, it is the family of the murderer Cain (for whom, 'when you till the ground, it shall no longer yield to you its strength') which is presented as the sponsor of a range of significant innovations. The Cainites build the first city, discover the working of metals, introduce the technique of nomadic herdsmanship, and are the first to invent musical instruments. (Gen. 4:12–22). Difficulty and suffering play roles in stimulating men to perform their God-given task. Development proceeds; but, in a post-Fall world it is not costless.

Although man is depicted as the lord of created things, exploiting resources to serve the needs of a dynamic economy, the Pentateuch requires him to show respect for environmental issues. Nature is the handiwork of the Creator, displays the majesty of the Lord and, as such, possesses an autonomy which commands attention. Hence, for example, in the book of Deuteronomy (which is an exposition of legal precepts in an historic setting) one of the laws of war reads:

> When you besiege a city for a long time, making war against it in order to take it, you shall not destroy its trees by wielding an axe against them; for you may eat of them, but you shall not cut them down. Are the trees in the field men that they should be besieged by you? Only the trees which you know are not trees for food you may destroy and cut down that you may build siege-works against the city that makes war with you until it falls. (Deut. 20:19—20).[6]

Many of the precepts of Deuteronomy deal directly with the regulation of economic relationships. Conformity with these precepts in administering the land and other resources given Israel by the Lord is the means whereby the scarcity problem is solved. 'There will be no poor among you,' it is affirmed, 'if only you will obey the voice of the Lord your God, being careful to do all this commandment which I command you this day.' (Deut. 15:4—5). The commands extend to regulation of consumption habits (14:3—21 and 22:5, 11), productive activity (22:9, 10 and 24:4), and to the distribution of both output and productive factors. Those in need, for example, are to be assisted through tithe claims (14:28, and 26:12), and participation in festivals (16:11, 14). In sabbatical years, debts are to be cancelled, and slaves liberated with capital to commence an independent existence (15:2 and 12).[7] In buying and selling, the same standard measure is to be used at all times (23:19—20), and in lending, certain items are not to be taken as security on a loan (24:6, 10—13). The taking of interest on loans to foreign traders is

---

[6] This passage is also a prime illustration of the teleological bias and willingness to employ rational economic calculus which are characteristic of much Jewish thought and practice. Even in the heat of battle, there must be a definite end or purpose to be served in destroying one tree. Again, the cost of creating a potential shortage of food is too high when considered against the benefit of easier conquest of the city. On the teleological outlook and economic rationalism of Jewish thought, see Werner Sombart, *The Jews and Modern Capitalism*, (1911; Collier Books, N.Y., 1962) pp. 248—54.

[7] This latter precept is supported as a quite reasonable one on strictly commercial grounds: 'It shall not seem hard to you, when you let him go free from you; for at half the cost of a hired servant he has served you six years.' (15:18).

expressly permitted, but it is forbidden in the case of lending
to a fellow Israelite, whether the loan be made in the form of
money or goods (23:19—20).[8]

Both the books of Exodus and Leviticus also condemn
interest charges levied on countrymen (Ex. 22:25, and Lev.
25:35—37). In these instances the prohibition seems to be
confined to consumption loans to the poor. The nineteenth
chapter of Leviticus contains precepts dealing with organisation of agricultural production, care of the poor, wage
payment, consumption habits, and sale of goods. The
twenty-fifth chapter deals with the institution of the year of
jubilee, the fiftieth year, in which existing economic relationships are to be thoroughly revised. In that year the land is to
lie fallow, landed property reverts to its former owners, slaves
are emancipated, and there is a remission, or at least a
suspension, of debt obligations.[9] Underlying this prescription
of periodic, peaceful revolution in the pattern of ownership
and control of resources (land, capital in the form of slaves,
rights to future income) is the view that men are simply
stewards or administrators of those resources on the Lord's
behalf. 'The land shall not be sold in perpetuity,' says the
Lord, 'for the land is mine; for you are strangers and
sojourners with me.' (Lev. 25:23). The conception of the
meaning of economic activity outlined in Genesis persists in
Leviticus.

The Prophets
The ideas of the books of the Torah were based on the
experiences of the Hebrews as a nomadic people before
1000 B.C. After their settlement in areas of Canaan, they
eventually felt a need to appoint a king, first Saul, and later
David (1005—970 B.C.) and Solomon (970—930 B.C.). This
change in political structure reflected a tendency to adopt
manners and mores of surrounding Canaanite groups, and as

[8] The individual who may be charged interest is referred to as *nokri*, i.e., foreigner,
not *ger*, i.e., resident alien.
[9] On the significance of the institution of Jubilee, see Eli Ginzberg, 'Studies in the
Economics of the Bible', *Jewish Quarterly Review*, Vol. 22 (4) (Apr 1932)
pp. 343—408.

part of this process the traditional religious ideals based on the Covenant of Sinai began to lose their grip on sections of the Jewish people. In the period before the fall of Jerusalem and the beginning of the Babylonian exile in 586 B.C., reaffirmation of the earlier tradition was undertaken by a series of social and religious reformers, the Prophets. One of the first of these was Amos who taught between 790 and 750 B.C.

Amos attacked those who ignored the Law with respect to the significance of individual wealth and the duty to care for the poor (Amos 4:1; 6:4—6). His sentiments are echoed by Isaiah (58:3—8). Amos condemns the sharp practices of retailers (8:4—6), but unlike Aristotle, he does not go so far as to advocate the abolition of the activity altogether. Rather more Socratic in tone is the condemnation by Isaiah (c. 760 B.C.) of foreign trading contacts. Like Plato and Aristotle, the prophet sees these as avenues through which local society can be corrupted (Is. 2:6—8). Another Platonic note is struck by a later prophet Habakkuk (c. 602 B.C.) who argues that usury is a major source of social instability as debtor turns against creditor in internecine strife (Hab. 2:6—7). Since both prophet and philosopher were expounding policies to restore traditional values in the midst of societies in the process of disintegration, such a coincidence is not entirely surprising.

In 538 B.C., Cyrus, the conqueror of Babylon, permitted those Jewish exiles who wished to return to make their way back to their homeland. The temple at Jerusalem was restored in 515 B.C., and during the next century a series of social and religious reforms were introduced in Judea by Nehemiah, a former official at the Persian court of Artaxerxes, and by Ezra who was given a special commission from the Persian king to exercise religious authority in the region. The Wisdom Literature of the Old Testament, which stems mainly from the post-exilic period, canvasses a wide range of economic issues. The width of the range may be due in part to Jewish experience in Babylon where many came to own land and capital and were engaged in commerce on a large scale. Later, after the conquests of Alexander and the subsequent rule of the Ptolemies in Palestine, the impact of

Hellenism on Jewish thought and practice may help account for the broader scope.

Wisdom literature

The old vision of man's economic activity as expressed in the Torah remains. Psalm 8, for example, celebrates his lordship of creation, while Psalm 112 (111) extols the righteous man as the freely distributing steward of the goods that have happened to come into his possession. The same psalm also affirms that 'wealth and riches' are the mark of the God-fearing man, a not unreasonable inference from the notion of long standing that the key to the solution of the scarcity problem lies in conformity to the Lord's commands. This inference is brought under intensive scrutiny however, in the book of Job which debates the problem of the suffering of just men. Job's friends adhere to the tradition that suffering is a punishment for non-conformity, whereas Job asserts it is not. But, in the end, Job's sufferings prove transitory, and as a righteous man his fortunes are restored so that he has 'twice as much as he had before ... fourteen thousand sheep, six thousand camels, a thousand yoke of oxen, and a thousand she-asses' (Job 42:10–12).[10] This is entirely in keeping with the dynamic proposed in the earliest chapters of Genesis.

Entrepreneurship, and especially commercial risk-taking, is commended as a characteristic of the Lord's administrator in the book of Ecclesiastes (11:1–6). Written towards the end of the third century B.C., this book is a direct attack on the wisdom of making the solution of the scarcity problem a focal point of human activity. It offers one of the strongest possible contrasts with the Hesiod–Robbins approach to be found in Old Testament literature. The Preacher writes:

> He who loves money will not be satisfied with money; nor he who loves wealth, with gain; this also is vanity. When goods increase, they increase who eat them; and what gain has their owner but to see them with his eyes? Sweet is the sleep of a labourer, whether he eats little or

[10] Modern Biblical criticism suggests that this ending is a later addition. In the original, the problem which Job poses for the traditional equation of riches and righteousness remained unresolved.

much; but the surfeit of the rich will not let him sleep. (5:10—12).

Instead of the accumulation and disposition of resources to satisfy increasingly expanding personal ends, the Preacher proposes repeatedly that men focus on work itself as the source of satisfaction in life. 'Behold, what I have seen to be good and to be fitting', he states, 'is to eat and drink and find enjoyment in all the toil with which one toils under the sun the few days of his life which God has given him, for this is his lot.' (5:18). Absorption in work for its own sake is the rational response to the goal of maximising personal welfare. 'Enjoy life', he continues, 'in your toil at which you toil under the sun. Whatever your hand finds to do, do it with your might; for there is no work or thought or knowledge or wisdom in Sheol, to which you are going.' (9:9—10). Pleasure in work, rather than in the end products of that work is God's gift to man. Even the accumulation of capital, whether in the form of goods, or money, or slaves, is a vain pursuit. Those who happen to possess capital are encouraged to employ it in active support of business ventures and should not be dissuaded by the possibility of financial loss. (11:1—6).

In general, the Preacher's analysis of the human condition is designed to discount the significance of use-values as the end of rational economic activity. As such, it is linked closely to the understanding of economic life outlined by Genesis. Relief of scarcity pressures may or may not flow from man's work, but that is not the central issue. It is from the work itself, from commitment to the role given man by God in relation to other created things that meaningful subjective value is derived. The whole approach is supportive of the type of mentality which, as was mentioned in Chapter 2, Karl Marx ascribed to the modern capitalists. Not use-values, but rather 'the restless, never-ending process of profit-making alone,' said Marx, is what the capitalist aims at. Again, the approach is quite anti-Aristotelian, and at a great remove from the conceptions of economic life to be derived from the poetry of Hesiod or the teaching of Sophists.

Elsewhere in the Wisdom Literature there are many

examples of a strong work-ethic which contrasts sharply with
the attitude of the Socratics. 'Do you see a man skilful in his
work?', asks the book of Proverbs (22:29), 'he will stand
before kings; he will not stand before obscure men.'[11] At the
same time, as in Ecclesiastes, the pursuit of an abundance of
possessions is seen as vain, or as invoking the wrath of the
Lord. Satisfaction of personal economic needs will come as a
by-product of diligence in carrying out the original command
to Adam. Distortion of the goal of economic activity into the
solution of a personal ends—means dichotomy leads to failure.
'He who tills his land will have plenty of bread, but he who
follows worthless pursuits will have plenty of poverty. A
faithful man will abound with blessings, but he who hastens
to be rich will not go unpunished.' (Prov. 28:19—20).

In Ecclesiasticus, the wisdom book of Ben Sirach, which
was written by a scribe of Jerusalem about 190—180 B.C.,
work, even arduous labour, is recognised to be a creation of
the Lord (7:15). 'Stand by your task (or 'covenant') and
attend to it,' the author advises, 'and grow old in your work.'
At the same time, the reader is warned to avoid concern with
the question: 'What do I need, and what prosperity could be
mine in the future?' (11:20—3). As in Ecclesiastes, while
industry is encouraged, parsimony is opposed. From the time
of Adam Smith, at least, economists have been led to think
of these two activities as very closely related. However, for
the later authors of the Old Testament they are quite distinct
categories. Of parsimony Sirach writes: 'Riches are not
seemly for a stingy man; and of what use is property to an
envious man? Whoever accumulates by depriving himself,
accumulates for others; and others will live in luxury on his
goods. If a man is mean to himself, to whom will he be
generous? He will not enjoy his own riches.' (14:3—5).

Subsequent chapters of Ecclesiasticus display very strong
affinity with the attitudes of the Greek philosophers on
aspects of economic activity, an affinity which indicates the
degree of penetration of traditional Hebrew thought by
Hellenistic culture at that stage. As in Plato and Aristotle,

---

[11] See also Proverbs 6:6—11; 10:4, 15; and 24:30—4. On the social ideas of
Wisdom literature, see Ernest Barker, op. cit., Part II.

there is a deep suspicion of the market economy. 'A merchant can hardly keep from wrongdoing,' it is stated, 'and a tradesman will not be declared innocent of sin. Many have committed sin for a trifle, and whoever seeks to get rich will avert his eyes. As a stake is driven firmly into a fissure between stones, so sin is wedged in between selling and buying.' (26:29, and 27:1—2.)[12] Later, the reader is warned never to consult 'with a merchant about barter or with a buyer about selling.' (37:11). However, at the same time, one is encouraged to be unashamed of success in business dealings; taking profit in traffic with merchants; and keeping accurate and comprehensive business records (42:3—7). Clearly, Socratic teaching, although present here, is not fully assimilated or is consciously rejected in part.

The pursuit of money is singled out for special condemnation (31:5—7), specialisation in economic activity is recommended (11:10), the existence of an extensive system of borrowing and lending is depicted as a prime source of internal social disruption (29:4—7, and 16—18), the dependence on others which poverty brings means a sub-human existence that 'cannot be considered as life' (40:28—9), and then, the Greek influence evident in each of these postures is confirmed by the use of a clear-cut distinction between work and leisure. 'The wisdom of the scribe', writes this scribe, 'depends on the opportunity of leisure; and he who has little business may become wise. How can he become wise who handles the plough, and who glories in the shaft of a goad?' (38:24—5). Having adopted this Aristotelian position, the author goes on to claim that craftsmen, blacksmiths, potters, and all who 'rely upon their hands' are cut off from the acquisition of wisdom. Yet, like Aristotle, he must admit these to places in the social order, for 'without them a city cannot be established, and men can neither sojourn or live there,' (38:32). But further, in an intellectual step which transcends the thought of the philosopher and indicates the very considerable gulf which exists between Greek thought

---

[12] This attitude persisted for many centuries in the mainstream of Christian thinking, and as in shown in Chapter 6 began to be dispelled by Saint Albert the Great, Saint Thomas Aquinas, and their contemporaries in the thirteenth century A.D.

and even this strongly Hellenistic Hebrew document, the scribe adds that manual workers: 'keep stable the fabric of the world, and their prayer is in the practice of their trade.' (38:34).

No one phrase better summarises the difference between Greek and Jewish conceptions of the significance of economic activity.

The New Testament

The most influential set of writings in the history of Western thought, the twenty-seven 'books' of the New Testament, displays strong parallels with earlier Jewish assessments of the scope and meaning of rational economic behaviour. The existence of such parallels is emphasised by many modern Christian commentators, who depict the Economic Problem as the challenge to build up the order of created things in accord with a divinely patterned historical dynamic. For example, a document of the Ecumenical Council of Vatican II (1963–5) states:

> For man, created in God's image, received a mandate to subject to himself the earth and all that it contains, and to govern the world . . . This mandate concerns even the most ordinary activities. For while providing the substance of life for themselves and their families, men and women are performing their activities in a way which appropriately benefits society. They can justly consider that by their labour they are unfolding the Creator's work, consulting the advantages of their brother men and contributing by their personal industry to the realization in history of the divine plan.[13]

Against such a statement, however, many others from authoritative Christian sources can be cited which depict economic activity in a very different light. Frequently, over the centuries, that activity has been assessed more in accord with the retreatist philosophies of the Hellenistic era than with the Jewish tradition. The most notable instance of this

---

[13] 'Pastoral Constitution on the Church in the Modern World', in Walter M. Abbot (ed.), *The Documents of Vatican II* (N.Y., The American Press, 1966) p. 232.

is the monastic movement which advocated simplicity of life and minimal involvement in economic pursuits. Productive activity, for example, was seen by the founders of monastic orders as having its rationale simply as a means of giving their foundations the necessary degree of self-sufficiency to make them independent of surrounding social institutions, and as a guard against the moral dangers of idleness. Hence, the forty-eighth section of the Rule of the Roman-born Benedict of Nursia (c. A.D. 480—547) reads:

> Idleness is the enemy of the soul. And therefore, at fixed times, the brothers ought to be occupied in manual labour; and again, at fixed times, in sacred reading . . . But, if the needs of the place or poverty demand that they labour at the harvest, they shall not grieve at this: for then they are truly monks if they live by the labour of their hands, as did also other fathers and the apostles.[14]

This post-Socratic retreatism tempered by an element of Hesiodic realism concerning self-sufficiency, was based, in the opinion of its advocates, on explicit injunctions of the New Testament.[15] It is quite possible then, to draw more than one assessment of the nature of rational economic behaviour from its pages. Despite the strong parallels, there are also significant divergences from Jewish attitudes on the question. In fact, reviewing the literature of Europe prior to what some

---

[14] 'The Rule of St Benedict', in Henry Bettenson (ed.), *Documents of the Christian Church* (London, Oxford University Press, 1963) p. 171. The persistence of the Benedictine attitude is illustrated by the later Rule of St Francis, approved in 1223. Section five of the latter also stresses the prevention of idleness and adds that the brothers should work in such a way that 'they do not quench the spirit of holy prayer and devotion to which other and temporal activities should be subordinate.' The brothers are forbidden to draw wages in the form of 'coin or money'. op. cit., p. 181. It seems paradoxical that, in practice, the regime of monasticism can be claimed to have contributed much to the process of economic development in many areas of Europe.

[15] Where possible, the Old Testament also was invoked. For example, Dom Leclercq notes that his monastic predecessors were very fond of quoting Ben Sirach's Aristotelian position on the relationship of wisdom to the opportunity for leisure (Ecclesiasticus, 38:24). The monastic ideal was freedom from work in the ordinary sense, and pursuit of leisure, albeit busy leisure (*negotiosissimum otium*), in which the major emphasis was on contemplation. Consult, Jean Leclercq, *The Love of Learning and the Desire for God: A Study of Monastic Culture* (N.Y., New American Library, 1962) p. 73.

historians call the 'Albertino–Thomist revolution' in Christian thought in the thirteenth century, it would appear that
the divergences were to prove of greater importance than the
similarities.

The books of the New Testament were written between
about A.D. 30 and A.D. 130. Their language is Koine (or
'common') Greek, the vernacular of the eastern portion of
the Roman Empire of the period. These writings can be
grouped in four categories: (1) the four Gospels, dealing with
the actions and words of Jesus of Nazareth; (2) the book of
Acts, which concerns the activities of his immediate followers; (3) the 21 epistles or letters, from prominent figures to
certain groups among those followers; and (4) the Apocalypse, the only prophetic book in the collection, which is a
circular message to seven of the early Christian communities.

Synoptic gospels

Throughout his boyhood and youth, Jesus of Nazareth
thoroughly imbibed the teachings of the Jewish holy books.
In addition, he was exposed to a range of non-Jewish
influences present in the quite cosmopolitan region of
Palestine in which he lived, Galilee. There, the cities were
mainly Greek, the countryside Jewish, and striking through
the area was the major trading route which linked Damascus,
Syria, and Mesopotamia with Egypt. As a craftsman, he was
poor, although in a better economic position than most of
the local peasantry and unskilled day labourers, and his
teachings were directed at the poor as well as those with
wealth or power.[16]

Most significantly, the vast majority of those who initially
took up his new conception of the plan of the God of Israel
were themselves poor. Given their insignificance as individuals in terms of local power structures, and given the
dominance of centralised decision-making by the occupying

---

[16] For a treatment of contemporary social conditions consult Werner Förster,
Palestinian Judaism in New Testament Times (Edinburgh, Oliver and Boyd,
1964). Another very useful exposition is J. L. McKenzie, 'The Jewish World in
New Testament Times', in Bernard Orchard, and others (eds), *A Catholic
Commentary on Holy Scripture* (London, Nelson, 1953) pp. 728–41.

power of Rome, early Christians saw little opportunity of influencing the prevailing pattern of social and economic organisation through direct action. Hence, they did not elaborate on the implications of their leader's message for the day-to-day operations of that organisation. Unlike the Socratics, they could not hope to aim at the erection of ideal city-states, nor were they in the position of a Moses handing down guidelines for the business of a nation. These earlier forms of incentive for investigation of specific economic issues were absent in their case. Further, Christ had conveyed to them the vision of a cosmopolitan community of all men, transcending limitations of regional or even national social structures. Such vision did not translate readily into programmes for reform on anything save an individual or specifically localised basis.

In the Synoptic Gospels (those attributed to Matthew, Mark, and Luke), the traditional Jewish theme of man as the administrator, or steward, of God-given resources is given considerable prominence. Among the illustrations of the theme are the diptych concerning the faithful and unfaithful servants (Matthew, 24:45—51), and the Parable of the Talents (Matthew, 25:14—30). The emphasis here is on the efficient use of material and physical resources in the furtherance of the Lord's plan. Risk-taking is enjoined, and interest earned on commercial loans seems to be approved. It is suggested also that the measure of individual success or failure in any enterprise is not established in absolute or impersonal terms, but rather is related to the varying degrees of opportunity offered for participation in the work involved. The scale of value with respect to work-effort is not established by reference to the magnitudes of output.

At the same time, and with an even greater stress than is present in earlier Jewish literature, concern with the use of resources to solve personal ends—means dichotomies is depicted as a wasteful preoccupation. In the Sermon on the Mount, for example, Christ states: 'You cannot serve God and mammon (i.e., 'money,' or wealth in the sense of something deposited). Therefore I tell you, do not be anxious about your life, what you shall eat or what you shall drink, nor about your body, what you shall put on. Is not life more

than food, and the body more than clothing?' (Matthew,
6:24–5).

Then, reaffirming the validity of Deuteronomy 15:4–5
(quoted above), Christ argues that the solution of scarcity
difficulties will flow as a by-product in communities where
there is a genuine attempt to adhere to the Lord's plan. 'But
seek first his kingdom and his righteousness,' he goes on, 'and
all these things shall be yours as well.' (Matthew, 6:33).

Like Aristotle and Ben Sirach, Christ affirms the superiority of contemplation, or intellectual activity involving detachment from the mundane, to absorption in a daily round of
physical and administrative labours. This preference emerges
quite clearly in the narrative of Martha and Mary (Luke
10:38–42). The latter, who has elected to listen to Christ
rather than attend to urgent household duties, 'has chosen
the better part.' Martha's devotion to the mundane is not
condemned as worthless, but it is not recorded that Christ
positively affirmed its worth. There is no equivalent here, for
example, of Sirach's view that, for manual workers, 'their
prayer is in the practice of their trade.' Elsewhere in the
Gospels, of course, as in the case of the story of the Good
Samaritan, those who devote money, time and physical effort
to the relief of human distress are praised. Yet this praise
cannot be said to amount to affirmation of a strong
work-ethic as encountered in passages of the Old Testament
extending back to Genesis.

There is an important difference of emphasis then as
between the Old and New Testaments, on the status of
commercial and industrial pursuits in relation to the divine
plan. The relative neglect by Christ of the issue of that status
is due, perhaps, to an element in his thought which has
impressed a number of modern biblical scholars, namely, a
conviction concerning the impending destruction of Jerusalem and a suggestion that the destruction would be
followed after a short interval by the end and transformation
of the entire existing order of created things.[17] If this was

---

[17] Consult, for example, G. R. Beasley-Murray, *Jesus and the Future, an
Examination of the Criticism of the Eschatological Discourse, Mark 13, with
Special Reference to the Little Apocalypse Theory* (London, Macmillan, 1954).
At one point in Mark's gospel (13:32), Christ explicitly reserves knowledge of the

Christ's view, and it certainly seems to have been that of most of his immediate followers, then it is understandable that little weight would be placed on engagement in economic development. In the brief time remaining, there was little the current generation could do to improve upon the results of past efforts to carry out the dynamic function bestowed on Adam with respect to Creation. The urgent, pressing need was to prepare oneself and others for the wholesale transformation shortly to occur. As Albert Schweitzer has observed, Jesus' ethic 'is oriented entirely by the expected supernatural consummation.'[18]

Epistles

The orientation emphasised by Schweitzer, which was crucial in helping determine the manner and timing of the emergence of economic analysis in the theological literature of Europe, is quite evident in various of the apostolic letters. It is present, for example, in the epistle to the Hebrews. Since he is writing for a Jewish audience, the author at one point quotes Psalm 8:4—6, to assist his argument. In this psalm, man's dominion over and responsibility for tending created things is celebrated. Yet the epistle writer in his quotation omits the surrounding verses of the psalm (verses 3, 7 and 8) which refer to specific natural objects — the moon, stars, sheep, fish. Commenting on the omission, a modern biblical analyst writes, 'Verse 7c, though an authentic part of the psalm, was omitted by the author, who has no interest in showing that man (Son and sons) is over the visible creation subject to angels, senescent and doomed to disappear. What he wants to show is that man is over the future world which

---

timing of the final consummation to his Father alone. 'But of that day or that hour no one knows,' he states, 'not even the angels in heaven, nor the Son, but only the Father.' In the Jewish prophetic tradition, however, prediction of a day of wrath, of justice or of judgement, was bound up with the theme of a destruction of Jerusalem. Preaching within that tradition and to his fellow Jews, it is understandable that the ideas of cosmic transformation and fall of Jerusalem would be intermingled in Christ's discourse.

[18] A. Schweitzer, *The Mystery of the Kingdom of God* (London, A. and C. Black, 1914) p. 100.

alone has abiding reality.'[19] Here, the new vision of a
permanent role for man in a transcendent order completely
overshadows the significance of his role in contributing to a
visible and temporal order.

The apostle Paul, too, in the letters attributed to him, does
not appear interested in exhorting his followers to pay
attention to the progress of the world in which they live.
They are to respect its political arrangements, work quietly at
their daily round of tasks, do good in the sight of other men,
and act peaceably at all times. In his first epistle to the
Corinthians, for example, where he considers the conduct
appropriate to 'these present times of stress' (7:26—31),
Paul's advice is that 'those who have to deal with the world
should not become engrossed in it.' He offers this advice
'because the world as we know it is passing away', and in the
conviction that 'our time is growing short'. Among the
specific directions given is that 'those whose life is buying
things should live as though they had nothing of their own.'

The writings of Paul, as a whole, suggest a quietist, if not
an outright retreatist attitude to economic engagements. The
sentiments expressed contrast markedly, for example, with
those current among certain groups of Christians in the
nineteenth century. Hence, writing of the Pauline ethic
against a background of capitalistic activity in a Protestant
culture, Johannes Weiss states:

> Yet we still miss here, as in the preaching of Jesus,
> express statements and attractive instruction for the
> ethical idealization of common labor ... this highly
> tensioned religious idealism has as its consequence a sort of
> alienation from the world, or rather an indifference to the
> interests of everyday civil life. Creative and elaborately
> planned enterprises, e.g., those of modern industry or
> wholesale business with its keen desire to open up new
> countries, could not thrive on this soil where the impulse
> of gain is tied down ... There is no discussion as to
> whether there are any worldly aims at all to which a
> Christian may devote himself with burning zeal, or

[19] John F. McConnell, *The Epistle to the Hebrews* (Collegeville, Minn., Liturgical
Press, 1960) p. 18.

whether the earning of money as a selfish purpose can possibly be permissible for him. These questions lie outside his field of vision.[20]

Johannine literature

An abrupt change in the early apostolic field of vision was occasioned by the onset of systematic persecution of Christians by Imperial Rome, and as a result the ground was laid for a fresh Christian assessment of economic activity. The documents which most clearly express the new approach are the Apocalypse of John of Patmos and the Gospel attributed to the same author. These were composed about A.D. 100, after the persecutions launched first by Nero (about A.D. 65) and then on a greater scale by Domitian (about A.D. 95). The political and social order with which the earliest groups of Christians were prepared to coexist had turned against them, so it was no longer possible to maintain a posture that Christians could continue to be indifferent as to the way that order functioned.

In the face of this first, major crisis for the Christian church as an institution, the author of the Apocalypse essays the first comprehensive statement of a Christian theology of history. Most significantly, the end of the world is not portrayed as imminent.[21] Rather, links are forged between Christian conceptions and the Jewish understanding of the future course of temporal affairs as the unfolding of a divine plan in which 'the people of God' (the Hebrew nation or the Christian church) play an active role. Hence, as Yves Congar points out, 'we get the cosmic praise of Apocalypse V, 13, which is none other than the realisation of the Old

---

[20] Johannes Weiss, *Earliest Christianity: A History of the Period A.D. 30–150*, Vol. II, (1897, English translation 1937; N.Y., Harper and Row, 1965) p. 593. For a similar assessment by a contemporary writer, see Yves M. J. Congar, *Lay People in the Church* (London, Chapman, 1959) pp. 380–2.

[21] 'When the Roman Empire first unleashed its full might against the infant Church under Nero it must have seemed the very end of everything, even of the world itself; surely now Jesus would appear upon the clouds in judgement upon the Roman eagles and in salvation for his persecuted faithful. But Peter and Paul died, and so did many others, and still the end of the world did not occur . . . By this time, a more complete understanding of eschatology (doctrine of the last things) was possible.' Dominic Crossan, *The Gospel of Eternal Life: Reflections on the Theology of St John* (Milwaukee, Bruce, 1967) p. 155.

Testament, which so often associates all nature with the de-
liverance of the redeemed.'[22] Again, whereas Israel acquired
power, authority and responsibility on earth through the
Sinai covenant, so, the Apocalypse suggests, by their adherence to a new covenant, i.e., Christ, Christians are made 'a
kingdom and priests to our God, and they shall reign on
earth.' (5:10). Here then, the conception of the Economic
Problem outlined in Genesis is reaffirmed as relevant for the
new people of God.

The same affirmation is a dominant theme of the Gospel
of John. Neither the retreatism of the post-Socratic philosophers nor the Pauline indifference to problems of economic
organisation is enjoined. Instead, as H. Richard Niebuhr
suggests, John 'finds room for affirmative and ordered
response on the part of created man to the creative, ordering
work of God; even though the creature may go about his
work unwillingly as he tills the ground, cultivates his mind,
and organises his society, and though he may administer
perversely the order given him with his existence.'[23] Underlying John's view is the conviction that whatever has been
created is good, since 'all things were made through him, and
without him (i.e., Christ), was made nothing that has been
made' (John 1:3). Further, unlike the other Gospel writers,
John stresses the point that the final transformation of the
order of creation has already commenced.[24] The Christian,

[22] Y. M. J. Congar, op. cit., p. 82.
[23] H. Richard Niebuhr, *Christ and Culture* (N.Y., Harper, 1951) p. 192.
Elsewhere, Professor Neibuhr notes that this line of thought is a significant element
in the doctrine of the religious reformer John Calvin (1509—64), op. cit.,
pp. 217—8. This suggests that if the thesis of Max Weber concerning an intimate
relationship between Calvinism and the advent of the economic world of
capitalism is accepted, then the Johannine outlook is relevant to an explanation
of the origins of aspects of modern economic thought and practice. Further, as
St John's approach is linked closely to' that found in the Old Testament, the
Jewish assessment of the meaning of economic activity must also be taken into
account in such an explanation.
[24] 'The Synoptics situate at the end of time such things as judgment, the return of
Christ, becoming sons of God (Mt 25:31; Lk. 6:35, 20:35—6). John, without
denying the truth of this, emphasises that these things have already begun: his
eschatology is in part already realised. (Cf. Jn. 3:18; 5:24—5; 7:12; 9:16;
10:19—21; 12:31—3; 14:1—3, 18—20; 17:3).' Raymond E. Brown, *The Gospel of
St John and the Johannine Epistles* (Collegeville, Minn., Liturgical Press, 1965)
p. 13.

as the Lord's administrator, is participating in a developmental process leading up to the establishment of an entirely new form of society.

The Fathers of the East

In the two centuries immediately following the Apostolic Age, intellectual leadership of the Christian Church was provided mainly by writers steeped in Hellenistic philosophy and Greek educational practice. Outstanding among these were: St Justin Martyr (c. 110–65), who was the first to attempt a philosophy of Christian thought; the Athenian-born Clement of Alexandria (c. 150–215); Origen (c. 185–254), a pupil of Clement and a professional teacher of grammar; and St Athanasius (c. 297–373), an Alexandrian who defended orthodoxy against the doctrines of Arianism and promoted monasticism as the ideal form of Christian living. During the fourth century, these were followed in the East by St Cyril of Jerusalem (c. 315–86); by the three Cappadocians – St Basil the Great (c. 331–79), St Gregory of Nyssa (c. 330–95), and St Gregory of Nazianzus (c. 330–89); and by St John Chrysostom (c. 344–407), a lawyer of Antioch whose fellow citizens dubbed him 'Golden-mouthed' (*Chrysostom*) and 'Great Teacher of the Earth'.[25]

The assessment of the nature of the Economic Problem by these men shows little affinity with that of the Pentateuch and the Johannine writings. Rather, interpreting the Scriptures with minds heavily conditioned by Hellenistic philosophy, they adopt a minimalist-retreatist position on economic activity that is similar to the outlook of their Cynic and Stoic contemporaries. Justin, and to a greater extent Clement, are significant exceptions to this general tendency which was to help stifle movement towards systematic

[25] The creative impetus in Greek theology seems to have waned during the fifth century. However, a notable later figure is Dionysius the Pseudo-Areopagite who wrote in the fifth century and was to have a strong influence on the thought of St Thomas Aquinas, among others. Later still, St John of Damascus (c. 676–749), sometime chief revenue officer of the Caliph of Damascus, employed Aristotelian logic and philosophy in his theological works. His compendium, *Fountain of Wisdom*, especially its third section, *The True Faith*, attained a status in the Greek Church akin to that of Aquinas' *Summa* in the West.

economic analysis in Europe for many centuries. The major, historical vehicle for the continuance of Hellenistic retreatism through the middle ages and even beyond, was monasticism. As Dom Leclercq observes, monastic culture 'is a patristic culture, the prolongation of patristic culture in another age and in another civilization.'[26] In theory, if not always in practice, the monastic understanding of economic life discouraged serious scholarly endeavour in economics.[27]

The retreatism of the majority of the Fathers of the East is illustrated vividly by their treatment of the role of work in human existence. Given their Cynical or Stoic predispositions, the passages of the Book of Genesis in which work is portrayed as an activity commanded by God posed important problems. This command they endeavoured to explain away by positing that 'it is through idleness that man learned all evil.' The rationale of any engagement in productive endeavour is a reduction of the proportion of time in any one life which could be given over to occasions of sin. St John Chrysostom, for example, is prepared to apply this rationale even to pre-Fall Adam in a state of innocence. 'God commanded man to till and keep it (Paradise)', he rationalises, 'in order to prevent him from becoming haughty through having everything too much to his liking (for it is through idleness that man learned all evil).'[28] He continues that, 'if he were altogether without toil, man (Adam) would forthwith have fallen into laziness from too much leisure.'

St Basil the Great, too, interpreted the mind of the Creator as having designed work simply as a guard against idleness, and this gloss, so tenuous in terms of Jewish and much other

[26] Jean Leclercq, op. cit., p. 113.

[27] Certain tendencies in medieval monasticism ran counter to this negativism. Among these were the retention of a humanist outlook and a sense of history. Also of significance was a horror of Nature 'in the raw'. See, op. cit., pp. 135—7, and 226—7. However, these tendencies were not strong enough to overcome attitudes derived from non-Christian philosophers. There was some substance in the jibe of the apostate emperor Julian concerning the early monks, that these men were the Cynics of the Christian world. That substance persisted into the middle ages. Compare monastic attitudes with, for example, Epictetus on 'finance and ways and means', in Epictetus, *Discourses*, 3, 22, 83—4.

[28] From Maurus Wolter, *The Principles of Monasticism*, trans. B. A. Sause (St Louis, Herder, 1962) p. 498. This volume, pp. 457—577, contains an extensive collection of patristic and monastic passages on work.

Christian understanding, was repeated by generation after generation of monastic commentators. Some even went so far as to portray work as an institution created as a punishment for original sin. For example, John of Tritheim, abbot of Sponheim (d. 1516), wrote that, 'the all-powerful God inflicted this penalty (work) upon his creature Adam for the transgression of the original command, assuring him that in the sweat of his brow he should produce his food from the earth with his hands.' [29]

A somewhat more positive approach to the role of work was adopted by Origen. The fact of human need is a divine ordinance, he believes, designed to give man the opportunity to use his rational capacities. In the absence of a scarcity problem, those individuals not attracted to contemplative pursuits would lack incentive to realise their potential. The obligation to work then, is bound up with a God-given opportunity to exercise that faculty which distinguishes man from other forms of creation. Origen goes on (*Contra Celsum*, IV, 76) to celebrate the innovations which have flowed from this divine arrangement. In the face of the need for food, human ingenuity has developed systematic agriculture, carpentry and metal-working skills for the production of agricultural implements. The requirement of having shelter has led to expansion of skills in providing clothing and buildings, and the latter, in turn, has stimulated the emergence of architectural science. Finally, 'the demand for useful things' has given rise to the arts of navigation and maritime trade. This catalogue of Origen looks back to those of the

---

[29] Op. cit., pp. 498—9. While such attitudes deprecated concern with the problems of rational organisation of productive activity, at the same time they enjoined devotion to whatever task happened to be at hand. Thus, St Basil recommends that 'everyone should be devoted to his own trade, applying himself to it enthusiastically and accomplishing it blamelessly with ready zeal and careful attention, as if God were the overseer, . . .' op. cit., p. 534. The contrast between the practical economic achievements of monks and their contribution to economic analysis becomes more explicable in the light of this fundamental duality of approach. The dualism was resolved, in practice, by a rational organisation of monastic communities under abbots who were obliged to take on the very range of concerns which, as monks, they were supposed to eschew. The model for organisation was an idealised Greek *polis*, and the original moving force was the legislation of St Basil. On the latter, see Charles Norris Cochrane, *Christianity and Classical Culture* (London, Oxford University Press, 1957) pp. 341—2.

Athenian dramatists. However, for the Christian writer,
economic development through innovatory activity has
occurred because of the operation of divine providence, not
despite the wishes of the gods.

The major dissenting voice in the midst of the flight of
most of the Eastern Fathers from economic enquiry was
Clement of Alexandria. In his attempt to synthesise the
Hellenistic and Christian worlds he had resort to the vision of
Plato, a more sympathetic framework for systematic investigation of economic activity than those afford by post-
Socratic philosophies. His approach to the Economic Problem is fundamentally Socratic. 'The best wealth', he writes,
'is to have few desires.'[30] However, concern with the
multiplication and allocation of resources to serve those
desires cannot be neglected entirely. 'The possession of the
necessities of life', it is claimed, 'keep the soul free and
independent if it knows how the use earthly goods wisely . . .
We must be busy with material concerns not for themselves,
but for the body, the care of which is required by the very
care of the soul, to which all things must tend.'[31]

Like Plato and Aristotle, Clement is ready to condemn
certain types of economic activity as akin to warfare.[32]
Nevertheless, 'it is not at all forbidden to busy oneself with
an unworldly mind with worldly things according to the will
of God.'[33] In his treatise, *Who is the Rich Man That Shall Be
Saved?* he confronts directly the retreatist, Christian ascetic
who finds the only rational approach to economic activity in
non-involvement with possessions, and hence, allocation of
those resources that might accrue to him personally. To
divest oneself of possessions, Clement argues, can be a most
irrational form of behaviour:

> For neither great nor worthy to be desired is the state of
> one so lacking in possessions that he does not have
> wherewith to live; for if it were, then that whole swarm of
> proletarians, derelicts and beggars who live from hand to

[30] *The Pedagogue*, II, 3.
[31] *Stromata*, IV, 5.
[32] *The Pedagogue*, I, 12.
[33] Op. cit., III, 11.

mouth, all those wretched cast out upon the streets, though they live in ignorance of God and of his justice, would be the most blessed and the most religious and the only candidates for eternal life simply because they are penniless and find it hard to live, lacking the most modest means.[34]

Rational behaviour, in Clement's opinion (as in those of Aristotle before him and Aquinas much later), involves personal retention of ownership of accumulated material wealth, allied to use of that wealth as if it were the property of the community at large. A person who deprives himself of the basic necessities of existence is open to distraction 'from the duties of seeking his own perfection'. Those individuals who command resources cannot escape the obligation of deliberate and careful concern with problems of efficient allocation to meet their own needs and those of their fellows. Clement continues:

We must not cast away riches which can benefit our neighbour. Possessions were made to be possessed; goods are called goods because they do good, and they have been provided by God for the good of men: they are at hand and serve as the material, the instruments for a good use in the hand of him who knows how to use them. If you use them with skill you reap the benefit from them.[35]

To a greater extent than Plato or Aristotle, Clement emphasises that the manner in which an individual utilises resources under his control has a broad social dimension. Underlying the new degree of emphasis is a particular understanding of the meaning of property ownership. Although property titles can be vested in individuals, the community as a whole has a claim on what the property may yield in excess of satisfaction of its owner's needs. 'God', writes Clement, 'has given us the right of use, but only within the limits of necessity; and he has ordained that this use be in common. It is therefore wrong that one should be in luxury

---

[34] *Quis dives salvetur?*, XI. Concerning the significance of this treatise see Ernest Barker, op. cit., pp. 424–30.
[35] Op. cit., XIV.

while the many are in distress . . .'[36] Neither complete
communalisation or absolute autonomy of the individual
with respect to possessions will afford the best basis for
maximising welfare in the economy as a whole. The most
desirable form of organisation is that combining private
ownership and communal use.

The Fathers of the West

Most of the early Latin Christian literature is African in
origin, and the outstanding figure in this tradition is the
Numidian-born Aurelius Augustinus (354–430) whose writings were to have a profound impact on European social
thought. St Augustine is the first of the Fathers to look
towards the creation of a new, non-classical culture. Before
him,

> all the Fathers, whether Greek or Latin, regarded ancient
> civilisation as the only possible type of culture. They could
> not conceive of any other form any more than they could
> visualize a political organization other than the Roman
> Empire. Hence the attitude towards ancient civilization is
> critical rather than constructive. They criticize and correct
> but they do not look forward to building up a new
> culture.[37]

Because of his new vision, Augustine opened up the
possibility of a fresh assessment of economic life that was not
restricted to Greek or Roman models. The assessment
implied by his work has affinities with that of the Book of
Genesis and St John the Apostle and it looks forward to
aspects of the social thought of the reformer John Calvin. St
Thomas Aquinas too was strongly influenced by Augustine,

---

[36] *The Pedagogue*, II, 12; see also III, 6. Use in common is also advocated by
St John Chrysostom in his discussion of the morality of riches (*Patrologia Graeca*,
Vol. 62, cols 562–4). He asks: ". . . but is it not wrong to hold in exclusive
possession the Lord's goods, and to enjoy alone that which is common? Are not
the earth and the fullness thereof the Lord's? If, therefore, our possessions are the
common gift of the Lord, they belong also to our fellows; for all the things of the
Lord are common.' St Basil adopts the same position (*Patrologia Graeca*, Vol. 31,
cols 273, 278). For a discussion of the Fathers on property, consult John A.
Ryan, *Alleged Socialism of the Church Fathers* (St Louis, Herder, 1913).

[37] Frank P. Cassidy, *Molders of the Medieval Mind* (1944; Port Washington, N.Y.,
Kennikat, 1966) pp. 149–50.

although, since St Thomas devoted little attention to the development of a philosophy of history, much that was novel in his predecessor was neglected.[38]

Before Augustine

Among the most important precursors of St Augustine in the West were: Tertullian (160–240), a prominent Carthaginian lawyer, converted first to orthodox Christianity, then to the doctrines of the Montanist sect, and later to form a sect of his own devising; St Cyprian of Carthage (c. 200–58); and Lactantius (c. 250–330), an African teacher of rhetoric. Nearer Augustine's own day were: St Hilary of Poitiers (c. 310–67); St Ambrose of Milan (c. 340–97); and the great literary pedagogue and ascetic, St Jerome (c. 340–420). A particular work of interest is *The Shepherd* by Hermas who lived in Italy and wrote in Greek. The author is thought to be the brother of Pope Pius I (140–55).

The assessment of the meaning of economic life by Tertullian offers little ground for the development of systematic economic analysis within the context of Christian thought. Tertullian seeks to emphasise the opposition between a Christian way of life and involvement in the concerns of secular society. 'Whatever may be the customs of the society in which the Christian lives, and whatever the human achievement it conserves, Christ is seen as opposed to them, so that he confronts men with the challenge of an "either–or" decision.'[39] Tertullian does not rule out completely the possibility of a Christian involving himself in commercial pursuits. Yet business activities imply acquisitive behaviour based on the sin of covetousness, and covetousness is a type of idolatry. Such vocations cannot be regarded as fitting for those who wish to be servants of the true God.[40]

---

[38] In the monastic tradition, some of St Augustine's writings were accorded the greatest respect. However, there was relative neglect of those aspects of his thought which posed problems for the pre-Christian conception of economic analysis the monks continued to foster. Consult J. Lerclercq, op. cit., p. 104 and pp. 222–3.

[39] H. Richard Niebuhr, op. cit., p. 40.

[40] See Tertullian, *On Idolatry*, XI. Commercial practices, notably bargaining processes, are seen as being characterised by deceitful behaviour.

Surveying contemporary secular society, Tertullian declares that 'we are now a burden on the world, there are
barely enough of the essentials for us, our needs have become
more acute, and there is a cry of complaint on the lips of all
men, for nature can no longer sustain us.'[41] This situation
has come about, he declares, despite the fact that 'the world
itself, as it appears to our eyes, becomes more refined and
progresses from day to day.' To explain this seeming
paradox, and to rationalise his fundamental despair concerning the human condition, he has resort, as did the Reverend
Thomas Malthus in the nineteenth and his middle-class
popularisers in the twentieth centuries, to the bogey of
excessive population. Further, like his modern counterparts,
he looks to 'epidemics, famines, wars, and the earth's opening
to swallow whole cities' as means whereby the dilemma
might be resolved.[42]

In such a world a science devoted to investigation of more
efficient means of solving existing scarcity problems or to
uncovering the bases of future economic growth, loses much
of its rationale. The fruits of applying its findings must
always be blighted by the forces unleashed by the sin of
Adam. Belief in the doctrine of 'population explosion' is a
secularised expression of belief in a doctrine of pervasive
original sin from the effects of which the ratiocinations of
economists offer little hope of escape. The zeal, amounting
to religious fervour, with which twentieth-century economists' conceptions of growth and development are attacked
by contemporary, secular Tertullianists finds a counterpart in
the reaction of some of the elements in early Christianity to
the Roman world as they found it.

A rather different reaction is evident in the second-century
writings of Hermas. For him, human history is not to be
understood in terms of recurrent cycles characterised by
sequences of economic growth, overpopulation, chaos, and
then re-emergence of growth. Instead, it is a progression
marked by 'the gathering together of all the spiritually living
elements throughout mankind into a new spiritual society.'[43]

---

[41] *De Anima*, XXX, P. L. II, 700.
[42] Ibid.
[43] Christopher Dawson, *The Dynamics of World History*, ed. J. J. Mulloy (1956;
N.Y., New American Library, 1962) p. 236.

This view of history is a more extensive application of that of the Jewish writers of the Old Testament. History is a process of building up the community of the people of God, the latter conceived of in a much broader sense than 'the Hebrew nation'. However, this new view retained certain affinities with the general assessment of the Economic Problem offered by the Pentateuch.

For Hermas, as Igino Giordani points out, 'riches are the property of God. Man is merely their administrator and he must administer them according to the will of their owner, that is, he must invest them in good works in order to reap the profit in that which is his true country.'[44] Exercised correctly, command over resources can yield spiritual benefits to the administrator while it serves the material needs of society as a whole. Material goods, Hermas emphasises, are of divine origin, and his attitude concerning their potential use 'christianizes property, labor, finance, money and even capitalism, insofar as we may use the term in speaking of those times.'[45]

While these sentiments approach the Jewish religious assessment of economic activity, they lack the growth and development dimensions which are present in the thought of the earlier writers. Probably, this is due, in the main, to the influence of early Christian expectations concerning the end of the world. Hermas' treatment of history, according to Christopher Dawson, 'shows how the primitive Christian sense of an imminent end led to a foreshortening of the time scale and distracted men's attention from the problem of the future destinies of human civilization.'[46] Hence, Hermas advocates that Christians do not concern themselves with investment in fixed capital such as 'edifices and homes' or in landed estates. His ideal economy is one essentially stationary, but not so stagnant as to be unable to provide all its members with an existence above the poverty line. The dynamic in the life of Christians is not to be too closely identified with their

---

[44] I. Giordani, *The Social Message of the Early Church Fathers*, (Paterson, N.J., St Anthony Guild Press, 1944) pp. 263–4.
[45] Op. cit., p. 261. See, for example, the advice of the angel to Hermas at the conclusion of the work. As in the Old Testament, the man who administers resources with wisdom and humanity 'will live and shall be prosperous in his life.'
[46] C. Dawson, op. cit., p. 237.

citizenship in an earthly city. Rather, their energies are bent
to serving the demands of membership of another city, a
spiritual kingdom.[47]

A much greater willingness to recognise the relative claims
of the requirements that might be attached to earthly
citizenship is evident in the *Divine Institutes* by Lucius
Caelius Firmianus Lactantius (c. 250–330). Written after the
Edict of Milan (A.D. 313), whereby Christianity was made a
licensed cult of the Roman Empire under Constantine, this
work represents the first attempt by a Western intellectual at
an orderly presentation of Christian theology.[48] The fifth of
its seven books deals with the problem of justice, and in it
the author looks forward to a progressive improvement of
economic conditions in a society which combines Christianity and traditional elements of Romanism. In fact, as C. N.
Cochrane indicates, he anticipates 'that peculiar mixture of
pagan humanitarianism and Christian sentiment which goes
by the name of Christian socialism, a compound in which the
real virtues of either element are largely neutralized by the
other.'[49]

Lactantius' attempt at establishing a common ground for
both spiritual and socio-temporal commitments of the
individual might be expected to have produced a fresh
assessment of economic life within the Christian tradition.
However, as Cochrane's statement suggests, no new outlook
was actually engendered. Lactantius achieved no genuine
synthesis of the elements with which he worked, and much
that was novel in Christianity, as compared with classical
culture, was de-emphasised by him in the interests of
harmonising the two outlooks.[50] His version of Christianity
presented no real challenge to the existing political and
economic orders of the Roman world. This early affirmation

---

[47] Hermas, *Pastor*, Sim. I.
[48] Consult Otto Bardenhewer, *Patrology*, trans. T. J. Shahan, (St Louis, Herder,
1908) p. 205, and Ernest Barker, op. cit. pp. 460–72.
[49] C. N. Cochrane, op. cit., p. 196. The author adds: 'From the fate which
overtook this liberal-social-democratic programme (when applied by Constantine),
it is possible to forecast the probable outcome of analogous movements in
modern times.'
[50] Consult J. Danielou, 'Patristic Literature,' in Jean Danielou and others,
Historical Theology (Harmondsworth, Penguin, 1969) pp. 88–9.

of a fundamental agreement between Christ and contemporary culture failed to yield any meaningful counter to
the retreatist theme in much Patristic economics.[51]

Among the critics of Lactantius' version of Christian
doctrine was the fiery Jerome (c. 340–420). Educated in
Rome, but heavily influenced by the writings of the Eastern
Fathers, and by Eastern monastic practice, St Jerome is an
oustanding champion of the retreatism they advocated. He
makes their doctrine of work his own. 'In Egypt', he
explains, 'the monasteries make it a rule to receive none who
are not willing to work; for they regard labour as necessary not
only for the support of the body but also for the salvation of
the soul, lest the mind stray into harmful thoughts.'[52]
Hence, he advises: 'Always have some work on hand that the
devil may find you busy.'[53] In addition, he is vociferous in
his condemnation of accumulated wealth. Like Karl Marx
and David Ricardo, Jerome considers the question of income
distribution primarily in its static aspects. 'All riches come
from iniquity,' he writes, 'and unless one has lost, another
cannot gain. Hence that common opinion seems to me to be
very true, "the rich man is unjust, or the heir of an unjust
one".'[54] The tendency in Jewish thought to equate riches and
righteousness is, of course, completely negated here.

Any idea of mutual gain from trade, whether domestic or
international, seems to be quite absent from Jerome's
thought. In his commentary on Isaiah, for example, he
declares that 'one man does not accumulate money except
through the loss and injury suffered by another.' Commenting on Micheas he writes: 'Now, however, the rich abound
not so much in riches as in injustice, since all riches, being a
spoliation of others, are born of injustice.' Despite these
sentiments, however, Jerome does not completely deny that
command over resources might be a socially useful function
performed by some individuals. John A. Ryan points out that
against the passages cited above, others can be set which

[51] For a study of some other attempts at establishing a Christ-culture agreement,
see H. Richard Niebuhr, op. cit., Ch. 3.
[52] *Patrologia Latina*, Vol. 22, Col. 1079.
[53] Op. cit., Col. 1078. See also, Vol. 25, Col. 155.
[54] Op. cit., Vol. 22, Col. 984.

suggest support for a measure of private ownership of property.[55]

Jerome seems to envisage some legitimate social function for wealth when he is commenting, not on the Prophets, but on the Wisdom literature of the Old Testament. Here, he has less scope for employing the philosophies of Greece to wrench Christian conceptions of the significance of economic activity away from their biblical foundation in the Jewish understanding of the issue. Pagan ascetical outlooks as expressed in early monasticism are tempered by the consideration that 'A wise man with riches has greater glory than one who is wise only. Some need wisdom and others, riches; and he who is wise and not rich can indeed teach what is proper, but sometimes he cannot perform what is asked.'[56] He continues in this vein that 'wealth is not an obstacle to the rich man if he uses it well, nor does want make the poor man more praiseworthy, if in the midst of his filth and poverty he does not avoid sin.' The example of Abraham indicates that it is not entirely out of the question that the rich can be righteous.

Augustine

Most of the conflicting tendencies concerning economic life in the Greek, Old Testament, and New Testament understandings are represented in the writings of St Jerome's contemporary, Augustine. However, the latter's thought transcends the conflict to suggest the possibility of a new way of considering economic and other historically-conditioned phenomena.[57] Educated in Carthage, a professor of rhetoric at Milan, baptised a Christian when aged thirty-two, and subsequently, bishop of Hippo in his native Africa, Augustine was subject to all the major intellectual and emotional currents of his era.

[55] J. A. Ryan, op. cit., pp. 71–8.
[56] *Commentary on Ecclesiastes*, as quoted in op. cit., p. 75.
[57] Comparing Jerome and Augustine, Jean Danielou writes: 'Apart from his work as a translator, Jerome is greatly indebted to the Greek world. With St Augustine, by way of contrast, we are faced with a new creation, where the Christian West is displayed in the mind of a genius. It is from Augustine onwards that Latin Christian thought definitely branches off to take its own course.' J. Danielou, op. cit., p. 119.

His work of most immediate significance for economics, the *XXII Books of St Aurelius Augustine the Bishop on the City of God against the Pagans*, itself was occasioned by a contemporary event of revolutionary proportion. In the year 410 Alaric and the Goths sacked Rome, and between 413 and 426 Augustine set about rebutting the charge that the fall of Rome was due to the Empire's embracing the God of the Christians. The result was the formulation of a general vision in which 'the course of human history from the fall of Adam through successive ages of time is regarded as part of an unending progress.'[58] Secondly, in this work and the earlier *Confessions*, he revolutionised the classical conception of human personality and set the evolution of the individual personality at the centre of the historical dynamic. The person as essentially a shell or mask, the pliable subject of external pressures (as discussed above in Chapter 2), is no longer a being who can represent human nature in its full dimensions. Instead, there emerges modern European man.[59] Thirdly, in the *City of God* 'the Patristic Church, which did not think to be other than "a society within a society" and could not hope to change the world, comes of age and takes social responsibility. The *City of God* . . . was the first great attempt to relate the eschatological Christianity of the New Testament to culture, and a first grasp in the Church's groping toward a full social ethic.'[60]

The implications of these changes for a new approach to the scope and meaning of economic activity, and to economics as a science, are best illustrated with reference to Socratic conceptions with which Augustine was very familiar, and which strongly influenced his social thought. As was outlined in Chapter 2, Socratic involvement in economic analysis was based on a concern with the nature of the good (happy) life. This is also a basic preoccupation for Augustine. In one of his sermons, for example, he states: 'if I were to ask

[58] F. P. Cassidy, op. cit., p. 145.
[59] On Augustine's revolutionary treatment of personality, consult C. N. Cochrane, op. cit., p. 386ff.
[60] Thomas J. Bigham and Albert T. Mollegen, 'The Christian Ethic,' in Roy W. Battenhouse (ed.), *A Companion to the Study of St Augustine* (N.Y., Oxford University Press, 1955) p. 393.

of you why you believe in Christ and why you have become
Christians, everyone would answer truthfully by saying, "For
the happy life." Therefore the pursuit of the happy life is a
goal common to philosophers and Christians.'[61] Further,
answers to this question could only be formulated meaningfully for the Socratics in a social context. Likewise, for
Augustine, the relevant answers were heavily conditioned by
the inescapable reality of man's membership of an earthly
city (a *res publica*). Men were obliged to come together in a
polis, according to Plato and Aristotle, because of lack of
economic self-sufficiency, and the same holds true of the
citizens of Augustine's cities. The basic rationale of civil
authority, he argues, is the maintenance of 'a common
agreement among men regarding the acquisition of the
necessaries of life', or, in another phrase, 'the combination of
men's wills to attain the things which are helpful to this
life.'[62]

Although satisfaction of human economic need is at the
basis of civil society, Augustine, like the Greek philosophers,
does not believe that the individual can best solve the scarcity
problem through application of a science devoted to the
multiplication and allocation of resources. Rather, a more
rational course to pursue is restriction and reorientation of
wants.[63] This is not to say that Augustine, any more than
the Socratics, regarded poverty as a condition admirable in
itself. At one point, in fact, he goes so far as to state that to
own and control an abundance of resources 'without cleaving
to them is much more admirable than not to have them at
all.'[64]

---

[61] Quincy Howe (ed.), *Selected Sermons of St Augustine* (London, Gollancz,
1967) p. 91.
[62] *De Civitate Dei*, XIX, 17.
[63] 'For as for riches and high rank, and all other things in which men who are
strangers to true felicity imagine that happiness exists, what comfort do they
bring, seeing that it is better to be independent of such things than to enjoy
abundance of them, because, when possessed, they occasion, through our fear of
losing them, more vexation than was caused by the strength of desire with which
their possession was coveted? Men are not made good by possessing these
so-called good things, but, if men have become good otherwise, they make these
things to be really good by using them well.' *Epistula*, CXXX, II, 3.
[64] *De Moribus Ecclesiae Catholicae*, XXIII, 42. The same underlying principle is
applied to patterns of consumption. See *De Doctrina Christiana*, III, 12.

Despite these parallels, however, there is a profound difference between the Augustinian and the Socratic appreciations of the conditions for the solution of the problem of scarcity. The fundamental, and quite radical, difference is that for Augustine, the solution is something which may be approximated, but never achieved, over time. The elements of approximation and temporality are inevitably present for any one individual or any one community at any single moment of his or its existence. There is no hope of a 'final solution' by, for example, the erection of an ideal city-state peopled by just heads of households pursuing the golden mean of temperate living. Approximate solution is a matter of historical progression; of an on-going creative effort; and, of the orientation of the will of individuals.

As for Karl Marx, conflict is an inevitable ingredient in the progressive search, but Augustine, convinced of the autonomy of the individual personality, cannot be drawn into any forecast of an earthly paradise such as Marx's more restricted vision of the dimensions of conflict made possible. There is some shape to human history given by the Father's act of Creation, the Son's manifestation of his manhood in the historical figure of Jesus of Nazareth, and in the promise of an end with a new heaven and a new earth such as provided by the Johannnine literature. 'Scripture,' he states in *De doctrina Christiana* (Lib. III, c. 10), 'is a history of the past, a prediction of the future and a delineation of the present.' However, Augustine is no adherent of any doctrine of inevitable progress in secular history.

The African bishop invites his Christian contemporaries to renewed explorations in economic analysis by refocusing on 'the great problem of Plato's *Republic* — how to apply the simple rule of justice, giving "to each his due".'[65] At the same time, he offers them a much broader and far less static frame of reference for that analysis than that provided by a Greek *polis*. For Augustine, a community, i.e., 'a people', is not a group brought together by accidents of birth and locality. Rather, 'a people is an assemblage of reasonable beings bound together by a common agreement as to the

[65] Edward R. Hardy, Jr, 'The City of God', in R. W. Battenhouse, op. cit., p. 274.

objects of their love.'[66] Such a community too can progress
or regress, depending on the changing perception of the
quality of life sought by its members. 'It will be a superior
people,' Augustine continues, 'in proportion as it is bound
together by higher interests, inferior in proportion as it is
bound together by lower.'[67]

Productive and distributive activities for a community such
as this have their rationales in contributing to the progressive
approximation of that quality of life which is appropriate for
men made in the image of their Creator. The composition
and distribution of community output ought to be determined by their utility with respect to that end. In any given
historical circumstance, however, rational organisation of
economic life is not fully attainable. Conflict is inevitably
present. The principle of ordered harmony such as Plato
sought for society is seen by Augustine to be under constant
challenge. True justice (*vera justitia*) is an attribute of God's
kingdom only, and the justice of any *res publica* can be
merely an image or approximation of the truth.

The major disturbing element in society is the tendency of
many persons to treat output as an end instead of as a means.
Some men insist on worshipping or 'serving' those things
which are 'the works of their hands' instead of using them as
vehicles for a more meaningful mode of existence.[68] 'Use the
world,' Augustine urges, as an alternative,

> let not the world hold you captive. You are passing on the
> journey you have begun; you have come, again to depart,
> not to abide. You are passing on your journey, and this life
> is but a wayside inn. Use money as the traveller at an inn
> uses table, cup, pitcher, and couch, with the purpose not
> of remaining, but of leaving them behind.[69]

Augustine does not adopt the retreatist attitude to
economic involvements, as do many of his Patristic predecessors. The possibility of movement towards more rational

---

[66] *De Civitate Dei*, XIX, 24. Nationality, to Augustine's way of thinking, is a
matter of the individual person's mind and will.
[67] Ibid.
[68] Op. cit., VIII, 23.
[69] *In Joann. Evangel.*, XL, 10.

conduct of economic relationships is always present. The achievement of justice in those relationships is not a question of imposing some blueprint for social order, but an on-going process dictated by the degree to which individuals are capable of using instead of being used by, the material results of production.[70]

There is room within the Augustinian theory for the thought that mathematics, logic, and natural science, the fine arts and technology, may all become both the beneficiaries of the conversion of man's love and the instruments of that new love of God that rejoices in his whole creation and serves all his creatures. The Christian life can and must make use not only of these cultural activities but of 'the convenient and necessary arrangements of men with men' — conventions regarding dress and rank, weights and measures, coinage and the like.[71]

The possibility of economic growth as a legitimate human aspiration is also opened up by Augustine's new appreciation of personality. Time, for Augustine, is personality-relative. Its measure is not located in external events but in the individual consciousness.

> This new theory of time which St Augustine originated [observes Christopher Dawson] also renders possible a new conception of history. If man is not the slave and creature of time, but its master and creator, then history also becomes a creative process. It does not repeat itself meaninglessly; it grows into organic unity with the growth of human experience. The past does not die; it becomes

[70] The reverse case is depicted as follows: 'For when those things are loved which we can lose against our will, we must needs toil for them most miserably; and to obtain them, amid the straitnesses of earthly cares, whilst each desires to snatch them for himself, and to be beforehand with another, or to wrest it from him, must scheme injustice.' *Enarrationes in Psalmos*, VII, 16.

[71] H. Richard Niebuhr, op. cit., p. 215. Augustine's basic approach to these matters is indicated by the following statement: 'Knowledge which is used to promote love is useful, but in itself and separated from such an objective, it turns out to be not only useless but even harmful.' *Lib. II, ep. 55, ad inquisitiones Januarii* s.39. Also, acts based on love without knowledge are to be avoided. He repeats the logion of the *Didache* (I, 5—6) against carelessness in the distribution of material aid: 'Let the alms sweat in your hand until you know to whom you are giving.'

incorporated in humanity. And hence progress is possible,
since the life of society and of humanity itself possesses
continuity and the capacity for spiritual growth no less
than the life of the individual.[72]

With Augustine, the command of the Lord of the Book of
Genesis for man to involve himself in a developmental
process is made relevant to the Christian, not only the
Jewish, condition.

Despite the wide-ranging influence of Augustine's thought
in later centuries in Europe, his novel conception of the
scope and meaning of economic activity does not seem to
have exercised a decisive impact on the mainstream of the
development of economic analysis. One reason for this was
that 'His application of his social principles was critical rather
than constructive, and though the applications are brilliant
they are not systematic. The conditions of the early fifth
century did not stimulate St Augustine or anyone else to
undertake a work of social construction.'[73] Again, 'Social
responsibility in Augustine never achieves the absoluteness of
a command from the God whose Kingdom breaks into and
transforms history.'[74] Unresolved ambiguities in Augustine's
social thought left later thinkers free to emulate some aspects
of his assessment of economic life while ignoring others.

When a definite movement towards the re-emergence of
economic analysis began in the writings of the theologians of
the thirteenth century, certain particular observations by
Augustine were to prove highly influential. Among these

[72] C. Dawson, op. cit., p. 312. On this same point, consult C. N. Cochrane, op.
cit., p. 440. He points out that for Augustine, 'time is anything but otiose. But to
say that time works wonders is really to say that men work wonders in time. It is,
indeed, through their consciousness of spatio—temporal movement that they are
enabled to see themselves directly and actually, as lords of creation, . . .'
[73] Edward R. Hardy, Jr, op. cit., p. 274. With St Augustine on his death-bed,
barbarian hordes were beseiging the walls of the very town, Hippo, in which he
lay.
[74] T. J. Bigham and A. T. Mollegen, op. cit., p. 393. The Yale theologian H.
Richard Niebuhr, op. cit., pp. 215—17, traces Augustine's failure to go on to
develop new, positive economic and sociological analyses to his adherence to a
theological doctrine of predestination in which 'the elect' are irrevocably
differentiated from 'the damned'. The similar failure of the Reformer John Calvin
is also noted.

were his guarded approval of the activities of merchants, his relation of mercantile profits to compensation for expenditure of labour, and the linking of market evaluation of goods to subjective understanding of personal need.[75] However, it cannot be said that St Thomas Aquinas and his contemporaries worked in terms of the full framework for economic analysis which a thorough appreciation of Augustine suggests. In particular, they neglected the possibility of an economics of growth.

The Albertino—Thomist revolution which engendered medieval economic analysis relied on a doctrine of the concordance of nature and grace. By stressing this concordance, they allowed little scope for the conflict which Augustine found inherent in any given social situation. Through a playing down of the role of such conflict, the schoolmen were able to minimise the function of time in the resolution of social problems. Their novel vision of a just, Christian order of society, here and now, masked, as had an analogous vision for Plato and Aristotle, the dynamics of the problems they were endeavouring to solve. In consequence, the growth aspects of economic issues which the Augustinian vision made relevant were lost.[76] When they eventually emerged, it was to be in terms of a non-scholastic and non-Augustinian conception of society. Growth was envisaged as a function of aggrandisement of national states, and economic enquiry was to

[75] On the latter, see *De Civitate Dei*, XI, 16.

[76] On the strong contrast between Augustinian and Thomistic thought Reinhold Niebuhr writes: 'Aquinas, in fact, constructed his theory of the natural law upon classical, and primarily Aristotelian, foundations. It was the weakness of both classical and medieval theories that they assumed an order in history conforming to the uniformities of nature ... Augustine was wise in avoiding the alleged solution of a natural law theory, which was the basis of so much lack of realism in both the classical and the medieval period, and which can persist today long after the Aristotelian idea of fixed form for historical events has been overcome, ...' Niebuhr concludes: 'It is in fact something of a mystery how the Christian insights into human nature and history, expressed by Augustine, could have been subordinated to classical thought with so little sense of the conflict between them in the formulations of Thomas Aquinas; ...' R. Niebuhr, *Christian Realism and Political Problems* (London: Faber, 1954) pp. 126—7. It should be remarked that Neibuhr here appears to overlook the fact that Aquinas paid some attention to the relationship of historical progression to social behaviour, particularly in his treatises on the Old Law and the New Law.

regress to the status of a tool of that aggrandisement instead of a tool in the quest for social justice. The conception of economics fostered by the Greek Sophists was to pre-empt the field of investigation of growth and development in the hands of the writers called 'mercantilist'.

5 Three Legal Traditions: Rabbis, Romans and Canonists

The role of the social visions of major religious thinkers and philosophers in shaping the course of economic thought generally excites more interest than the seemingly more mundane contributions of legists. Yet it is an inescapable fact that European economic analysis owes a great deal to legal enquiry of earlier ages. The contribution of the Roman jurists in this respect is often acknowledged. Less frequently, the evolution of the legal system of the Christian church of the Latin rite is deemed relevant. Because of sketchy historical evidence and communication problems amongst researchers, the Jewish tradition based on the *Mishnah* tends to be neglected almost completely. This chapter offers some preliminary insights concerning the economic aspects of these bodies of legal thought and, while recognising that much detailed work remains to be done, indicates some of the areas of impact on the predisposition of analytical economics as it began to emerge in scholastic debate.

The Mishnah

Approximately 100 years after the writings of St John the Apostle, Rabbi Judah the Patriarch (c. A.D. 135—220) completed in Galilee a collection of oral law in the Jewish tradition coming down from the Scribes and Pharisees. This collection is the Mishnah, and its roots extend back to at least the first half of the second century B.C. In Jewish religious literature only the Scriptures take precedent over it, and it formed the basis of both the Babylonian and Palestinian Talmuds. Together with the Gemera, a later commentary on it, the Mishnah has continued to serve as a key source of reference for Jews of orthodox persuasion throughout succeeding centuries. Given its central role in shaping Jewish thought and behaviour, and given the influence of orthodox Jewish mores on the development of Western culture, the economic thought in the Mishnah must be taken into account in any attempt to trace the course of European economic enquiry in general.[1]

In the Pentateuch, we have seen, economic activity is regarded as an aspect of the exercise of stewardship on behalf of the Creator, and economic enquiry is part of the investigation into the correct conduct of the office given to man. The Mishnah does not alter this basic stance. However, to a much greater extent than the earlier writings, it enters into detailed consideration of the conduct of man's office. Operating within the previously established conception of the Economic Problem, the Mishnah proceeds to one of the types of economic enquiry that conception requires. The framework of discussion is predominantly legalistic, with emphasis on a case-study approach rather than a systematic presentation of general principles. It is in the course of these case studies that particular economic relationships are classified and analysed. The Mishnah does not concern itself directly with examination of functional relationships between economic variables. It does not set out to explain how prices or outputs are determined or why levels of employment or profit can increase or decline. Rather, it aims at clarifying what is actually involved in processes such as buying and selling, borrowing and lending, or exercising command over resources. As such, it represents a most significant movement towards better understanding of the realities of economic life.

[1] Concerning the impact of Jewish thought and practice during the middle ages, for example, the noted historian Salo W. Baron writes: 'In the feudalistic medieval world the Jews were perhaps the most "liberal" economic group, not only as a result of their forced inventiveness in the struggle for economic survival, but paradoxically, also because of their staunch adherence to tradition. What the "reception" of Roman law at large meant to the German or French economies of the early modern period was accomplished on a minor scale by the Jews acting within the earlier medieval economy under the legal requirements of talmudic law, which was likewise basically formulated under the semicapitalist civilization of the Hellenistic and early Roman Empires.' S. W. Baron, *Ancient and Medieval Jewish History* (New Brunswick: Rutgers University Press, 1972) p. 252.

Ranging over the entire field of legislation of the Pentateuch, the Mishnah is divided into six 'orders' or sections, each of which is devoted to an area of law relating to Jewish observance. In the first order, 'Zeraim' ('Seeds') there is consideration of the welfare provisions set out in Deuteronomy and Leviticus. However, of greater interest in terms of economic analysis is the fourth order 'Nezikin' ('Damages') which includes discussion of property damage and transfers of money and goods. Within the fourth order, the two sub-sections, 'Baba Metzia' ('The Middle Gate') and 'Baba Bathra' ('The Last Gate'), are particularly important.

Exchange and price
The analytical approach of the Mishnah to economic issues is well illustrated by the variety of passages in which acts of exchange are dealt with. Consider the following:

> Gold acquires silver, but silver does not acquire gold; copper acquires silver, but silver does not acquire copper. Disused coins acquire current coins, but current coins do not acquire disused coins. Unminted metal acquires minted metal, but minted metal does not acquire unminted metal. Movable property acquires coined money, but coined money does not acquire movable property. Movable property acquires other movable property. Thus if the buyer had drawn fruit into his possession from the seller but had not yet paid him money, neither may retract; but if he had paid him money but had not yet drawn the fruit into his possession from the seller, either may retract. (Baba Metzia, 4:1–2).[2]

Here, an act of exchange is characterised essentially by the buyer's actually taking possession (drawing) of the goods involved. The buyer's payment of money to the seller does not of itself define the act. In law, according to the Mishnah, it is the seller's parting with possession of a commodity which gives him a title to money, rather than the buyer's

---

[2] This and other passages quoted below are from *The Mishnah*, trans. Herbert Danby (London, Oxford University Press, 1933, reprinted 1972).

parting with money which gives him a title to the commodity. 'Consequently,' as Herbert Danby points out, 'the problem arises in an exchange of coins (gold for silver, etc.), which is the commodity whose drawing makes the purchase valid, and which is the medium of payment whose 'drawing,' i.e., passing into the other's possession, does not constitute the essential element in exchange? The answer is: The less current and less convenient medium constitutes the 'commodity' and the more current and the more convenient medium constitutes the purchasing medium.'[3]

The basic principle defining an exchange transaction is repeated in the Shebiith (10:9): 'All movable goods are legally acquired only by the act of drawing them into the purchaser's possession.' Elsewhere, a variety of refinements is added. The case of sale of immovable property is dealt with as follows:

> Property for which there is security (immovable property) can be acquired by money or by writ or by usucaption; and that for which there is no security can be acquired only by the act of drawing. Property for which there is no security in conjunction with property for which there is security can be acquired by money, by writ, or by usucaption, and imposes the need for an oath also on property for which there is security. (Kiddushin 1:5).

Account is taken of the fact that an exchange may be undertaken by written deeds of sale, and the conditions under which a deed can be written up and the information it must contain to specify the transaction are defined. (Baba Bathra, 10:3, and Gittin, 3:2). Also defined is onus of proof in the event of dispute over whether or not payment and transfer of goods have occurred: 'Rabbi Judah says: He that has possession of the produce, his hand is uppermost.' (Shebuoth, 7:6). Even the relative status of buyer and seller during the period of time when measurement of the quantity of goods concerned in a transaction is in progress is a matter for attention. (Baba Bathra, 5:7—8).

---

[3] Op. cit., p. 353.

In this latter passage, and elsewhere,[4] commodity prices are treated as variables subject to sudden fluctuation. Price formation is depicted as occurring through a competitive, communal marketing process, and individual exchange transactions are to be entered into only with full knowledge of the prevailing state of the market:

> No bargain may be made over produce before its market-price is known. After its market-price is known a bargain may be made, for even if one dealer has not the produce another will have it . . . A bargain may be made to pay for wares at the cheapest rate that prevails at the time of delivery. Rabbi Judah says: Even if the bargain was not made to pay for wares at the cheapest rate, he may say, 'Give me the wares at such a price, or give me back my money.' (Baba Metzia, 5:7).

It is recognised here, however, that certain legitimate transactions may be made in the absence of full knowledge and a perfect market. These are wholesale deals made with a producer for agricultural products held in stock, e.g. olives in the vat, or purchases of products intended to serve towards further production. The latter goods, which the Austrian economist Eugen von Böhm-Bawerk (1851–1914) was to designate as 'intermediate products', or 'social capital', include 'the clay-balls of the potter', 'lime as soon as the limestone is sunk in the kiln', and manure.

Guardianship, loans, and deposits

As can be seen from the above, the Rabbis are able to make firm analytical distinctions between fixed capital and other articles, between social capital and finished products, and between the competitive market conditions that can be approximated in retailing but less readily in wholesaling.[5] A wide variety of monetary obligations is also the subject of categorisation: secured and unsecured loans, book debts to retailers, hiring charges, and fines (Shebiith, 10:1–9). Various modes of wage payment are distinguished (Baba Metzia,

[4] See, for example, Baba Metzia, 5:9.
[5] Clear differentiation of wholesaling and retailing functions is found also in Demai, 2:4.

9:11), and productive activity is classified into thirty-nine main types of task (Shabbath 7:2). A major area of analysis is concerned with degrees of control over and responsibility for resources, apart from the control and responsibility flowing from outright ownership. There are four types of non-owner controllers: an unpaid guardian, a borrower, a paid guardian, and a hirer (Baba Metzia, 7:8).

All craftsmen, for example, who are using the materials owned by another in their workshops are regarded as the paid guardians of those materials. This means the craftsmen can retain the materials as pledges against payment for their work, but, at the same time, they are financially responsible if the materials are lost or damaged. Then, when the work is finished and it is indicated that the owner can pay for it and remove it from the workshop, the status of the craftsmen changes to that of unpaid guardians who are no longer responsible for loss. Again, the receiver of a pledge on account of a loan is regarded as the paid guardian of the pledge. However, Rabbi Judah argues that a distinction is to be made between loans of goods and money loans. The lender is a paid guardian only in the case of loans of goods. In money loans he is an unpaid guardian of the pledge. The reasoning here, according to Herbert Danby, is that by lending goods, 'the lender is thus saved the loss from decay which he would otherwise suffer, and that this advantage is equivalent to receiving hire for the pledge's safe-keeping.'[6] Yet another dimension to the issue of the status and degree of discretion of the guardian of a pledge is added by Abba Saul. He contends that a guardian may hire out the pledge of a poor man if the income accruing from the hire is greater than the cost of depreciation of the object when so used. The net return serves to help decrease the poor man's debt (Baba Metzia, 6:6–7).

The type of reasoning employed with regard to pledges is applied to the case of deposits of money, although here there is evident division of opinion among the Rabbis. Recognising that the purchasing power of a sum of money can alter during the period over which it is deposited, they are divided on the issue of the criterion for valuation of the deposit on return to the depositor, if the sum has been used in business

[6] Op. cit., p. 358.

transactions by the person to whom it was entrusted. According to the School of Shammai, 'if a man put to his own use what had been left in his keeping,' he is obliged to repay the sum at its original value if that value has fallen in the interim. Alternatively, if its value has risen, he is obliged to repay the sum's new worth. Others disagree:

> And the School of Hillel say: He must restore the deposit at the same value as when he put it to his own use. Rabbi Akiba says: At its value when claimed. If a man had expressed his intention of putting the deposit to his own use, the School of Shammai say: He is forthwith liable, and the School of Hillel say: He is not liable until he has put it to his use, . . . (Baba Metzia, 3:12).

The controversy over deposits is also significant for the attempt which is made to reason in terms of the economic function rather than the general social role of a person. With the Socratic philosophers, it was seen, persons were regarded as householders and citizens. These social categories were deemed sufficient to serve for the analysis of economic activity. Hence, for example, there was no significant distinction between the householder in his economic function as consumer and in his function as producer or distributor. However, such a distinction is offered in the Mishnah. Householders, as householders, are not to be thought of as businessmen, although there is some doubt in the case of small, family-run retailing. It is argued:

> If a man left money in the keeping of a money-changer and it was sealed up, he may not make use of it and, therefore, if it was lost he is not answerable for it; if the money was loose he may make use of it and, therefore, if it was lost he is answerable for it. If it was left in the keeping of a householder, he may not make use of it whether it was sealed up or loose; if, therefore, it was lost he is not answerable for it. A shopkeeper is to be deemed a householder. So Rabbi Meir. Rabbi Judah says: A Shopkeeper is to be deemed a money-changer.' (Baba Metzia, 3:11).[7]

[7] See also Meilah, 6:5.

Income and work
An outstanding feature of the economic thought of the
Mishnah is the concern with differentiating forms of income
– interest, profit, rent, and wages. Profit, as a return on a
speculative business venture, is distinguished from interest, as
follows:

> What is usury ('neshek') and what is increase ('tarbith')?
> It is usury ('neshek') when a man lends a 'sela' (four
> 'denars') for five 'denars,' or two 'seahs' of wheat for
> three; because he is a usurer ('noshek,' i.e. one who bites).
> And what is increase? When a man increases his gains in
> trafficking with produce. How? If one man bought wheat
> from another at a golden 'denar' (twenty-five silver
> 'denars') the 'kor' when such was the market price, and
> then wheat rose to thirty silver 'denars' the 'kor', and he
> said 'Deliver me my wheat since I would sell it to buy wine
> with the price,' and the other said, 'Let thy wheat be
> reckoned to me at thirty 'denars,' and thus thou has now a
> claim on me for wine to that value!' – although he has no
> wine. (Baba Metzia, 5:1).

In the text immediately following this, the difference
between usury and a legitimate rental charge on fixed
property is noted, and subsequently (5:8–11) alternative
ways in which a lender may attempt to take usury are
detailed. During this discussion, Rabban Gamaliel is cited as
rejecting the view that loss of liquidity itself represents a cost
which warrants a legitimate return by way of interest
(5:10).[8] Elsewhere, the case is considered of a purchase of
fixed capital made under conditions which give the seller the
option of repurchasing at any time over one year at the price
the buyer has given. This would seem to put the buyer in

[8] The prohibition concerning interest-taking applied only within the community
of Israelites. 'Money may be borrowed from gentiles on usury and lent to them on
usury, and the same applies with a resident alien.' (Baba Metzia, 5:6). This
suggests that the Rabbis recognised that there was a sound economic base for
interest charges, but that the ancient commands of Leviticus or Exodus were still
binding on the people of the Lord in their mutual dealings.

potential receipt of usury, having had the use of the capital
for a time plus the return of the sum originally spent if the
seller decides to exercise his option. The decision is: 'This is a
kind of usury which is yet not usury.'[9] The thinking here
seems to be that the purchaser was not intending to earn
interest, since the option of repurchase was that of the seller.
Also, there is the fact of the uncertainty to which the buyer
is subject in such a contract. This may justify compensation
akin to the compensation one can take in speculative business
ventures of uncertain outcome. (Arakhin, 9:3).

Profit-taking is carefully distinguished not only from
interest-earning, but also from the receipt of income by way
of wages. This is illustrated by the discussion of business
partnerships involving active and sleeping partners. In certain
circumstances the former is to receive a return for his effort,
a wage, which is distinct from any share of the surplus
which the business venture may yield. At the same time, it
would seem, the size of the surplus is not determined until
the cost of the sleeping partner's original investment has been
deducted from gross takings and credited to him. The
relevant passage reads:

> None may set up a shopkeeper on the condition of
> receiving half the profit, or give him money to buy
> produce therewith on the condition of receiving half the
> profit, unless he is paid his wage as a labourer. None may
> set another's hens to hatch out his eggs on the condition of
> sharing the profit, or give another calves or foals to rear on
> the condition of sharing half the estimated loss or gain,
> unless he is paid his wage for his labour and the cost of
> food. (Baba Metzia, 5:4).

It is added that where the inactive partner contributes
capital, e.g. a cow or an ass, which provides some services of
exclusive benefit to the active partner, as distinct from the

---

[9] Further, returns on loans to improve the productivity of agricultural land
already subject to rental charges are seen as legitimate when they are earned in the
form of an offer by the tenant of the land to pay increased rental. (Baba Metzia,
5:5).

partnership itself, that benefit can replace the right to wage payment.[10]

While the Mishnah's exploration of particular features of economic activity is much more intensive than that of the Bible, it does not seek to add to the general assessment of the scope and meaning of work to be found in the Old Testament. Certain scattered observations, however, are relevant to this broader issue, notably that contributed by a fifth generation rabbinical teacher, Simeon b. Eleazar (c. A.D. 165–200). In a series of queries which echo the words of Jesus of Nazareth (Matthew 6:26–30), Rabbi Simeon asks: 'Hast thou ever seen a wild animal or a bird practising a craft? — yet they have their sustenance without care and were they created for naught else but to serve me? But I was created to serve my Maker. How much more then ought not I to have my sustenance without care?' (Kiddushin, 4:14).

Whereas Christ posed the same questions to endeavour to persuade his listeners, during the Sermon on the Mount, of the irrationality of concern with the problem of scarcity, Rabbi Simeon finds such concern rational in a fallen world. 'But I have wrought evil,' he explains, 'and so forfeited my right to sustenance without care.' Accompanying texts from other Rabbis recommend the pursuit of a 'cleanly craft' to meet the need of subsistence, while at the same time warning that it is the craftsman's degree of moral worth rather than his skill that will determine whether or not he attains wealth. Of all crafts, it is command of the Law which is most beneficial, 'for a man enjoys the reward thereof in this world and its whole worth remains for the world to come.' (Kiddushin, 4:14). Care in attainment of knowledge of the Law, and care in the strict observance of it offer the best means of dealing with scarcity issues.

[10] On hours of work, working conditions, and non-wage benefits for wage earners, Rabban Simeon b. Gamaliel's dictum is cited: 'Everything should follow local use.' (Baba Metzia, 7:1). The clear emphasis of the Mishnah is that the appropriate minimum return to hired labour is governed by local custom and will vary accordingly. Centuries later, the English economist David Ricardo (1772–1823), whose orthodox Jewish parents sent him as a child to school in which the Talmud was studied, also supported the idea that the minimum return to hired labour was determined by local custom. See J. A. Schumpeter, *History of Economic Analysis* (N.Y., Oxford University Press, 1959), pp. 664–5.

Later development and impact

The history of economic enquiry in the Jewish religious
tradition does not cease with the Mishnah. Further investigation was to be undertaken by the commentators on the
Mishnah whose views were given permanent shape in the
Gemara during the sixth century. These two compilations
were combined to form the Talmud which, in its Babylonian
version especially, remained as the central point of reference
for the conduct of orthodox Jewish life. Later still, the
wide-ranging legal code of the scholar Maimonides
(1135–1204) included among its fourteen books three given
over almost exclusively to questions concerning economic
activities.[11]

While the thought in this tradition is extremely sophisticated,[12] the analysis of economic matters remains subordinate to, and merely a tool of, legal enquiry. It does not
seek to penetrate the determination of economic variables in
the manner suggested by Greek thinkers, e.g. Aristotle's
treatment of value, or Xenophon's observation that the
extension of the division of labour is limited by the size of
the market. Again, although it covers many facets of
economic life, it does not attain to the concept of 'the
economy' such as began to emerge in the writings of the later
scholastic doctors. Further, it is difficult to gauge with any
certainty the degree of influence it exerted on the development of the mainstream of Western economic thought.
Before the thirteenth century, the vast majority of Jewish
people were located in areas dominated by Islamic culture.[13]
Yet, throughout the middle ages they seemed to have played
a significant role in the commercial life of towns in, first,
southern and later, northern Europe. In addition, for long

[11] For a study of Maimonides' economics, including comparisons with the
thought of Aristotle and of medieval Christian theologians consult Salo W. Baron,
'The Economic Views of Maimonides', op. cit., pp. 149–235.
[12] Werner Sombart remarks that, 'Some of the Rabbis speak as though they had
mastered Ricardo and Marx, or to say the least, had been brokers on the Stock
Exchange for several years, ...' *The Jews and Modern Capitalism*, (N.Y., Collier,
1962), p. 291.
[13] An outstanding example of economic enquiry in the Islamic context is Ibn
Khaldun, *The Muqaddimah: an Introduction to History*, trans. Franz Rosenthal, 3
vols (N.Y., Random House, 1967).

periods in many areas of medieval Europe, as Salo Baron has observed, 'Not only orally but often in widely circulating pamphlets and treatises, the Jews were in a position to discuss frankly the differences between their own and the Christian attitude to life. In few modern countries . . . would men be allowed to speak their minds so freely and in a way so clearly running counter to the established order and the interests of its dominant group.'[14] Given such a degree of freedom, and given the importance of the Jewish presence in trade and finance, it is reasonable to suppose that Talmudic economic thought cannot be discounted as a force in the gradual emergence of economic analysis in Christian Europe.

The Roman law tradition

One of the most crucial of all the elements in the making of European social thought is the influence of legal reasoning in the Roman pattern. Its importance stems from the long political dominance of Rome as an imperial power, revivals of Roman models for the establishment of law and order in later regimes, and the outstanding quality of the analytical work it embodied. Roman law, and its extensions, have a very special significance for economics, since

> to the end of the eighteenth century, most of the writers on economic questions were, if not businessmen, either clergymen or lawyers by profession: the scholarly training of these two types of economists was largely provided by the Roman and the canon law and so there was a natural avenue by which the concepts, the spirit, and even, perhaps, some mannerisms of the Roman jurists entered the field of economic analysis.[15]

[14] S. W. Baron, op. cit., p. 266.
[15] J. A. Schumpeter, *History of Economic Analysis* (N.Y., Oxford University Press, 1959) p. 70. Outside the work of the jurists, Roman literature has little to offer by way of insights into economic issues. Cultured men of letters rejected economic analysis as unworthy of their concern. (Consult, for example, Cicero, *De Officiis*, 2, 24, 87.) Some wrote treatises on farm management which are of marginal interest for economics. For the latter, see, for example, F. Harrison, *Roman Farm Management in the Treatises of Cato and Varro* (N.Y., Macmillan, 1913).

This tradition offers no comprehensive assessment of the nature and significance of the Economic Problem as was attempted by Hesiod or Aristotle, or by the writers of the Pentateuch and the Johannine literature of the New Testament. Again, within it, economics does not attain the status of a distinct field of study in which, to use a Schumpeterian phrase, 'the How and Why of economic mechanisms' are the loci of interest. Rather, economic enquiry, as in the Mishnah, remains the servant of legal analysis. Economic issues are explored to the extent felt necessary to elucidate the manner in which institutionalised justice might be achieved in particular areas of human intercourse. Because, at its height, trading activity within the Roman Empire was extremely lively and commercial practices reached levels of considerable sophistication, concern with justice and social order obliged Roman lawyers to consider some economic issues in depth. Their explorations were to prove most influential.

The first codification of Roman law occurred about 450 B.C. in response to unrest among the *plebs*, those inhabitants of the region who were liable to taxation and military service but were not classified as Roman citizens at that time. The result was the Twelve Tables, a code that was never to be replaced entirely by later legislative enactment. About 366 B.C., an office, that of *Praetor urbanus*, was established to administer the law of the Twelve Tables with respect to those who were recognised as Romans. Then, about 242 B.C., because of the increasing volume of dealings by Romans with foreigners, and between foreigners within the expanding political orbit of Roman dominion, a *Praetor peregrinus* was created.

The latter's province involved consideration of the relevance of the *ius gentium*, the relevance of the general principles of law common to all races and nations, to particular instances of litigation.[16] Through such consideration, Roman law was forced out of reliance on merely local

---

[16] *Ius gentium* is distinct from *ius civile* and *ius naturale*. Also, it should not be identified with the term 'natural law' as the latter was used by St Thomas Aquinas, and after him by innumerable European philosophers of law. On these distinctions consult A. P. D'Entrèves, *Natural Law: an Historical Survey* (1951: N.Y., Harper and Row, 1965) pp. 28—9, 59—60.

custom and tradition. It was obliged to search for significant generalisations that would capture the essence of the seemingly different understandings of what constituted justice in given litigious situations involving men of differing backgrounds. A venue was established for genuinely scientific investigation of legal issues, and many prominent Romans were thereby encouraged to give their leisure over to a unique, new intellectual pursuit of some substance and challenge. M. Antistius Labeo, for example, was moved to give public lectures on jurisprudence, while about A.D. 30 Masurius Sabinus founded a law school.

The classical period of Roman law may be said to date from those years in which the Empire under Domitian was forcing Christians to reassess their understanding of the meaning of social realities in the face of official persecution. About that time, P. Jeventus Celsus, who participated in the conspiracy against Domitian (A.D. 94), began preparing his *Digesta*, a legal work in thirty-nine books. Subsequently, the emperor Hadrian commissioned Salvius Julianus to bring into order the various rulings of the *Praetor urbanus* and the *Praetor peregrinus*. The resulting codification was the *Edictum Hadrianum* (A.D. 129), and this signalled the end of the development of Roman law by way of praetorian decision. Thereafter, the law developed through the work of practising jurists, and by imperial edict.

It is in the writings of the jurists, whose period of activity is coincident with that of the compilation and promulgation of the Jewish Mishnah, that analyses of direct interest to economists are undertaken. The jurists were divided into two main schools of opinion: the Proculians, who followed Labeo, and the Sabinians. One of the most influential of the Sabinians was Gaius whose *Institutes*, an introduction to the principles of Roman private law, was written between A.D. 138 and 180. Other leading figures were: Q. Cervidius Scaevola; Papinian (d. A.D. 212), a pupil of Scaevola and possibly the most outstanding of the jurists; Domitius Ulpianus (d. A.D. 228); Julius Paulus, a contemporary of Papian; and Modestinus (d. A.D. 244), a pupil of Ulpian. These latter were mainly of Proculian persuasion, and, in time, this school's views were to dominate.

The work of these men may have had little impact on later thought if it had not been for the initiative of the Christian Byzantine emperor Justinian (483–565). In 533 he published and made law a systematic collection of the Roman juristic literature in the form of a *Digest*. To this he allied a *Code* (529 and 534) which dealt with statute law, as against the non-statute law of the *Digest*. These were supplemented by an up-dated version of the *Institutes* of Gaius, and by a variety of later statutes promulgated by his own regime, the *Novellae Constitutiones*. Together, the four collections comprise the *Corpus Juris Civilis* which had a profound effect on the development of both civil and ecclesiastical law in Europe.[17]

The evolution of Roman–Byzantine law did not come to a sudden halt with Justinian. However, among the later developments, the most important for the history of economic thought appears to have been the revival of Roman law studies centred on Bologna in the twelfth century. The leading spirit here was Irnerius (c. 1050–1130) who founded a school of law in 1084. His glosses to the *Corpus Juris Civilis* came to command a wide following, and his *Summa codicis* is the first medieval system of Roman jurisprudence. Irnerius and his successors, in seeking to apply the principles of Roman law to current conditions, were faced with the problem that 'early capitalism had invaded the medieval structure, upsetting the existing social order as well as the traditional price system.'[18] Their responses to that problem led to significant extensions of the scope of economic

---

[17] "If the autocracy played a basic role in maintaining the strength of the Byzantine state, it was law which bound together Byzantine society. And it is the Roman law, codified by the Byzantine Emperor Justinian and transmitted via Italy to the West which is perhaps Byzantium's chief practical legacy to the modern world." Deno J. Geanokoplos, *Byzantine East and Latin West: Two Worlds of Christendom in Middle Ages and Renaissance* (N.Y., Harper and Row, 1966) p. 34. In the sixth century, a good deal of Italy was recaptured from the barbarians. Ravenna became a centre for the dissemination of Roman–Byzantine law. It fell to the Lombards in the eighth century. Three centuries later, European economic development out of the static conditions of the early middle ages began in the towns of northern Italy, and Lombards played a prominent role in the movement. Ravenna was one of the focal points of the new growth.

[18] Edgar Salin, 'Just Price', *Encyclopedia of the Social Sciences* ed. E. R. A. Seligman and A. Johnson, Vol. VIII (N.Y., Macmillan, 1932) p. 505.

discussions within the legal tradition they fostered, and these extensions in turn were to influence the economic analysis undertaken by St Thomas Aquinas and subsequent theologians. According to some historians, it was these lawyers, together with some of the canonists, who played the leading role in giving early capitalism its fundamental social and moral justification. John F. McGovern, for example, writes:

> Jurists had been expounding tenets of a revised economic outlook as early, and, in most instances, earlier than spokesmen in other genres . . . the lawyers desired chiefly to attain three ends with their new approach to wealth and commercial activity. The commentators in the genre of law preferred a private sector which would be vibrant and competitive; they wished the state to conserve resources and, if possible, to increase them; finally, canonists and civilians felt that governments should retain a strong fiscal posture.'[19]

Sale and barter

In the second and third century writings of the Roman jurists, considerable attention was given to specifying the scope and meaning of a contract of sale (*emptio-venditio*). Its specification was the subject of controversy involving the two leading schools of legal opinion, the Proculians and the Sabinians. According to the latter, there was no important distinction to be made between exchange of goods by means of barter (*permutatio*) and *emptio-venditio*. Such a position corresponds to that adopted by Aristotle in his discussion of exchange justice, and to the view which the authority of Adam Smith helped impress on orthodox economic analysis in the nineteenth century. However, the Proculians disagreed, and their arguments proved decisive for both Roman and scholastic thought.

The Proculians affirmed that the presence of money and money price made a vital difference in acts of exchange. Given their presence, a transaction could exist in which there was a definite seller, the person willing to part with goods,

[19] J. F. McGovern, 'The Rise of New Economic Attitudes in Canon and Civil Law, A.D. 1200–1550', *The Jurist*, Vol. 32, No. 1 (Winter 1972) p. 50.

and a definite buyer, the person willing to part with money.
In the case of barter, however, both parties to the transaction
are simulatenously both buyer and seller. Hence, Ulpian
writes: 'We must understand by "buyer" anyone who
acquires a thing for a (money) price. In the case of exchange
("sed si quis permutaverit") both parties are to be considered
as being in the position of both buyer and seller.'[20] Money is
no mere middle term which veils what is essentially a barter
relationship between two parties. The presence of money
prices makes for a fundamental qualitative change in economic relationships.[21]

The leading features defining a contract of sale are set out
in the *Institutes*. Here, it is laid down that

> A contract of sale is concluded as soon as the price has
> been agreed, although it has not been paid and even no
> earnest has been given ... The price must be settled, for
> without a price there can be no sale. And it must be
> definite ... Further, the price must be in money ... Once
> a contract of sale has been concluded, the risk of the thing
> sold is at once on the buyer, although the thing has not yet
> been delivered to him ... For the seller is unaffected by
> anything that occurs without malice or negligence on his
> part.[22]

Such a conception of sale seems to be in conflict with that
according to the Mishnah. In Rabbinical law, the determining
factor is delivery of the goods concerned to the buyer, risk of
loss or damage to the goods up to that point devolving on the
seller. However, the clash of conceptions is more apparent
than real, at least by the time of Justinian codification. The
above conditions concerning incidence of risk and the key
role of agreement as to price, are held to apply only to sales

---

[20] *Digesta,* Book 21, Tit. 1, Lege 19. This, and other passages concerning sale, are
taken from the collection and translation by F. De Zulueta, *The Roman Law of
Sale* (Oxford, Clarendon Press, 1945).
[21] Much of the inadequacy of Aristotelian economic thought, and of that of
Adam Smith and some of his successors into the twentieth century, might be
traced to the failure to appreciate this basic point. The early controversy on the
issue is reviewed in the original *Institutes* of Gaius, Book 3, s.139—s.141. See also
the statements by Paulus, *Digesta,* 18, 1, 1.
[22] *Institutes,* 3, 23: 'De emptione et venditione'.

involving the transfer of specific objects, e.g. this particular
horse, this entire stock of wine. Where the objects are
non-specific, e.g., a horse of the seller's choosing from his
herd, or a cask from his wine stock, risk remains with the
seller and sale is completed only on delivery of the object
into the buyer's possession.[2 3]

Price

In the Roman discussions of sale, the process of price formation is depicted as an exercise in bargaining between individual
sellers and buyers. Paulus, for example, writes that 'In buying
and selling natural law permits the one party to buy for less
and the other to sell for more than the thing is worth; thus
each party is allowed to outwit the other. It is the same in
letting and hiring.'[2 4] Ulpian too adopts the same approach,
but he seeks to draw some line between legitimate and
illegitimate exercise of bargaining skill.[2 5] The most extensive
exposition of the view that prices are determined through a
series of approximations ending in negotiated compromise is
found in the *Codex* of Justinian. The relevant section reads:

> The mere fact that you allege that the land was sold at
> somewhat too low a price is no ground for the recission of
> the sale. Indeed, if you had considered the nature of
> buying and selling, and the fact that a buyer approaches
> the contract with the desire of buying cheap and a seller
> with that of selling dear, and that only after much

[2 3] Hence, the *Codex,* 4, 48, 2, reads: 'Assuming agreement for the sale of wine at
a definite price for each jarful, then, until delivery of the jars, the sale still
remained imperfect and the risk of wine going off was not on the buyer, provided
he was not in default in the matter of carrying out the measurement. But where,
as you allege is the case, the whole of the wine laid down in the warehouses was
sold irrespective of measurement and the keys were delivered to the buyers, there
was a perfected sale, and any loss that has occurred owing to the wine going off
concerns the buyer. All this applies to sales not of wine only, but also of oil or
corn or the like, supposing that the goods have either deteriorated or been
completely lost.' Cf. *Digesta,* 18, 1, 35 and 18, 6, 1. Also see *Fragmenta Vaticana,*
16.
[2 4] *Digesta,* 19, 2, 22.
[2 5] Ulpian states: 'What a seller says in order to puff his wares is to be considered
neither as a statement nor as a promise. But if it was said in order to deceive the
buyer, it must be held that, though here too there is no action for contravention
of a statement or a promise, there is the action *de dolo* [i.e., an action for fraud
or misrepresentation].' *Digesta,* 4, 3, 37.

chaffering, during which the seller gradually reduces his demand and the buyer increases his offer, do the parties with difficulty agree to a definite price, you would undoubtedly realize that neither good faith, which is the guardian of the contract of sale, nor any rational ground allows of a contract definitely consented to, whether at once or after haggling over the price, being rescinded for the reason you give: . . .[26]

Passages such as those immediately above concentrate on the making of price in individual contracts. There is little recognition of a wider world of market consensus outside the face-to-face bargaining of particular buyers and sellers. Admittedly, Paulus refers to selling 'for more than the thing is worth', and the section of the *Codex* just quoted goes on to speak of a parcel of land having a 'true value at the time of the sale'. However, these references remain vague. The fact that buying and selling can be communal activities, and that there may be an unique and objectively ascertainable market price at any one time and place are considerations which enter only when the question of injury, and so the possibility of action for damages by one of the contracting parties, is raised. Hence, there is some recognition of the making of prices in markets when the jurist Pomponius considers damages caused by late delivery of articles contracted for sale. He argues that a seller of wine who has not supplied at the due delivery date may be liable 'for the value of the wine either at the date of contract or at that of judgement, whichever is the greater and according to the value either at the place where the thing is sold or at that where the action is brought, whichever is the greater'. Where delay is due to the buyer, 'the prices current in the place where action is brought should not be regarded, but those current in the place at which delivery is due.'[27]

As it stood, the Roman jurists' theory of price as the outcome of individual bargaining was plainly inadequate, even in its own day. The crucial step promoting evolution towards a more adequate theory of price was not taken until

[26] *Codex*, 4, 44, 8: Idem AA. et CC. Aureliae Euodiae (A.D. 293).
[27] *Digesta*, 19, 1, 3.

the issue of the nature of the just price (*iustum pretium*) was posed. This was a Christian innovation, and it was brought to the fore by the doctrine of laesio enormis embodied in the Justinian *Code*.[28] According to this doctrine, if the bargained price in the sale of land represented less than half the true value of the land, the seller could later rescind the contract unless the buyer agreed to pay an additional sum, so as to make the price a just one.[29] Initially, this principle was confined to protection of the seller of land alone, but gradually it was extended to cover the positions of both buyer and seller in many types of exchange of goods and property against sums of money. The extension was mainly the work of medieval Romanists after Irnerius.

The tendency of Romanist thought on price in the twelfth and thirteenth centuries demonstrated that an adequate treatment of issues of justice in commercial transactions required the development of criteria for assessing whether or not a price was fair and, less obviously, an understanding of the forces which could combine to determine market evaluations. Among the criteria which emerged for assessment of pricing justice were: the most commonly requested price; the estimation of those living in the locality; the price of close substitutes; and the income that might be expected to accrue through use of the object of the sale for productive purposes.[30] Prevailing market price then, came to play a

---

[28] Some students of Roman law used to attribute this innovation to the Emperor Diocletian on the grounds that the *Code* itself seems to suggest he was the promulgator of the relevant rescripts. However, as De Zulueta observes, the rescripts show signs of having been interpolated and are contradicted by certain post-Diocletian constitutions. Zulueta concludes: 'It is practically certain that this doctrine, which is known as that of "laesio enormis", is not due to Diocletian; Justinian himself may be its originator.' op. cit., pp. 19—20.

[29] *Codex*, 4, 44, 2; and, 4, 44, 8. The actual term, *laesio enormis* seems to have been used first by the Post-glossator Cinus (1270—1333). A detailed discussion of these passages in the *Code* is undertaken by Kenneth S. Cahn, 'The Roman and Frankish Roots of the Just Price of Medieval Canon Law', *Studies in Medieval and Renaissance History*, Vol. 6 (1969) pp. 13—18.

[30] For an excellent discussion of this phase of the Roman tradition consult John W. Baldwin, *The Medieval Theories of the Just Price: Romanists, Canonists, and Theologians in the Twelfth and Thirteenth Centuries* (Transactions of the American Philosophical Society, New Series, Vol. 49, Part 4, 1959) p. 22ff. The above set of criteria was put forward by Odofredus (d. 1265), the eminent professor of Roman Law at Bologna.

paramount role in the medieval approach to commercial justice, but the Romanists themselves do not appear to have penetrated to any great extent the factors involved in the play of market forces. One reason for this failure may have been the lack of any obvious support for speculation on the subject of the nature of economic value in the ancient legal tradition on which they drew.

Value

Adopting a pragmatic approach to pricing, the Roman jurists had not sought to link their consideration of sale to any attempt at formulation of a definite theory of value. Their range of vision was quite different from that of Aristotle. However, there was another aspect of their thought apart from analysis of *emptio-venditio*, which had some bearing on the future development of value theory. This aspect was examination of the bases of ownership, or, more specifically, the natural methods of acquiring the ownership of single items of tangible property. One method recognised by the Roman lawyers was *specificatio*, and this recognition was a fundamental element in the background of the emergence of a labour theory of value in Europe.

Acquisition by *specificatio* occurred when one person by expenditure of his skill and labour converted the property of another into a new form, e.g. *A* made a ship with *B*'s wood. This title to ownership was not established without some controversy.

> The Sabinians thought that the raw material was the thing to be considered, and that the owner of the material was the owner of the product; the Proculians that the product belonged to the maker (G. ii. 79). Justinians took a middle course (*media sententia*). If the thing could be reduced to its former state (as a statuette made by *A* out of *B*'s brass), it belonged to the owner of the materials; if it could not be so reduced (e.g. *A* has made wine out of *B*'s grapes), the maker became owner, paying compensation.[31]

[31] R. W. Leage, *Roman Private Law* (London: Macmillan, 1909) p. 129. Justinian added that if *A* makes a new product partly by means of *B*'s and partly by means of his own materials, it belongs to *A*.

The status given the expenditure of labour in this analysis
was not lost on the medieval schoolmen and, as is outlined in
the next chapter, provided the background against which the
philosopher John Locke was able to transform a long-
standing theory of property into a theory of value. In this,
Locke had additional support not only from other aspects of
the thought of his scholastic predecessors but also from that
of the Roman lawyers. For the latter, in a *societas*, a business
partnership, 'a man's skill or labour is often equivalent to
money', so whereas investment of capital justified the sharing
in profits by some of the partners, the claim of others could
depend solely on expenditure of labour.[32]

Another type of insight on the subject of value was offered
later thinkers by the Roman treatments of reparations for
damages and the division of inherited property. In both cases,
according to the *Digest*, an underlying principle to be applied
is that 'The values of things are not to be calculated from the
sentiment or interests of individuals, but by the general view
(commonly).'[33] Here, there is a positive affirmation of the
idea that the determination of value is the result of a social
process. It is the outcome of the establishment of a
consensus, rather than a direct function of private, individual
preference.

When Christian Romanists began to explore the nature of
the just price, these passages on damages and inheritance
were employed as offering an answer to the general question
of its derivation. Direct reliance on them is found, for
example, in the discussion of *laesio enormis* by the authoritative Bolognese lawyer, Francesco Accursius (1182–1260).
Unlike most previous jurists he confronts explicitly the
problem of establishing the just price. Community evaluation
is put forward as the measure of a commodity's true worth,

[32] Op. cit., p. 301. An early Christian reference to labour as a title to the
legitimate possession of property is made by the influential St John Chrysostom
(c.344–407). In the midst of an attack on the retention of inherited personal
riches (*Patrologia Graeca*, Vol. 62, cols 562–4), he exempts the Old Testament
figure Jacob from his strictures. Chrysostom's ground for the exemption is that
Jacob's 'wealth was received as the reward of his labour'. See also St Augustine's
reference to property as 'the fruit of just labour' in *Patrologia Latina*, Vol. 38,
col. 650.
[33] *Digesta*, 9, 2, 33; 35, 2, 63.

and the relevant principle from the *Digest*'s treatment of damages and inheritance is cited as lending the support of legal tradition for his position.[34]

Accursius' teacher Azo (d. 1230), working from certain hints in the Justinian *Corpus*, opened up an approach to the problem of capital evaluation which was developed by later Romanists. As Kenneth Cahn has observed:

> Drawing upon a Justinian rule concerning public sales of property made for the purpose of paying debts owed to the community (*Codex*, 4, 44, 16), he (Azo) suggests that the value of property can be established from the quantity of its returns. A price thus established is just (*iustum*). Other legists, almost immediately, added a degree of precision. Value, they said, was to be assessed from the income derived from the property over a twenty- or fifty-year period — presumably they meant by capitalizing income at a certain rate. This procedure was drawn from the *Novellae* of Justinian (120, 9 pr., and 7, 3 par. 1) and was suggested in the early part of the thirteenth century by Laurentius Hispanus, Johannes Teutonicus, Tancredus, and Vincentius Hispanus.[35]

The relationship of this line of thought on value to the emphasis on communal estimation is taken up by Accursius. This leads him to distinguish between fixed capital and other types of saleable object. Expected future return is a major determinant of capital value. This is not the case with mobile commodities, like grain, which are commonly traded. Their values are objectively established by current market forces.[36]

Money

The influence of Roman law on the economics of the medieval schoolmen was not confined to questions of price, value, property ownership and income. The tradition was instrumental also in shaping their perception of the nature of money. The most extensive single statement on this latter

[34] Accursius, *Commentariis*, C.44, 4, 2.
[35] K. S. Cahn, op. cit., pp. 46–7.
[36] Op. cit., p. 49

issue in the *Corpus Juris Civilis* was from Paulus. He wrote:

> Sale originates in barter. For in early days there was no
> such thing as money nor were there distinct terms for the
> merchandise and the price, but according to his occasions
> and needs a man would barter what was useless to him for
> what was useful, since it commonly happens that what one
> man has in superfluity another lacks. But since the
> coincidence was not always readily found, that when you
> had what I wanted I had what you were willing to take, a
> material was selected which, when given a permanent value
> by the State, might obviate the difficulties of barter, by
> providing a uniform measure. This material, when stamped
> by the mint, serves for commerce and conveyance, on
> account not so much of its inherent qualities as of its
> quantity, so that things exchanged are no longer both
> called merchandise, but one is called the price.[37]

When St Thomas Aquinas and his contemporaries were
able to read translations of Aristotle's *Ethics* and *Politics*,
they found that his view of money confirmed that in the
Corpus. Particularly, there was the same, strong non-metallist
emphasis in both. For Paulus, as for Aristotle, money is
essentially a creature of the law, gaining its rationale 'not so
much of its inherent qualities' but by State fiat. Money too,
the schoolmen learned from Paulus, must be distinguished
from merchandise. Any 'commodity' aspect which money
might possess is incidental to its role in economic life.

On and beyond the Aristotelian parallels, there was the
Roman classification of money as *res fungibiles*, things which
cannot be regarded normally as consisting of distinct,
individual units. Like corn or wine, one money quantity held
in a particular stock or balance was not significantly different
from the same quantity in another balance. Again, there was
the Roman distinction between things not lost by use, e.g. a
house, and things which were so lost, e.g. wine and food (*res
quae usu consumuntur*). Following the jurists' division, the
medieval schoolmen argued that money was in this second

[37] *Digesta,* 18, 1, 1.

category. A sum of money could perform only a single act of use-service for its owner. In performing that act, it was lost to him. Inevitably, in use, the ownership of money was transferred.[38]

Interest

The Roman distinctions concerning money and merchandise, fungibles and non-fungibles, consumptibles and non-consumptibles are at the very core of the scholastic treatment of interest payment. The direct observations of the jurists themselves on the phenomenon of interest were also to prove crucial for the manner in which this key aspect of economic analysis was to be approached.

In Roman law, the need for interest payment could arise in two of the four main types of real contract. The four types were: *mutuum*, a loan for consumption; *commodatum*, a loan for use; *depositum*, transfer of an object for safe-keeping into the custody of another; and, *pignus*, a mortgage. Interest might be associated with a *mutuum* if that contract was linked to a second, and also with a *depositum irregulare*. The *mutuum*,

> was a loan for consumption of res fungibiles (e.g., money, wine or grain). Necessarily, therefore, the borrower became dominus or owner, and his obligation is to restore not the thing lent but its equivalent in value. The mutuum being the descendant of the ancient law nexum was a contract stricti juris (the liability of the parties was measured exactly by their promises); hence, the borrower was, by virtue of the contract itself, only bound to return the exact equivalent of what he received without interest, even though he was in default (mora), i.e., had failed to repay at the proper time. The only means of securing

[38] In J. T. Noonan, *The Scholastic Analysis of Usury* (Cambridge, Mass., Harvard University Press, 1957) pp. 38–9 a similar view of money is noted as present in canon law from about 1180. Its origin is the palea *Ejiciens* written by a heretical author of the fifth or sixth century. This particular statement concerning money may have been even more influential in shaping scholastic attitudes than were their adaptations of Roman categories concerning 'things'.

interest was to get the borrower to promise it by a separate
contract, the verbal contract known as stipulatio.[39]

Stipulatio involved the borrower's taking on of an obligation
by giving a formal answer to a formal question put by the
lender concerning the matter of the loan.

Depositum irregulare applied when one party transferred a
res fungibilis to another for safe-keeping, with the understanding that the keeper became the owner and was obliged
to restore only the equivalent in value of the money or other
fungible deposited. However, if there was delay in the
depositary's returning the money at the agreed time (*mora*),
the depositor could claim interest by the *actio depositi
directa*. In this case, there was no need for *stipulatio* to be
present.

With both *mutuum* and *depositum*, the essential feature of
the contract was that when the agreement was made initially,
one of the parties to it, the lender or the depositor, had done
everything that he was obliged to do under the contract. He
had fulfilled his obligations by a transfer of something which
was his own to the possession of another. He was not in a
position to damage the other party with respect to the
contract, although the borrower or the depositary could
damage him, e.g. through delay in repayment.

This emphasis concerning the incidence of potential
damage affected profoundly the direction of exploration for
possible economic bases for interest payment during the
middle ages. Given the Roman law background, scholastic
writers were led to look for such bases in circumstances
applying to the lender rather than the borrower of money.
Irrespective of the use to which the borrower put the money,
he might be liable for payment of interest if the lender had
incurred damages by his action. Whether or not the borrower
employed a money loan for consumption or production
purposes, and whether or not he reaped large or small profits,

[39] R. W. Leage, op. cit., pp. 266–7. It is also relevant to note that logically, no
usufruct could be associated with the loan of res fungibiles like money. A
usufruct is the right of using property that belongs to another, provided that the
substance of the property remains unimpaired. The latter proviso could not apply
to things like wine, corn, or money which were destroyed or lost in use.

were irrelevant considerations. It was how his actions affected the lender that was the relevant matter.

The schoolmen's development of interest theory was also influenced by the Roman jurists' discussions of damages in the case of consensual contracts (contracts that are formless but reasonable), like sale. The Roman tradition allowed that a buyer might be able to recover his purchase money with interest in circumstances where the commodity bought had latent defects or was not delivered. Again, a seller may be able to claim interest when a buyer is late in making payment.

Ulpian's view on actions *ex venditio* for recovery of payment by a seller from a buyer is that interest will be due. He argues that 'The following things are recoverable in this action. In the first place the price for which the thing was sold. Next interest on the price from the day to delivery: for since the buyer enjoys the thing, it is only fair that he should pay interest on the price. We are to hold possession to have been delivered even if it be revocable at will: for all we need consider is whether the buyer has the power of taking the fruits.'[40] This passage is particularly significant for the contrast it presents with the approach to interest-taking in real contracts. Here, it is not the damage done the seller, but rather the gain made by the buyer which affords the rationale for enforcing an interest charge. Ulpian's analysis is lent support by another section of the *Digest* which states: 'If a buyer is late in paying the price, he will have to pay the seller interest only, not every profit that the seller might have made had the buyer not been late, for example if the seller was a trader and could have made more than the interest by trading.'[41] Despite the fact that the seller has suffered damage through loss of possible profit in excess of the sum due him at the prevailing interest rate, he is not to be compensated for the excess

Rather more consistent with the treatment of damages and of interest in real contracts is the analysis of compensation to

[40] *Digesta*, 19, 1, 13.
[41] Op. cit., 18, 6, 20(19).

buyers in instances of non-delivery of purchases of capital goods, like slaves. In Roman law, a slave was not a *persona* but a *res*. Further, as an object which was not consumed in use, a slave, unlike money, could not be classified as *quae usu consumuntur*, nor was he a fungible. The present, capital value of a slave is influenced by the rate of depreciation to which he is likely to be subject, and the expected value of the services which will flow from his employment.[42] Factors such as these are to be taken into account where a buyer of a slave has suffered damage through non-delivery in a contract of sale. Hence, Neratius argues, 'I am bound to make good to the buyer not only what I have myself acquired through him (the slave sold), but also all that the buyer would have acquired if the slave had already been delivered to him.'[43] In like manner, Paulus, considering an *actio empti* involving slaves, approves of the principle that the action cover 'the buyer's whole interest in not being deprived of the slave.'[44] Not only potential profit forgone, but also, in some circumstances, a profit which ceases to be taken, Paulus could be suggesting, is relevant to the assessment of damages.[45]

Paulus goes on immediately to contend that if the liability of a seller is very much in excess of the price paid originally by the buyer, it is unreasonable to suggest that the seller be obliged to make compensation to the full amount of current capital value. A slave of little value at the time of sale may have acquired skills in the interim, which acquisition, and

---

[42] For example, in considering actions for redhibition and for reduction in price of slaves, an edict of the curule aediles states: 'The buyer must, however, make good to the seller all the following: any deterioration of the slave which has occurred since the sale and delivery and has been caused by himself or his household or his procurator, also anything born from or acquired through the slave since the sale, also any other thing that went with the slave as an accessory on the sale and any profits that have come to the buyer therefrom.' op. cit., 21, 1, 1. See also, op. cit., 21, 1, 24 and 21, 2, 8.

[43] Op. cit., 19, 1, 31.

[44] Op. cit., 19, 1, 43. 'Actio empti' was the most common action by which a buyer could enforce his rights. In this instance, the buyer has had possession of the slave but is obliged to give him up because the seller did not have the right to make the sale.

[45] Paulus' discussion is not free from ambiguity. It is not entirely clear whether he thinks historical cost of maintaining capital or cessation of receipt of income due to the capital is the relevant factor.

hence appreciation of value, could not be foreseen. Since there is an inevitable expectational element in any evaluation of capital, both the *Digest* and the *Code* place a practical limit on a seller's liability of double the purchase price.[46] However, the basic, general principle remains: 'If the thing sold is not delivered, an action lies for damages, that is for the buyer's interest in having the thing: this sometimes exceeds the price, where the buyer's interest exceeds what the thing is worth or what it was bought for.'[47]

While Paulus may be suggesting that a profit which ceases is relevant to assessment of damages in the case of sales of capital goods, he denies the relevance of profit potential thwarted by non-delivery in sales of *res quae usu consumuntur*. He writes:

> When the seller is responsible for non-delivery, the damages must take account of the whole loss of the buyer, provided it is directly connected with the thing. Thus, the fact that he might have traded with the wine and made a profit should not come into account, any more than the fact that because of the non-delivery of corn which he had bought his household has suffered from starvation: he recovers the value of the corn, not that of slaves who have died of starvation.[48]

This denial is in marked contrast with the development of the mainstream of scholastic thinking on money loans in later centuries. Profit forgone, under the title of *lucrum cessans* was to become a major ground on which interest could be taken in a money loan. A lender who might have employed the money profitably in trading activities was 'damaged' by transfer of the sum concerned to a borrower. Interest was a form of compensation for the injury suffered.

Canon law

The revival of Roman law studies through which the medieval theologians were made familiar with the economic ideas of the jurists, was accompanied by the development of a

---

[46] Op. cit., 19, 1, 44; and *Codex*, 7, 47, 1.
[47] *Digesta*, 18, 1, 1.
[48] Op. cit., 19, 1, 21.

systematic, scientific approach to canon law. Appreciation of this legal tradition too is crucial to an understanding of the evolution of medieval social thought and practice. The maintenance of justice in the dealings of individual church-men and of the vast, complex organisation to which they belonged, was an issue which occupied the professional attention of a host of the best minds of Europe for many centuries. Canonists applied themselves to the task of translating Christian moral theory into rulings concerning the objectively desirable forms of conduct in the social life of Christians. As a result, they were obliged to analyse the economic aspects of life in contemporary society.

Before Gratian

The canon law of the Church of the Latin rite is heavily indebted to Roman law precedents.[49] However, its early substantial content was provided by decrees of ecumenical councils such as those held at Nicaea (A.D. 325) and Chalcedon (A.D. 451). With these were allied decrees of various provincial church councils, and the rulings and letters of the popes in Rome. That the churchmen were quite prepared to depart from the provisions of Roman civil codes is illustrated by Canon 17 of Nicaea I. The canon reads:

> Many clerics motivated by greed and a desire for gain, have forgotten the scriptural injunction, 'he gave not his money to usury,' and instead demand a monthly rate of one per cent on loans they make; therefore this holy and great council decrees that in future anyone taking interest or in any way whatsoever dealing in usury and demanding his fifty per cent profit or seeking some similar way of earning money is to be deposed and removed from his order.[50]

[49] The extent of this debt, evident still in church law of the twentieth century, has been explored in a continuing series of articles by Bernard F. Deutsch. See B. F. Deutsch, 'Ancient Roman Law and Modern Canon Law', *The Jurist*, Vol. 27 (1967) pp. 297–309, and subsequent issues of the same journal.

[50] *Conciliorum Oecumenicorum Decreta* (St Louis, 1962), 13. At the time, Roman civil practice permitted a maximum legal interest rate of 12 per cent p.a. on money loans and 50 per cent p.a. on loans in kind. An example of a later, similar council ruling, but this time extending to laymen as well as clergy, is the

This particular canon, the sentiments of which were to be repeated in decrees emanating from a number of other councils through to the middle ages, is of special importance in the history of economic analysis. It was an authoritative step in the foundation of a tradition which gave a peculiar cast to canonical economic thought. When the medieval jurists came to attempt the systematisation of church law, they found themselves equipped with 'individual pieces of legislation directed against specific evils. From these texts, which defined usury and attacked the evils of speculative sale, the Decretists produced a generalised theory embracing the whole realm of buying and selling. Beginning with the specific canons of ancient Canonical and Carolingian legislation they produced the beginnings of an economic analysis.'[51] From the very outset of the development of canon law as a scientific study, the problem of interest payment is placed at the centre of the economic dimensions of the enquiry. If the view of the Austrian economist Eugen von Böhm-Bawerk (1851–1914) is accepted, namely, that the problem of interest is the central issue in economic investigation, then the canonist bias was a potentially very fruitful one for the development of economics.

From at least the fourth century onwards, clerical scholars throughout Europe undertook the compilation of collections of canons for the guidance of bishops and other clergy. This work was carried on in a decentralised fashion, and there was little opportunity for the emergence of a standardised code. Some of these collections had limited circulation, while others gained a measure of authority in the conduct of church affairs in particular regions of Europe for lengthy periods.[52] Further, before the eleventh century, the collectors made little attempt at systematic arrangement of the

---

twentieth canon of the Council of Elvira: 'If a cleric is convicted of practising usury, he shall be disgraced and excommunicated. If, on the other hand, it is proved that a layman has indulged in usury, he shall be forgiven, but on conditions that he promises to stop the practice and not to repeat the offence, for if he persists in this sin, he will be expelled from the Church.'

[51] John W. Baldwin, op. cit., p. 41.

[52] A list of the more important collections is provided by Charles Duggan, *Twelfth-century Decretal Collections, and their importance in English history* (University of London, Athlone Press, 1963) pp. 12–13.

contents of their compilations and did not endeavour to reconcile the conflicting rulings given by the various ecclesiastical and civil enactments which they embodied. Thereafter, a trend to systematisation and reconciliation was begun, most notably by the widely influential *Decretum* of the Augustinian bishop Ivo of Chartres (c. 1040–1116).

In his *Decretum* Ivo draws on an extensive range of legal sources of considerable antiquity. Thus, as Kenneth S. Cahn has shown, his treatment of justice in matters of purchase and sale is derived from the rulings of the *Codex Theodosianus* (438), both directly, and as modified, in part, by transformations via the *Lex Romana Visigothorum* (506), eighth-century Bavarian law, and a ninth-century collection of capitularies by Benedictus Diaconus.[53] According to Ivo, if there is no fraud or violence in a transaction, the seller has no basis on which to seek rescission of a sale, since a sale cannot be rescinded simply on the grounds that the price was too low. Similarly, a buyer cannot take action on the grounds that he now believes the price was too high. Mutual agreement between individual buyer and seller is a valid mode of price determination when the original bargain has been struck in circumstances of free negotiation.[54]

This stress on the role of free bargaining is compatible with that found in the Justinian *Corpus*, but there is the same relative lack of emphasis on the relevance of communal market determinants of prices in just contracts. In Ivo's *Decretum* this lack is remedied elsewhere (Part VI, Chap. 259) by reference to a line of legislative tradition extending back at least as far as the Carolingian Empire of the late eighth and the ninth centuries. Then, the Emperor Charlemagne (742–814), relying to a considerable extent on earlier Church law, began the practice of issuing capitularies to regulate the conduct of economic life in his realm. These were in the form of directives to the *missi dominici*, travelling counts and bishops who together were responsible for inspecting and giving judgement on economic and other community arrangements throughout the Empire. The Caro-

---

[53] K. S. Cahn, op. cit., pp. 6–12.
[54] Ivo of Chartres, *Decretum*, Part XVI, Chaps 244 and 285..

lingian capitularies were to exercise a vital influence on the scope and content of later canon law, and, through that law, on the shape of the development of European economic analysis.

In the face of the widespread difficulties which the people of France were then experiencing, the emperor Carloman in 884 issued fourteen *capitula* which sought to remedy some of the problems. The thirteenth of these was directed at determination of the just price, and took the decisive step of equating that price with local market price. As repeated by Ivo and later influential canonists, this capitulary directed the attention of medieval scholars to the analysis of market phenomena in their quest for understanding of the roots of justice in economic relationships. According to the capitulary: 'Parish priests should amonish their flocks not to charge wayfarers more than the price obtainable in the local market. Otherwise, the wayfarers can complain to the priest who is then required to set the price with "humanity".'[55] The reference to market price here is much more general than any found in Justinian.

Carolingian legislation was also adamant that price formation should occur in markets that were freely competitive. Even attempts at speculative market operations which might lead to the creation of partial monopolies were outlawed by the Capitulary of Nijmegen in March 806. Promulgated at a time of severe famine, clauses 15 and 17 of this Capitulary stated:

> Those who by various manoeuvres dishonestly plan to amass goods of all kinds with the express aim of making money are acquiring ill-gotten gains ... All persons who at harvest time or when the grapes are gathered acquire corn or wine they do not need, but get simply through an underlying motive of greed, for instance buying a hogshead

[55] The fourteen capitula are reprinted in A. Boretius and V. Kraus (eds), *Capitularia Regum Francorum, M. G. H. Legum, Sec. 11* (Hanover, 1883), Vol. II, pp. 371–5. On the importance of this particular ruling for the future of economic theory, consult Raymond de Roover, 'The Concept of the Just Price: Theory and Economic Policy', *Journal of Economic History*, Vol. 18 (Dec 1958) p. 421; and K. S. Cahn, op. cit., pp. 41–2. The latter also discusses earlier Carolingian pricing legislation.

for two deniers and keeping it until they can sell it again for six deniers or even more, are guilty of what we call dishonest gain. If on the other hand, they buy it because they need it, so as to keep it for themselves or give it away to others, that is a business transaction [*negocium*].[56]

This early stress on free competition as the major pre-condition for the emergence of just prices was another element to be taken up and expanded in the canonist analyses. Not untypical are the opinions expressed in the *Liber Pauperum* of Vacarius (c. 1120–1200), who taught at Oxford and was employed as a legal consultant by Thomas à Becket. Vacarius attacks the formation of price-rings by dealers in wine and cloth and in the building and construction industry. At the same time, like most medieval jurists, he views trade unions as monopolies acting in restraint of trade. Yet, Vacarius does not believe in adherence to market price in every single transaction, and he makes a threefold distinction concerning types of price:

> One price is the true [*verum*] price, another the common [*commune*] price and yet another the special [*singulare*] price. The true price is the price for which the item is sold. The common price is the price for which it can be sold to anyone. The special price is found when something is worth more to one than to others. Consider the slave who is an excellent craftsman and who was sold to one who is a craftsman. The slave is worth more to him than to another who is not a craftsman.[57]

The Capitulary of Nijmegen is also of significance in shaping the canonical approach to the question of usury. In 789, Charlemagne had issued the *Admonitio Generalis* in which the prohibition against usury was extended to include all in his realm, laity and clergy alike. This was repeated in the difficult year of 806 in an expanded form which provided a very wide-ranging definition of usury. According to clause

[56] From Robert Latouche, *The Birth of Western Economy, Economic Aspects of the Dark Ages* (London, Methuen, 1961) p. 156.
[57] Francis de Zulueta (ed.), *The Liber Pauperum of Vacarius* (Publications of the Selden Society, Vol. XLIV, London, 1927) p. 150; see also p. 165.

11 of the edict: 'Usury consists in claiming back more than you give; for instance if you have given 10 "solidi" and ask for more back, or if you have given a hogshead of wheat and afterwards demand one extra.' 'Lending', continues clause 16, 'consists in providing something: the loan is fair and just when you claim back no more than you provided.'[58]

This sweeping condemnation of interest-taking in seemingly universal terms, found its counterpart in the *Hadriana*, the most authoritative collection of ecclesiastical laws in use throughout the empire of Charlemagne. Clergymen were prohibited by it from the receipt of usury, and laity so doing were accused of seeking *turpe lucrum* (shameful gain). In the opinion of Professor Noonan, it was this condemnation that constituted the cornerstone of later usury legislation.[59] Given this background, subsequent endeavours by some medieval schoolmen and their successors to develop a positive theory of interest were obliged to take the form of building a theory of permissible exceptions to the general prohibition of usury. It is in this respect that the long history of usury legislation finds its chief significance for the progress of economic analysis. While the ban on the taking of usury may have stifled some useful analytical initiatives in the economics of the scholastics, it also prevented them from too ready adoption of some of the fallacious theories of interest which dominated the mainstream of economic thought in the nineteenth and early decades of the twentieth centuries.

Gratian and after

The great watershed in the development of canon law as a systematic study came with the publication of the *Concordantia discordantium canonum* (generally called *Decretum Gratiani*). The work of an Italian monk, Johannes Gratian, who taught at Bologna, the compilation was undertaken between about 1140 and 1151. In the *Decretum*

> a great collection of ecclesiastical canons was constructed in a dialectical pattern. Given a problem in law, the arguments are marshalled first on one side, then on the

---

[58] From, R. Latouche, loc. cit.
[59] John T. Noonan, op. cit., p. 15.

other. The authorities for both points of view are carefully
arrayed, and from their differences and conflicts a harmony or synthesis is achieved . . . Coming at a moment of
crucial importance, summing up the best of well-
established traditions, and expressing them in the new
scholastic style, it swiftly captured the entire field of
ecclesiastical law, ousted the earlier compilations, and
became the standard text-book in the schools and the
principal authority in the courts. It marks the beginning of
the science of canon law.[60]

In the wake of publication of the *Decretum*, important
schools devoted to commentary on it evolved in Germany,
France and England, but the major centre of study remained
Bologna. Outstanding among the published commentaries
which emerged at the hands of the decretists were the *Glossa
Ordinaria* of Johannes Tuetonicus (c. 1215), and a *Summa* by
Huguccio of Pisa (d. 1210).

The decretists, like their Roman law contemporaries at
Bologna and other centres, were obliged to consider the
application of long-standing precepts in a new climate of
economic activity which was revolutionising town life, in
particular. At least by the year 1100, a strong trend to
rationalisation of productive activity and trading arrangements on a capitalist basis had become apparent. Traditional
economic morality was increasingly challenged by qualitative
changes of economic relationships in the course of a
developmental process which reached a peak about 1300.[61]

Through their work, the decretists helped create the more
liberal legal and social framework demanded by nascent
capitalism. One of their most important contributions in this
respect was to initiate a fresh Christian approach to the
question of property ownership.

[60] Charles Duggan, op. cit., pp. 15–16. See also S. Kuttner, 'Scientific
Investigation of Mediaeval Canon Law: the Need and the Opportunity',
Speculum, Vol XXIV (1949) pp. 493–501.
[61] On this trend see J. Gilchrist, *The Church and Economic Activity in the Middle
Ages* (London, Macmillan, 1969) pp. 7–10. Italian towns, first Venice and then
Pisa, Genoa, and Florence were at the leading edge of the new economic wave.
Flanders was also to become a significant area, and later, towns in England,
France, and Germany were to be linked in an expanding network of capitalist
commerce.

Around 1200 Decretists radically and momentously re-
vamped patristic teaching about property; henceforth,
private property was considered to be a sacrosanct
principle and the personal right of each individual because
it derives from natural law or is an inherent part of the 'ius
gentium' ... one can discern that St Thomas probably
obtained his views on private property from the lawyers,
especially Huguccio and Alanus.[62]

Moral and legal arguments were marshalled to protect the
private individual's accumulated wealth against arbitrary
seizure by governmental authorities, thus enhancing the
grounds on which traders and industrialists could hope to
build an expanding business with reasonable long-term
prospects for themselves and their inheritors.

The entrepreneur was to find support also from some of
the decretists in their tendency to liberate legal practice from
subservience to the letter of the law. Unwavering adherence
to ancient edicts (such as might appear to rule out new forms
of social organisation and to counter innovation) was
opposed by a line of canonist thought which sought to
promote the achievement of equity in disputed matters
rather than a merely just decision based on rigorous
application of existing statutes. Gratian himself was a moving
spirit in this regard. As Maurice Amen states,

> ... in the *Decretum* equity was a higher form of justice
> than could be attained through slavish observance of the
> rigors of the law. Equity was not static: it was a dynamic,
> living reality which always took into consideration the
> human condition. Gratian did not hesitate to make use of
> equity which was not written into the law, and his
> approach singled him out from the other canonists who
> were teaching at Bologna during the middle of the twelfth
> century.[63]

This liberal line was supported in the *Glossa Ordinaria*,
although it was opposed by Huguccio and by the influential

[62] John F. McGovern, 'The Rise of New Economic Attitudes in Canon and Civil
Law, A.D. 1200–1550', *The Jurist*, Vol. 32 (Winter 1972) pp. 42–3.
[63] M. Amen, 'Canonical Equity Before the Code', *The Jurist*, Vol. 33 (Summer
1973) p. 266.

Stephen of Tournai (1128–31) in his *Summa in decretum Gratiani*. These latter wished to maintain the more restricted view of equity associated with Roman law. Although under constant attack, the liberal line of Gratian continued to find authoritative adherents, most notably the outstanding canonist of the thirteenth century, Hostiensis (d. 1271).[64]

The economic thought of the decretists after Gratian provides evidence of a growing awareness of the realities of an enterprise economy. In contrast with the severe reservations concerning commercial activity in the Carolingian Capitulary of 806, it is contended that it is permissible for individuals to sell goods at higher prices than were paid previously. The circumstances which justify the practice are, necessity, improvement of the form or quality of the goods, incurrence of costs or the expenditure of labour in handling the goods, and the aim of supporting one's dependants through pursuit of a vocation in the world of commerce. The profits which honest merchants take can be quite legitimate forms of income.[65] According to the *Apparatus: Ius Naturale* (1210–15), even the clergy can sell at a profit providing they are well motivated, and have sold the items concerned at just prices. Profit is not confused with interest, the taking of which is forbidden. To establish the figure for a just price, it may be necessary to call on the judgement of a third party (*vir bonus arbitratur*). No criterion is offered here to be used as a basis for judgement, but about the same time Tancredus in his *Apparatus* (c. 1215) states that 'A thing is worth as much as it can be sold for ... but the value is to be established not by the affection of individuals, but by the community at large.'[66]

---

[64] Op. cit., pp. 276–7. Of Hostiensis' treatment of economic issues, J. W. Baldwin writes (op. cit., p. 42): 'The work of Hostiensis stands as the Canonist counterpart to the writings of Accursius and Odofredus in Roman law and the *Summa theologica* of Thomas Aquinas in theology.'

[65] For details, consult, J. W. Baldwin, op. cit., pp. 41ff. Gratian's *Decretum* itself is by no means as liberal, and tends to equate profit with usury. In addition Gratian follows the wide Carolingian definition of usury: 'whatever is demanded beyond the principal'.

[66] Quoted in op. cit., p. 54. About 1180 Simon of Bisignano in his *Summa* had employed the idea that 'a thing is worth as much as it can be sold for' as a guide to judgement as to whether or not usury is present in particular transactions. Also noteworthy in relation to the discussion of interest-taking is the use of the term *interesse* in the *Glossa Ordinaria*. On the derivation of this term and its significance in relation to *usura* see J. T. Noonan, op. cit., pp. 105–6.

From near the end of the twelfth century, a movement began within the ranks of the canonists which was eventually to take the lead in the progress of the discipline away from the commentators on Gratian. The latter had effectively systematised the analysis of early ecclesiastical legislation, and this facilitated the building of collections of modern case law. These collections were centred on decisions given in decretal letters issued by contemporary popes and their Curia. The problem of decretal codification began to overshadow the work of the decretists, and the change of emphasis in the discipline was signalled most clearly by the publication at Bologna of Bernard Baldi of Pavia's *Compilatio Prima* in 1191. This consisted mainly of decretal letters issued during or after the pontificate of Alexander III (1159–81) who himself had been a professor of canon law at Bologna and had published a commentary on Gratian. Other similarly structured compilations followed over the next four decades, and the practice culminated in the issue of the Gregorian *Decretales*. Compiled by St Raymund of Penafort (1175–1275) on the basis of papal decretals uttered after 1150, this collection became the cornerstone of canon law until the revision of 1917. It was declared definitive by Gregory IX's *Rex pacificus* of 1234.

The major figure in the history of economic analysis among the post-Gregorian canonists of the thirteenth century was Cardinal Hostiensis (d. 1271). After studies in Roman law and canon law at both Bologna and Paris, he taught in France and England and acted as ambassador of Henry III of England to Innocent IV. He was consecrated bishop in 1244, and was appointed Cardinal and Archbishop of Ostia in 1262. His major publications were a *Summa* (1250–61) and a *Commentaria super libros decretalium* (1271). In these he displays adherence to the liberal current in canonist thought as well as an unprecedented appreciation of the economic realities of the contemporary business world.

As noted above, he adopts the flexible approach of Gratian to the relationship of equity to the administration of justice in terms of the letter of existing law. In addition, he holds that ownership of property is natural, and can be acquired by individuals according to natural modes. Rulers, he affirms, cannot confiscate the goods of their subjects without very strong grounds for such action.[67] On the basis of the conviction that economic value is a variable determined in communal market places, Hostiensis undertakes an extensive analysis of sale.[68] Behind that analysis stands the findings of the medieval Romanists in their investigation of *laesio enormis*. Also, there is the fact of the incorporation in the *Decretals* of Gregory IX of Carloman's 884 capitula which equated a just price with that obtainable in the local market.[69]

On the problems of monetary dealings Hostiensis is of particular importance. Faced with the general condemnation of usury, he enumerates thirteen instances in which payment over and above the principal may be taken in the course of lending. One of these instances is *fidejussor*: where the guarantor of a loan is forced to agree to being party to a loan at interest, because of his obligation under the contract he may require payment of the interest from the person on whose behalf he has acted. Another instance is *vendens sub dubio*. Here, a seller may legitimately require a higher price than that current for a good sold on credit terms, providing there is doubt about the future price of the commodity. Hostiensis also allows for *poena conventionalis*, a penalty clause written into a contract that allows the creditor to be compensated if the debtor does not repay the principal of the loan on the date specified by the contract. Recognition too is given to *labor*, i.e. the work which a creditor may be obliged to undertake with respect to the giving of a particular loan.[70]

Beyond these cases, as Professor Noonan has observed, Hostiensis was the first authoritative figure to argue a ground for interest-taking from the beginning of a loan.[71] This ground, *lucrum cessans*, was, in the hands of later authors, to become the basis of the first theory of why in the absence of fraud, force, or delay, the rate of interest will not be zero. It will not be zero because a lender will legitimately ask for compensation for the profit he forgoes in not retaining

---

[67] Consult Richard B. Schlatter, *Private Property, the History of an Idea* (London, Allen and Unwin, 1951) p. 44.
[68] See J. W. Baldwin, loc. cit.
[69] The later wording is not quite the same, but the meaning is identical. See Gregory IX, *Decretals*, III, 17, C.1, C.I.C., Vol. II, col. 518.
[70] *Commentaria super libros decretalium, V De Usuris*, 16.

money for his own use in trading, but lending it to another.
'If some merchant', Hostiensis writes,

> who is accustomed to pursue trade, and the commerce of
> the fairs and there profit much, has, out of charity to me
> who needs it badly, lent money with which he would have
> done business, I remain obliged from this to his *interesse*,
> provided that nothing is done in fraud of usury ... and
> provided that the said merchant will not have been
> accustomed to give his money in such a way to usury.

Even though his debtor is in no way at fault, a merchant who
lends out of charity, although not habitually, can claim
interest.[72]

The lead which Hostiensis gave in this respect was taken
into the mainstream of scholastic economic doctrine in the
fifteenth century. Another of his innovations, the allowance
of *gratis dans* (a gift by the debtor) as an exception to the
usury prohibition, was to become basic to Florentine banking
practice. *Gratis dans* allowed payment of interest to bank
depositors at the discretion of the banker, no formal,
usurious contract for interest having been made. Despite the
absence of a legal undertaking, interest was paid for fear that
the depositors would transfer their funds to a rival bank. The
banker's 'gift' was not offered without a certain degree of
duress.[73]

---

[71] Hostiensis, loc. cit.

[72] By restricting the title *lucrum cessans* to non-habitual lenders, Hostiensis guards
against any seeming approval of professional money lenders. In insisting that the
loan be made out of charitable rather than business motives, he may be indicating
that in this instance where he approves interest payment, he has in mind the
requirements of equity rather than justice. A purely business transaction is
governed by the canons of justice and, traditionally, there is no ground for
interest provided by those canons. However, in the realm of relationships of
charity it is the dictates of equity (which he calls, 'justice sweetly tempered by
mercy') which are relevant, and these may permit the receipt of interest. For 300
years after Hostiensis those schoolmen who recognised the title *lucrum cessans*
generally added the requirement that the motive in lending be charity. To gain a
better understanding of the development of scholastic interest theory, it seems
important that research be undertaken which relates the attitude of various
writers on the incidence of *lucrum cessans* to their views on the relationship of
justice to equity. See, e.g., the remarks by Maurice Amen, op. cit., pp. 291–2
concerning the views of Francisco Suarez.

[73] Consult Raymond de Roover, *The Rise and Decline of the Medici Bank,
1437–1494*, (Cambridge, Mass., Harvard University Press, 1963) pp. 101–2.

The work of Hostiensis was contemporaneous with that of the theologian Thomas Aquinas and the Romanists, Accursius and Odofredus. Despite their skill, in terms of future impact, all three lawyers were to be quite overshadowed by the figure of Aquinas. Drawing on a wide range of sources, including the writings of the civilians and canonists, St Thomas' intellect was the one which moulded the analytical framework for economic and social enquiry in the centuries to come. Armed with the doctrine of the concordance of grace and nature, he provided Christian thinkers with fresh incentives for exploration of the problems of a just economic order, and, at the same time, he offered some bright, new analytical tools with which the task might be carried on.[74]

---

[74] In the foregoing discussion of canon law, nothing has been written concerning parallels or divergences between that legal tradition and the Jewish talmudic stream. The main reason for this lack is the fact that, in the English language at least, as Roman Ohrenstein points out ('Economic Thought in Talmudic Literature in the Light of Modern Economics', *American Journal of Economics and Sociology*, Vol. 27 (1968) p. 185), 'there is very little material on the socioeconomic doctrines of the rabbis.' Those interested in research in this area of medieval economics should consult references given in Professor Ohrenstein's article (pp. 185–96). See also the same author's 'Economic Self-Interest and Social Progress in Talmudic Literature', *American Journal of Economics and Sociology*, Vol. 29 (1970) pp. 59–70.

6 Saint Thomas Aquinas

As discussion intensified on problems of economic morality in the early part of the thirteenth century, theologians gradually entered into the field which canon lawyers and medieval Romanists had begun to explore. Their entry served to raise debate to new analytical heights. One of the prominent early contributors was St Albert the Great (1193–1280), a Swabian aristocrat who taught at Paris and Cologne, and who is generally regarded as the founder of the theological tradition associated with the Dominican order. However, it was the work of his pupil St Thomas Aquinas (1225–74) that was to prove definitive and establish a body of systematic thought that continues to exercise a profound influence on many European scholars today. One relatively minor element in that thought was analysis of aspects of economic life.

Born at Rocca Secca in the Kingdom of Naples, the son of Landulph, Count of Aquino, St Thomas began studies at an early age, first with the Benedictines at Monte Cassino, and later at the University of Naples. About 1240 he attempted to join the Dominican order, but was physically restrained from so doing by his parents who kept him in confinement for two years. Eventually, he escaped, was reunited with the Dominicans, and went on to Cologne and then Paris with his teacher, Albert the Great.

These studies brought him into contact with a flourishing world of learning. European scholarship had been able to emerge from the monastic refuges into which it had been driven by the instability and barbarism of earlier centuries. Students were able to move about now over a wide area, and they had the great advantage of Latin as an universal common language. Among the major centres of intellectual ferment were the universities of Paris and Oxford. Of such institutions, Joseph Schumpeter has observed that they 'enjoyed a large measure of freedom and independence; they gave more scope to the individual teacher than do the mechanical universities of today. They were a meeting ground of all classes of society; and they were essentially international.'[1] Aquinas' system of ideas was the outstanding product of that lively and cosmopolitan environment.

In 1252, St Thomas was appointed sub-regent in the Dominican *studium* at Paris. While teaching he took his doctorate at the University of Paris in 1257, and subsequently he lectured there and at a variety of other centres including Cologne, Rome, Bologna, and Naples. With his fame as a teacher growing, he was offered the Archbishopric of Naples in 1265, but he resisted such attempts to move him into administrative spheres and devoted himself to the scholarly business of research and publication. Through that research he endeavoured to synthesise a number of strands of earlier thought. On the one hand, there was the long, Christian tradition based on the Scriptures, the Fathers, and the insights of Roman thinkers. On the other, there was Greek Philosophy. Elements of Plato's thought had been absorbed within the Christian tradition in its early stages, but Aristotle had been 'rediscovered' only recently by medieval Europe through the medium of Jewish scholars and Arabian commentators like Avorres and Avincenna. In addition, in the foreground for St Thomas was the recent revitalisation of Roman law studies, the systematisation of canon law, and the new strength of theology itself as a research area. Among the most important of Aquinas' theologian predecessors were Hugh of St Victor (1096–1141), and Peter Lombard (1100–60) whose *Sententiarum libri quatuor* was adopted as the standard text for university courses in theology.

Because he was a theologian, St Thomas' main concern is the study of man in his relationship to his Creator. This study of necessity implies exploration of the relationships of man to man in society, since for Aquinas, as for Aristotle, man is a social being, and he works out his salvation in the context of

[1] Joseph Schumpeter, *History of Economic Analysis*, (N.Y., Oxford University Press, 1959) p. 77.

community. Justice in social relationships comes within the orbit of theological speculation, and like the philosopher, St Thomas is led to consider the morality of commodity exchanges and monetary practices. Some appreciation of the setting of economic discussion in St Thomas' thought is provided by its position in the structure of the most celebrated of his sixty works, the *Summa Theologica*, written between about 1265 and 1273. The *Summa* is a lengthy work in three parts, dealing with God and the creation, man and his nature (i.e. human acts), and Christ and the sacraments. The second section of the second part is concerned with particular human acts, and this involves discussion of the Cardinal Virtues, one of which is Justice. It is in the treatment of Justice that Aquinas enters into problems of commodity pricing and transfers of money sums.

Questions concerning money and interest, and value and price are focal points of economic enquiry in Aquinas' writings as in those of Aristotle. St Thomas is clearly indebted to the pioneering efforts of the Greek thinker on these subjects, but he aims at a greater degree of generalised treatment of them than Aristotle was able to attain. Particularly, he frees the discussion from some of the limitations imposed by the narrow institutional framework of the *polis*, the city-state concept that was at once the inspiration for Aristotle's economic analysis and the source of its most severe deficiencies. St Thomas reasons with a minimum of regard for the feudal system of his day. As Stephen Worland has observed, Aquinas

> largely disregards the institutional framework through which economic activity takes place and treats such activity simply as the conduct of private individuals ... Concentrating on questions of fundamental principle, he confines his economic investigation to a relatively high level of abstraction ... His conception of an economic system is that of a number of undifferentiated members of the human species held together by those basic institutions — private property, division of labor, exchange — which are 'natural' to man.[2]

[2] S. T. Worland, *Scholasticism and Welfare Economics* (Notre Dame and London, University of Notre Dame Press, 1967) pp. 8–9.

Undoubtedly, feudal conceptions have some bearing on St Thomas' economic thought. This factor is most evident in his treatment of money. Again, the economy of a medieval town is in the background when Aquinas comes to consider justice in commodity pricing. In such towns, markets were recurrent phenomena which could not be divorced from the life of citizens as consumers and producers, as Aristotle had thought possible in his social system. Merchants too, if not bankers, were gaining a measure of respectability amongst the citizenry, and could not be banished by the moralist as easily as the alien residents of Athens. This transition from the *polis* to the market towns of Aquinas' day was a potent factor in the revision of value theory. Nevertheless, while such institutional factors must be given their due, the fact remains that St Thomas' economic reasoning is very little in debt to the particular circumstances of the economy in which he lived. This lack of debt may help explain why his ideas remained so persuasive through the changing socio-economic patterns of succeeding centuries.[3]

The place of economics

St Thomas was not one to claim that the path to salvation for most men required them to embrace a life of poverty. Any virtuous life called for some measure of material support through access to goods and services. This point is made quite plain in the *Summa* (I–II, 4, 7c) where the role of 'external goods' is considered. Further, beyond the obvious need for subsistence, there was the fact that to perform certain types of virtuous act, e.g. charitable loans, the agent usually was obliged to command some surplus in excess of his subsistence requirements. Again, many persons might be obliged to hold possessions above the level necessary to ensure their own subsistence in order that they could carry out the functions

[3] A Latin edition of the writings of Aquinas is, St Thomas Aquinas, *Opera omnia*, 34 vols., ed. P. Maré and S. E. Frette (Paris, Vives, 1871–80). An English translation of his most celebrated work, the *Summa Theologica* (1267–73), was published in 20 volumes (London, 1911–25). There is also a translation of one of his commentaries on Aristotle, *Commentary on the Nicomachean Ethics*, (Chicago, Library of Living Catholic Thought, 1964). Selections from his writings of interest to economists may be found in *Basic Writings of Saint Thomas Aquinas*, ed. A. C. Pegis, 2 vols. (New York, Random House, 1945) and in A. E. Monroe *Early Economic Thought*, (Cambridge, Mass., Harvard University Press, 1924) pp. 52–77.

appropriate to their designated role in society. For these reasons, a healthy spiritual climate in the community demanded attention to the maintenance of a viable system of production and exchange. Such a system could be best ensured, according to Aquinas, on a basis of private ownership of property supplemented by market transfers. The state too may have to play a role from time to time in facilitating the distribution of goods. Private agencies might not always be able to bring about the achievement of the necessary standards of material welfare, and hence potential for virtuous living, for all sections of the community. Economic life then, is something which the theologian cannot ignore, and a study of it requires exploration of certain types of relationship between citizen and citizen, and between the citizen and the state.

Economic reasoning for St Thomas is integrated with moral philosophy and the establishment of legal precepts. Moral philosophy is seen as a discipline which deals with the actions of men as individuals, their conduct as members of households, and their behaviour as citizens. This third branch of moral philosophy is politics, and economics is included within it. Economic analysis is undertaken for the sake of determining appropriate standards in dealings between citizens. Above all, it is an aspect of the enquiry into justice. As Sir Alexander Gray has stated,

> If one word were sought to cover all phases of mediaeval economic teaching, it would probably be found in the idea of 'justice' ... We are brothers and should behave as brothers, respecting each other's rights and position in life. Each should receive that to which he is entitled. Justice, as the mediaevalist understood it, should be done. No one, under any circumstances, should take advantage of his neighbour. This is the sum and substance of mediaeval economic teaching.[4]

[4] A. Gray, *The Development of Economic Doctrine* (London, Longmans, 1959) p. 46. On Economics as a branch of Moral Philosophy, see Ernest Bartell, 'Value, Price, and St Thomas', *The Thomist*, Vol, XXV, No. 3 (July 1962) pp. 325–81. Of St Thomas' conception, Bartell observes, 'The economic decision is thus a voluntary moral act and so the branch of human knowledge that studies economic acts will be a branch of moral science. Moral science studies not the rational techniques of manufacturing proper to the mechanical arts, but rather it considers voluntary human acts as they are ordered to one another and to an end.' (p. 345).

Because it is concerned with justice, economic doctrine occupies a definite place within Aquinas' system of law. Law, in general, is conceived of as those rational precepts which enable human actions to be regulated in terms of the proper goals for the actions concerned. There are various types of law, and at the base is the type St Thomas calls 'Eternal'. This involves tendencies inherent in the behaviour of creatures. On this base is built Natural Law which consists of man's consciousness of inherent tendencies. The principles of natural law are thought to be self-evident and immutable with respect to their fundamentals, although there is scope for some alteration over time in their secondary aspects. These mutable, secondary aspects shade into another level of precept, the level of *ius gentium* or law of nations. It is at this level that generalisations concerning economic activity are located. Such generalisations are not self-evident, and precept can vary from society to society. Still more variable is positive law which attempts to apply natural law to particular cases and circumstances. Finally, in Aquinas' schema, there is divine law which consists of precepts given by divine revelation rather than human reasoning.

Justice in social life has three aspects according to St Thomas. First, there are the requirements of general justice which deals with the obligations of the individual to the community. Second, there is commutative (from *commutatio* — transaction) justice, governing the relationships of individual to individual. Third, the obligations of the community to the individual are matters pertaining to distributive justice. Aquinas' economic reasoning is associated mainly with the second of these three categories. Transfers of goods and money are largely matters in which relationships of individuals are involved. The morality of buying and selling, or of investing and lending concerns contracts, implicit or explicit, into which private parties enter on voluntary or involuntary bases. The conditions under which justice is obtained in those contractual associations are elucidated by means of economic analysis. This understanding of the role of economic analysis was to hold good throughout the subsequent centuries of the scholastic tradition. It is this vision of the scope of economics which binds the schoolmen's contributions together, despite the diversity of their solutions to particular problems considered within its orbit.

Money, interest and banking

St Thomas' exploration of the morality of commercial contracts, both formal and informal, required analysis of the nature of money, the bases of interest payment, and the roles of the merchant and banker. It also led to a most influential essay into the economics of price determination, the details of which are considered in the following section of this chapter. His conception of economics did not encourage investigation of the theory of production, and the absence of any serious treatment of the functions of real capital is one of the major deficiencies of his thought from the viewpoint of modern economics. Further, because he related economic analysis mainly to questions of commutative rather than distributive justice, Aquinas offers little by way of insight into the theory of income distribution.

The theologian's reasoning on money is dominated by two ideas. First and foremost, money functions as a medium for the exchange of commodities. He writes: 'Now money according to the Philosopher, *Ethics* V, 5, and *Politics* I, 3, was invented chiefly for the purpose of exchange and consequently the proper and principal use of money is its consumption or alienation whereby it is sunk in exchange.'[5] At the same time, money is a unit of account. It provides a common standard of value, a measuring rod for comparing the relative worths of exchangeable things:

> All other things from themselves have some utility: not so, however, money. But it is the measure of utility of other things, as is clear according to the Philosopher in the *Ethics* V, 9. And therefore the use of money does not have the measure of its utility from this money itself, but from the things which are measured by money according to the different persons who exchange money for goods.[6]

[5] *Summa Theologica*, II–II:78, 1. See also *In III primos libros politicorum*, Bk 1:6, 7, 8.
[6] *In IV libros sententiarum*, III:37, 1, 6. See also *In X libros ethicorum*, Bk V., Lect. 9. Earlier, St Albert had written: 'Now money equals all exchangeable goods just as the unit of a ruler by addition and subtraction equals all things ruled.' *In Librum V Ethicorum*, Tract. 2, cap. 10, no. 36.

The foregoing passage indicates the fundamental difference between money and commodities, according to St Thomas. The latter have utility 'from themselves', whereas money, in itself, has no utility. There can be no ground then, for the direct application of any general theory concerning the pricing and production of commodities to analysis of the economics of money. Money is a special case.

The sharp distinction between money and commodities is redrawn in the *Summa* (I–II, 2, 1), where St Thomas writes: 'For wealth is twofold, namely natural and artificial. Natural wealth is that which serves man as a remedy for his natural wants, such as food, drink, clothing, transportation, housing and the like; while artificial wealth is that which is not a direct help to nature, e.g. money, but is invented by the art of man.'

Medium of exchange

Because money is a medium of exchange it can be classified as a consumable, i.e. it is consumptible in use. When money is used by its owner to obtain goods it is lost to him. Ownership changes hands. This emphasis is found in the Roman law concerning bequests. Consumable things (*res quae minuuntur vel consumuntur*) are things which are extinguished and are intended to be extinguished by use. Money is included in this category. Of the four books of the *Corpus Iuris Civilis*, both the collection of views of leading Roman lawyers, the *Digest*, and the *Institutes*, containing rulings of the Senate, adopt this approach.[7] In consequence, St Thomas, following the Roman view, argues that the person who has obtained the legal right to use a particular sum of money must be seen as the lawful owner of that sum. To use money is to transfer its ownership, and one cannot give lawfully to another, property which is not yours to give. In law and morality, then, the ownership and use of money cannot be separated.[8]

The only exception to this identification of ownership and

[7] See *Digesta*, 7:5:2, 5, 6, 7 and 10. Also *Institutiones*, 2:4:2.
[8] See e.g. Saint Thomas, *Quaestiones disputatae de Malo*, Q. 13, art. 4c. This view of money is the cornerstone of Aquinas' main argument for the condemnation of usury as immoral.

use arises in circumstances where the use of money does not involve its consumption. A standard example of such circumstances is provided by the Roman contract dealing with the temporary transfer of a sum of money so that the recipient can use it for purposes of display (*ad pompam*). Because the contract does not permit the recipient to consume the money, in the sense of using it for exchange, no transfer of ownership is involved.[9] The owner can charge for the use of the money, although the contract also provides for full restitution of the sum transferred after an agreed period.

However, considered with respect to its primary end or purpose, money is consumed in use. It is something which performs a single act of use service. Its significance, life, meaning are summed up in the moment of its being exchanged. Although St Thomas does not refer to money as 'sterile', this popular medieval view reflects the analytical emphasis of Aquinas and his successors on the uniqueness of the service which the individual owner of money can derive from it.

Given this emphasis, an identification of money and physical capital which may yield a stream of services, is ruled out. The position of St Thomas as well as that of much later scholastics, is in sharp contrast with the view that eventually came to predominate outside the scholastic tradition. For example, their thinking is totally opposed to that of the French Renaissance jurist Charles du Moulin (Molinaeus) (1500–66). He wrote that '. . . the use and fruition of money not only consists in the first momentary expenditure or application, but also in the successive use of the wares or goods bought with it.'[10] One important consequence of the scholastics' stance was their ability to maintain a conceptual distinction between interest on money loans and returns to capital. With Molinaeus' approach, this distinction becomes blurred or inconsequential.

Another consequence of the stress on the act of exchange by St Thomas was his relative lack of regard of the significance which money may possess when held as a stock, i.e. in balances. Money yields a service in exchange, but it

[9] *Quaestiones Disputatae de Malo*, Q 13 and 15.
[10] *Tractatus commerciorum*, n. 530.

yields no direct service when held. Realisation of the presence of this latter service was a much later development in scholastic thought. Nevertheless, Aquinas did not completely ignore balances, as will be seen later.

Common standard, or unit of account

Acting as a common standard, money consists of a number of standard currency units. Units of the same denomination are not differentiated and can be freely exchanged for units of other denominations in fixed ratios. One unit can perform its social role as well as any other unit. For this reason the scholastics followed the Roman classification of sums of money as 'fungibles'. Fungibles are things which are not individually identified, but are identified only by reference to a class of objects.

As a result, the relevant contract for money loans was the Roman law contract of *mutuum*. This had always as its subject matter fungible things. The giving of a *mutuum* as defined in the *Institutes* of Justinian occurs in the loan of those things which are made up by weight, number, or measure, such as wine, oil, grain or money, and which one gives in weighing out, counting or measuring in such a way that they become the property of the receiver. In this contract, the borrower is obliged to repay only the exact amount of the fungible goods that he received. If he is to be obliged to pay something in addition to returning the principal, a second contract is required. The term used to describe such payment was *usura*.

While adopting the Roman law classifications concerning money and loans of money, St Thomas did not allow the lawfulness of *usura*. Nevertheless, he allowed that if the lender suffered some loss or damages due to the failure of the borrower to return the principal of a loan in the time and manner specified by the contract, then the lender was entitled to receive *interesse*. Most contemporary scholastic writers took a similar view.

As was seen above in Chapter 3, the right to compensation for delay in repayment was allowed by Plato. However, the scholastic approach to the matter evolved from Roman legal practice. The word *interesse* seems to have been coined by

Azo, the twelfth-century Bolognese canonist, to cover the phrase *quod interest*, damages due because of a default by one of the parties to a contract in Roman law. Incorporated into the *Glossa Ordinaria*, it became standard from about 1220.[11] The idea behind *interesse* was incidence of damage. It was the amount 'between' what the lender holds at the end of the loan period and what justice demands he should have. It was not a price for the use of money, but an indemnification for loss.[12]

The position of the lender, not that of the borrower, dictated whether or not there was some basis for payment over and above the principal of a loan. This Thomistic emphasis continued in the thinking of later scholastics. Whether the borrower used the money wisely or foolishly, whether he employed the money for purposes of consumption or production — these were irrelevant issues. One long-standing fallacy concerning the scholastic approach to lending is that it sought to differentiate loans for consumption purposes from those for production. Yet authoritative modern scholarship has shown that St Thomas made no such distinction.[13] Further, when his successors sought an explanation for the phenomenon of interest payment, the Roman law tradition and the authority of Aquinas led them to consider the significance of money in the hands of a potential lender, not its use by a borrower. By this emphasis, they were led to avoid any adherence to the type of simple productivity theory of interest which bedevilled classical economics in the early part of the nineteenth century.

Although Aquinas regards money, functioning as a common standard, a fungible to which the contract of *mutuum* is applicable, he believes, because it is a standard, that it is

[11] See J. T. Noonan, *The Scholastic Analysis of Usury* (Cambridge, Mass., Harvard University Press, 1957) p. 106, and J. Gilchrist, *The Church and Economic Activity in the Middle Ages* (London Macmillan, 1969) p. 279.
[12] H. Johnston, 'Some Mediaeval Doctrines on Extrinsic Titles to Interest', in Charles J. O'Neil (ed.), *An Etienne Gilson Tribute* (Milwaukee, Marquette University Press, 1959) p. 89.
[13] Consult Cardinal Joseph Van Roey, *De Justo auctario ex contractu crediti* (Louvain, 1903) pp. 282 ff; John P. Kelly, *Aquinas and Modern Practices of Interest Taking* (Brisbane, 1945) pp. 67—8; B. W. Dempsey, *Interest and Usury* (Washington, 1943) pp. 138—9; J. T. Noonan, op. cit., p. 56; and Herbert Johnston, op. cit., p. 88.

radically different from other fungibles. Money is not just
another type of merchandise. The special position which
money occupies for St Thomas has been remarked upon by
Joseph Schumpeter. He writes that Aquinas '... placed
implicit confidence in the proposition that the price of any
commodity that is chosen for the standard of value is unity
by definition.'[14]

This 'confidence' stems from the view that standards, to
perform their social function efficiently, must be established
and maintained by law. They cannot be left to determination
by the changing consensus of public opinion as, say, the
market price of commodities can be determined. Legal
authority sets the face value of money, and that face value
establishes its just price. The price of the common standard is
not determined by reference to the fluctuating quantities of
goods for which it can be exchanged. Money is a creature of
the law, a token or counter, the just price of which can be
altered only by legal enactment.[15]

St Thomas' legalism here is supported by Greek and
Roman authors and by the feudal conception of the
monetary system. Plato, as was seen in Chapter 3, believed
that the medium of exchange in his Republic should only be
a symbol or token sanctioned by the state. Aristotle accepted
his teacher's view. The philosophers were followed by the
influential Roman jurist Paulus for whom money's '... use
and power are derived not so much from its substance as
from its quantity [i.e. *tale*, the public price set on it].'[16]

[14] Joseph Schumpeter, op. cit., p. 94.
[15] Cf. John T. Noonan, op. cit., p. 52, 93–4. The idea of money as a fixed
measure provides a major ground for St Thomas' opposition to usury. The usurer
is guilty of attempting to 'diversify the measure' when he demands interest on a
sum of money loaned. He is endeavouring to ascribe two values to the one sum.
[16] On Paulus' monetary views see A. E. Monroe, *Monetary Theory Before Adam
Smith* (Cambridge, 1923) pp. 10–11 and M. Grice-Hutchinson, *The School of
Salamanca* (Oxford, 1952) pp. 21–2. Summarising these early approaches Charles
du Moulin in his *De Mutatione Monetae Tractatus* (1546) wrote, 'Money, insofar
as it is money, is not merchandise ... but measures the value of all things, as
Aristotle says in *Ethics* V ... This is proved by the origin and institution of
money. According to Aristotle ... men created money by common agreement, to
supply and represent necessary things, and that is why it is called numisma,
because it is the product of law, not of nature, and we have the power to alter its
value or to make it useless. The Jurisconsult [i.e. Paulus] is of the same opinion,
and says ... that (the value of money) resides not so much in its substance as in
its quantity; that is, in the public price set upon it, which has recently come to be
called its public and perpetual estimation.'

In the feudal conception, coinage was the property of the prince. He had the monopoly of its production and, as the owner of the currency, was the authority who determined its legal value. All weights and measures in the state were under his jurisdiction, and money was necessarily included. The prince was regarded as 'a measurer of the just proportion' owed by men to each other or to society as a whole. Because money is a yardstick or measuring rod employed in gauging the degree to which private and social obligations have been discharged, its status as a standard of reference was a matter in which the ruler's jurisdiction was decisive. Further, as Professor Estrup has observed, 'Since the coinage is nothing but a token, the value of which is fixed by the prince, the intrinsic value of the actual coinage is immaterial. The prince can fix the metal content of a given coin and its metal price independently of each other.'[17]

The tradition which stood behind St Thomas' view of money was one of non-metallism. Unlike some subsequent scholastics, he was not committed to the doctrine that money, to function correctly as money, must consist of a material that has value independent of its status as money. Metal content was an accidental, not an essential feature of the standard of value, so there was no ground for determining the just price of money in terms of a so-called intrinsic worth of its metal content. Irrespective of changes in purchasing power or metal content the just price of money remained unity in and by law.

Money in balance
So far, we have seen that St Thomas thought that money has no value 'from itself', and that it has economic significance only as a unit of account, a fixed standard of measurement, any multiple of which performs a single act of use-service for its owner in exchange. His attention is focused on money at the moment of transfer against the receipt of commodities, or at the expiry date of a loan. Yet, these major emphases do not lead him to neglect entirely the question of the

[17] Hector Estrup, 'Oresme and Monetary Theory', *The Scandinavian Economic History Review*, Vol. XIV, No. 2 (1966) p. 102. On this subject see also Gabriel le Bras, 'Conceptions of Economy and Society', *The Cambridge Economic History of Europe*, Vol. III (1963) pp. 561–62.

significance which money may possess when held as a stock or balance.

In his commentary on Aristotle's *Ethics*, he notes the philosopher's point that money can be held as a means of serving future consumption requirements, and that such a balance may be subject to alterations in purchasing power. He writes: 'Money, however, like other things is actually subject to change. One does not always get for it what he desires because it is not always equal, that is, it is not always of the same value. But money should be established in such a way that it is more stable in the same value than are other things.'[18] Whereas Aristotle chooses to deal with this latter problem by statutory price fixation. St Thomas is content to observe that changes of purchasing power should be kept to a minimum if money is to perform its exchange function adequately.

This recognition of fluctuation in the purchasing power of money balances would seem to be at variance with St Thomas' belief that money can be regarded as a fixed unit of account established by law. Yet, the apparent dichotomy here may be explicable in terms of the distinction between 'money of account' and 'coin in circulation' which developed in medieval Europe. Of this, F. P. Braudel writes,

> All prices, all accounting systems (even the most rudimentary) and all contracts — or at least almost all — were formulated in terms of an accounting unit, that is to say in a money which was 'not necessarily represented by metal currency', but which acted as a measure for the coin in circulation. Each country had its own particular version, with its subdivisions . . . all payments were a conversion into currency from prices formulated in a money of account.[19]

It seems possible that it was to money in the accounting sense that Aquinas referred when he declared money to be a stable measure set by legal enactment. The varieties of coinage in circulation could appreciate or depreciate together

---

[18] *In X libros ethicorum*, Bk. V, Lect. 9. See also *De Regimine Principum*, ii, 7.
[19] F. P. Braudel, 'Prices in Europe from 1450 to 1750', in E. F. Rich and C. H. Wilson (eds), *The Cambridge Economic History of Europe*, Vol. IV (1967) p. 378.

in terms of their command over particular commodities in greater or lesser abundance, but the exchange ratios between the different forms and denominations of coinage would remain fixed in terms of the legally established money of account. Since it was money in this latter sense that was relevant to contractual relationships, the legally fixed measure was the operative one in any analysis of their morality.

Another point at which Aquinas considers the status of money in balance is during his discussion of the restitution of stolen money in the *Summa Theologica*. He holds that a thief is bound to return to his victim a sum which includes compensation for the probable loss of profits experienced by the owner because of the theft. Here, a stock of money is seen as possessing the potentiality for gaining profits for its owner, just as seed has the potentiality of yielding a crop. 'One is held, however,' he writes, 'to give some compensation according to the condition of the persons and businesses . . . The sower of the seed in the field has the harvest not actually but virtually. In like manner, he that has money has the profit not actually, but virtually; and both may be hindered in many ways.'[20]

In this instance, St Thomas is considering money before it has been consumed in use by its true owner through exchange. As a stock in hand, it has the potential for being exchanged for goods and services, the employment of which by its owner may yield an eventual surplus over cost. Recognition of this potential also underlies Aquinas' treatment of compensation for delay in repayment of a money loan. The debtor is held to be obliged to return to the creditor a sum which includes the equivalent of the probable loss of profit incurred by the creditor because of the delay.[21]

These analyses of restitution and compensation are early examples of the scholastic practice of finding grounds for repayment of a greater sum of money than that initially transferred from one person to another, in the fact that one party experiences special financial disadvantages because of the transfer. Such disadvantages, under the titles of *lucrum*

[20] *Summa Theologica*, II–II:62:4:1, 2.
[21] *In IV libros sententiarum*, IV:15:1:5.

cessans and *damnum emergens*, were to become focal points for later attempts to explain the existence of a legitimate, positive rate of interest.

In Aquinas' thought, special financial disadvantage has a very restricted incidence. It can apply only in the case of a businessman who might have cause to use funds in exchange for commodities that can be employed to realise profit. Again, the discussion of compensation does not suggest that anything above the principal of a loan is payable before the agreed date of termination of that loan. Further, in both delay and theft, the loss of profit which gives an economic base for extra payment is a strictly involuntary loss. Voluntary sacrifice of probable profits by a lender, for St Thomas as for Plato, does not warrant a recompense such as an interest premium. 'For he who lent the money', Aquinas warns, 'ought to beware lest he incur damage for himself. Nor ought he who receives the loan incur loss from the stupidity of the lender.'[22]

There is one case in which the voluntary transfer of a money balance from one party to another can entitle the original owner of the money to a return greater than the original sum. The case is that of *societas* or business partnership, where two or more persons combine to pool money, labour, and skill for a common purpose. One person may merely contribute money to the partnership, and yet legitimately derive profits which could well exceed his original contribution in face-value terms. St Thomas writes: 'He who commits his money to a merchant or craftsman by means of some kind of partnership does not transfer the ownership of his money to him but it remains his; so that at his risk the merchant trades, or the craftsman works, with it; and therefore he can licitly seek part of the profit thence coming as from his own property.'[23]

Here, Aquinas, seems to be acknowledging the legal personality of a business partnership. It is a *ius fraternitatis*, a kind of brotherhood comprising those who have contributed elements which gave it life. The individual transferring money

[22] *Quaestiones disputatae de Malo*, Q. 13, art. 4, ad. 14.
[23] *Summa Theologica*, II—II:78:2, obj. 5.

to the partnership transfers it to an entity of which he is part. When the partnership uses the money, i.e. alienates it in exchange for goods, that entity is both the owner and user of the money, and the financial partner is part-owner of the goods obtained. When employment of those goods yields a profit, he is entitled to part of the return. The distinguishing mark of genuine membership of the brotherhood by the supplier of finance is his sharing in the risk of loss through the venture's failure. If he assumed no risk, he would not be a part-owner of the goods of the *societas*, and would merely be entitled to an eventual return of the same sum of money he gave originally.

The case of *societas*, then, is quite different from that of a mere money loan which, apart from the presence of delay in repayment to a businessman lender, warrants no surplus earnings on its principal. Aquinas is drawing a sharp division between loans and business investments, a division which was to continue to exert considerable influence on the future development of both economic theory and practice. Money in a balance has the *potential*, when held by a businessman, for profit earning. Voluntary sacrifice of that potential by lending does not warrant the return of a surplus. Where that potential is made actual through the purchase of productive factors by a legal personality in which the financier participates, then a profit can be taken. It can be taken also, if the financier sets up in business by himself as a sole trader.

Some commentators have argued that St Thomas achieves this distinction between interest on money loans and profit-earning in *societas* only at the expense of inconsistency in his theory of money.[24] Yet, this does not seem to be the case. Given that *societas* has legal personality, Aquinas is not obliged to depart from his basic belief that the use and ownership of money are indistinguishable. Further, given that profits result from employment of the commodities which the partnership purchases with an investor's money, there is no reversal of the Thomistic stand that money is something which has no value 'from itself'. Thirdly, it is not inconsistent to hold that money performs a single act of use-service, yet

---

[24] See, for example, J. T. Noonan, op. cit., pp. 143—45.

has some special significance as a stock or balance. St Thomas' view is at one with that of Leon Walras, whom many regard as the founder of modern monetary theory, when the latter writes: 'The need for money is nothing else than the need for the goods to be purchased with this money. It is the need for holding a stock.'[25] Both thinkers regard money as having a single use-service function, but they also recognise its stock dimension. Walras goes on to ascribe special value to money in balance because of the satisfaction it offers to its holder by way of enhancing his liquidity. St Thomas completely overlooks or implicitly rejects this liquidity-based value of a stock, and confines the special characteristic of a money balance to the profit potential it may have when destined for use in exchange for commodities by a business partnership or sole trader.

The status of banking

Despite his exploration of the functions of money, St Thomas does not enter into any thorough analysis of banking practices. Instead, like the vast majority of contemporary theologians, he was content to treat the vocation of banker as an unusual and morally suspect type of activity. The reason for this suspicion was the view of money as a form of artificial wealth which had no natural limit to its accumulation as was the case with commodities such as food, clothing, and housing. Dealers in money were prone to suffer serious personality deterioration in pursuit of gain. As Aquinas writes in the *Summa* (I–II, 2, 1): 'the desire for artificial wealth [of which money is a prime example] is infinite, for it is the servant of disordered concupiscence . . .'.

St Thomas was able to draw support for this position from both earlier Christian sources and from Aristotle. For the latter, professional bankers were engaged in an unnatural trade. Hence, when Aquinas came to comment on the philosopher's *Politics*, he observed: 'Likewise, the art of money or acquisition is natural to all men for the purpose of procuring food, or money with which to buy food, out of natural things such as fruits or animals. But when money is

---

[25] Leon Walras, *Economie politique appliqué* (1898) p. 95.

acquired not by means of natural things but out of money itself, this is against nature.'[26]

Further, St Thomas was led to apply Aristotle's condemnation of retail trade in general to the specific case of exchange banking. This application arose out of a mistranslation of the Greek term for retail trade. In William of Moerbecke's translation of the *Politics* he rendered the term as *campsoria*, which, in medieval times, designated the business of money-changing. Hence, as Professor Noonan points out, 'instead of being presented with a condemnation of all retail trade, which medieval Christian theologians would not have accepted, the early scholastics found in Aristotle only a condemnation of traffic in money; and themselves already suspicious of the "campsores", they found this highly natural.'[27]

Additional grounds for distrust of the morality of bankers was afforded by the belief that in their normal course of business they were involved constantly in the taking of usury. At that period, the most obvious form of banking operation was the exchange of currencies by money dealers who followed the round of fairs across Europe. Even in a major banking centre like Florence, the city's guild of bankers was known as the guild of money-changers (*Arte del Cambio*). In the transactions between money dealers (the *campsores*) and the merchants who gathered to trade commodities from fair to fair, extensions of business credit were often blended with the process of currency exchange. The one transaction might be both a loan, in a certain type of currency, and an exchange for another type of currency when the due date of repayment eventuated. Hence, the scholastic condemnation of interest-taking on money loans, in most circumstances, tended to be applied also to profit-earning in exchange banking. St Thomas, for example, when commenting on Psalm 5:5, 'Who has not given his money to usury', finds the verse applicable to 'the *campsores* who commit many frauds, and against the sellers of cloth and other goods'.[28]

[26] *In 111 primos libros politocorum*, I, 57.
[27] J. T. Noonan, op. cit., p. 47.
[28] Op. cit., p. 181. On the intimate relationship that could exist between an exchange transaction and an extension of credit, see Raymond De Roover, *The Rise and Decline of the Medici Bank, 1397–1494* (Cambridge, Harvard University Press, 1963) pp. 132–5.

Aquinas' attitude to banking activities did not carry over to those of merchants. Unlike Aristotle, he gave them definite approval, within certain limits. This approval represented a reversal of earlier medieval attitudes, and it enabled the scholastic followers of St Thomas eventually to find grounds for justification of aspects of banking. In these respects there are some bases for the claim that 'the very fact that St Thomas did incorporate the new entrepreneur and his profits, the market price and its justice, into the framework of Christian moral philosophy earns him the title of "pioneer of a liberal intellectual movement".'[29]

As late as the year 1078, a church council at Rome issued a canon which affirmed that it was impossible for either merchants or soldiers to carry on their trades without sin. They could not hope for eternal salvation, it was declared, unless they found other forms of employment. In line with this sentiment, the twelfth-century *Sentences* of Peter Lombard, which Aquinas used as a text in his early days of teaching in Paris, argued that while a merchant continued in that occupation, a confessor could not accept him as a penitent.[30] Such statements are quite in accord with Aristotle's position in which, it was suggested in Chapter 2, gain through mercantile operations was treated as akin to gain through military conquest. Both types of gain always can be achieved only through injury of another party.

By the thirteenth century, a number of theologians had begun to grasp the idea that merchants might perform some necessary social function. A willingness to defend them is evident in the writings of the British Franciscan, Alexander of Hales (d. 1245).[31] St Albert, too, in his commentary on Lombard's text, is willing to give merchants a place in the social order.[32] There is precedent then for St Thomas to argue, in his own treatment of Lombard's views, that a merchant might be able to undertake his business without committing sin. The merchant is warned, however, that this is not likely to be easy.[33]

---

[29] E. Bartell, op. cit., p. 378.
[30] *Sententiarum libri quatuor*, IV, dist. 16, qu 4, art. 2, quaestincula 2.
[31] *Summa theologica*, pars, II, in quis. III, tract. II, sect. II, Q. II, tit. III.
[32] *Commentarius in quatuor libros sententiarum*, Lib. IV, dist. XVI, art. 46.
[33] *Commentum in libros IV sententiarum magistri Petri Lombardi*, dist. 16, qu. 4, art. 2, quaestincula 3, obj. 1 and ad. 1.

A more positive approach to the vocation of merchant is taken in the *Summa*, a later work than the commentary on Peter Lombard. Here, Aquinas, is prepared to approve of merchants who are engaged in international or inter-regional trade.[34] These make good local commodity deficiencies and transfer surplus produce. This same approval is present in his *De Regimine Principum*, where St Thomas considers the means whereby a state can provide for its material needs. Self-sufficiency is put forward as a desirable national goal. He writes, 'The more dignified a thing is, the more self-sufficient it is ... A city therefore which has an abundance of food from its own territory is more dignified than one which is provisioned through trade.'[35] Nevertheless, he recognises that the activities of merchants are necessary quite often, even in 'perfect' cities. A well ordered society will employ their services in moderation.[36]

Leading theologians who were the immediate successors of St Thomas were ready to continue the process of extending approval of merchants, especially where they were engaged in international trade.[37] However, a transfer of this approval from merchant to banker was a much slower process. Within the Thomistic tradition proper, it did not occur in unambiguous terms until the advent of Thomas de Vio, Cardinal Cajetan (1465—1524), the authoritative Dominican commentator on St Thomas whose economic analysis is examined in the next chapter. He contends that since the vocation of merchant is morally permissible, the occupation of exchange banker which support the activities of merchants must also be socially justifiable. Aquinas' divergence from Aristotle in approving of merchants is used to counter his apparent agreement with the philosopher in condemning dealers in foreign exchange. It was not until 1499 that this counter-argument was proposed, and meanwhile, for the majority of theologians, many of the activities of the bankers remained under a deep cloud of moral suspicion.

[34] *Summa theologica*, II—II, qu. 77, art. 4, resp.
[35] *De Regimine Principum*, Bk. II, Ch. 3.
[36] Ibid.
[37] See, e.g., Duns Scotus (1265—1308) *Quaestiones in libros IV sententiarum*, dist. 15, qu. 2, no. 22, and Richard of Middleton (fl. c. 1290), *Quodlibeta*, quodlibet II, qu. 23, art. 1.

Value and price

The failure of the medieval scholastics to find a legitimate role for exchange bankers was closely associated with the absence of an appreciation of the existence of markets in money. On the other hand, recognition of the functions of merchants was related to an acceptance of commodity markets. With their thought, there is a clear shift from Aristotle's focus on setting the terms of trade between households, to the question of price formation through market consensus. However, like Aristotle, they approached the issue of commodity exchange as a problem of developing criteria for the establishment of justice in human affairs.

Aquinas writes in the *Summa* (II–II, Q. 77, art. 1): 'Purchase and sale are seen to have been introduced for the common utility of both parties, since one needs the goods of the other ... But what was introduced for the common good ought not be more of a burden on the one than on the other; and so the contract between them ought to be established according to an equality.'

Out of their concern with the nature of the just price emerged insights on the subject of value determination. Other insights, which were influential in moulding the development of later thinking on value, derived from their treatments of property, work, and income. In this section we consider St Thomas' contribution as regards his discussion of price and value. His other contributions are dealt with in the next section.

According to Aquinas, the just price of any commodity is its current market price established in the absence of fraud or monopolistic trading practices. This was also the view of Alexander of Hales and of St Albert. It is a price established by *communiter venditur*, the price generally charged in the community concerned, rather than the price dictated by the preferences or needs of any one individual in that community. In the immediate background of St Thomas' thought here are the similar positions on just price adopted by the canon lawyers and Roman law experts of the twelfth century and early thirteenth century.[38] Further back still is the

[38] Consult John W. Baldwin, *The Medieval Theories of the Just Price; Romanists, Canonists, and Theologians in the Twelfth and Thirteenth Centuries* (Transactions

Roman law of sale, and the principle that 'the price of things is not from the affection or utility of single persons, but from their common estimation.'[39] This is the tradition which underlies Aquinas' treatment of just price in his *De emptione et venditione*, written about 1262, and in the *Summa theologica* (II–II, qu. 77) some ten years later. In the former (a letter to the Dominican, James of Viterbo), for example, he employs a specific market price, the price of cloth at the Fair of Lagny, as the measure of the just price in a particular instance.

In the *Summa*, St Thomas declares that justice will not be done unless commodities are bought and sold at prices which correspond to the true worth or value of those commodities.[40] This statement sheds no light on the analytical issue of prime interest to economists, namely, the forces which he believes are at work in determining true worth or value. When this issue is faced, it is difficult to find a clear-cut response to it in Aquinas' writings. Passages may be cited which suggest that his thinking on value has a utility orientation. On the other hand, it has been affirmed that cost of production is the decisive consideration for him. Considerable controversy has been generated over the centuries by the ambiguities surrounding Aquinas' position.

When commenting on Aristotle's *Ethics*, St Thomas observes (Book V, Lect. 9) that the scale of values established by human estimates of the utility of commodities may differ markedly from the scale according to nature and creation. In creation, a pearl is a lesser thing than a mouse. Yet, because of human estimation the pearl is the more highly valued object. The price of things which are saleable is governed by their usefulness. The same generalisation on economic value is found in the *Summa* in a passage referring to St Augustine's *The City of God*. Although a horse is a lesser creature

---

of the American Philosophical Society, N.S., Vol. 49, Part 4, 1959) esp. pp. 21–57.

[39] *Digest*, 35:2:63.

[40] *Summa theologica*, II–II, qu. 77, art. 1: 'The value [*quantitas rerum*] of a thing that comes into human use is measured by the price given for it ... Therefore if either the price exceed the amount of the thing's value, or conversely, the thing exceed the price, there is no longer the equality of justice.'

than a slave, the former may sometimes command a higher price because it is deemed more useful in the circumstances.[41] Subjective estimate of utility then, provides the source or origin of value. Prices will reflect the market consensus of groups of individual preferences and subjective calculations concerning need. 'This one thing which measures all truthfully', he writes in his reflections on Aristotle's *Ethics* (V, 9), 'is need, because it embraces all exchange goods insofar as they are related to human need.'

Against the utility emphasis can be set those passages in the commentary on Aristotle's *Ethics* (V, 9), in which St Thomas considers the element of 'inequality of persons' in the workings of proportionate reciprocity according to the philosopher. It was shown in Chapter 3 that Aquinas believes that Aristotle is contending that goods will exchange in terms of the 'labour and costs' involved in their production. In addition, the commentator observes, 'the arts will be destroyed if prices are not so determined. Here, it might be said that St Thomas' comments on another writer should not be taken to commit him personally to a labour or cost of production theory of value. He is not expressing his own views. Yet this reading of Aristotle by Aquinas goes well beyond what is explicit in the original text. Aristotle's 'unequal persons', whose vocations are of differing moral worth or inherent skilfulness, are forsaken in favour of the inequality of their products in terms of cost. Again, the suggestion that prices must cover costs of production, if the productive processes involved are not to be discontinued, is by no means obvious in Aristotle's discussion. St Thomas seems to have grasped the notion that underlying the supply conditions for any market are the cost conditions within which the producers operate.

While he goes beyond Aristotle in linking market supply to cost, St Thomas does not go on to develop the implications of this insight for a general theory of price determination. As Professor Hollander points, out, Aquinas does not explain how market price can come to reflect normal

---

[41] *Summa theologica*, II–II, qu. 77, art. 2, ad. 3. Aquinas concludes: 'The price of saleable things does not depend upon their rank in nature ... but upon their usefulness to man.'

costs. Unlike Adam Smith, he does not trace through the consequence of a failure to cover supply price, or indicate the manner in which resources will move between occupations in response to relative profitability.[42] This failure may be due, in large measure, to the fact that Aquinas' discussion of the just price is related to his concern with commutative justice. The latter deals only with the relationship of one person to another, justice in a transaction between an individual seller and a single buyer in a particular market. Pricing is not considered in the wider context of the claims of distributive justice where the economic well-being of the community as a whole is a relevant reference point.[43] Because Adam Smith analysed pricing mechanisms in this wider context, he took account of the general consequences of a potential 'destruction of the arts'. He looked to mobility of labour and capital as means of correcting any departures from the requirements of commutative justice in particular markets, while at the same time, the welfare of the community as a whole was maximised through the same processes. Aquinas did not achieve such a synthesis in his treatment of the economic aspects of commutation and distribution.

Despite this failure, there are strong grounds for contending that St Thomas believed that both utility and cost of production were relevant in value determination. Certainly, he recognised that both demand and supply conditions influenced market prices. The role of demand is quite plain in his observations on the impact of human estimation on price. An illustration of his awareness of the relevance of supply is afforded by the discussion of marketing morality in the *Summa*.[44] Aquinas considers a case in which the purchasers of wheat are unaware of an impending increase in market supplies, although it is known to a seller. The theologian is in no doubt here that the market price of wheat will fall in response to the future influx on the supply side.

Given that St Thomas believed that prices were influenced by costs, some historians have claimed that he contended

---

[42] S. Hollander, *The Economics of Adam Smith* (London, Heinemann, 1973) p. 28.
[43] Cf., S. T. Worland, op. cit., Ch. 9.
[44] *Summa theologica*, II—II, qu. 77, art. 3, ad. 4.

that just price differentials should reflect the differences in social standing of various suppliers of products.[45] According to these commentators, Aquinas held that a just exchange system should also ensure justice in the distribution of income. A more worthwhile member of society, in terms of medieval social conventions, should receive a larger share of income than one of lesser rank, even though the latter was a productive member of the community. The former's services should be costed at a higher rate than those of the latter, if justice in distribution was to accompany justice in exchange. On this view, the just price of a commodity was not necessarily the prevailing market price, as suggested above, but rather a price which was geared to maintain the social status of the producer concerned.

In fact, St Thomas does not link the question of what the community owes the individual, i.e. distributive justice, to his analysis of justice in the exchange of commodities. Aristotle, as was seen in Chapter 3, may have been attempting to do this with his reference to the equation of 'persons who are unequal'. However, in his comments on Aristotle, Aquinas does not take up the philosopher's lead in this respect. Elsewhere, St Thomas makes it quite clear that, as far as market transactions are concerned, he is not prepared to differentiate between persons except as they act in a moral or immoral fashion in conducting those transactions. Price determination and social status are distinct matters: 'In a just exchange the medium does not vary with the social position of the persons involved, but only with regard to the quantity of the goods. For instance, whoever buys a thing must pay what the thing is worth whether he buys from a pauper or from a rich man.'[46]

The controversy and confusion surrounding this aspect of Aquinas' thought is a result of his failure to explore the possibility of the type of synthesis attempted by Adam Smith. In St Thomas' thought there is no guarantee that the achievement of justice in pricing will ensure justice in

---

[45] See, e.g., Hannah Robie Sewall, *The Theory of Value Before Adam Smith* (N.Y., Macmillan, 1901) p. 19, and B. W. Dempsey, 'Just Price in a Functional Economy', *American Economic Review* (Sep 1935) pp. 471–86.
[46] St Thomas Aquinas, *Quodlibetales*, Quodlibet VI, 10.

distribution. He does not confront the issue of the relationship of commutation and distribution which, as Professor Worland points out, is still a pressing issue in modern welfare economics.[47] It would appear that Aquinas believed that social status should not be taken into account in establishing commutative justice. However, for the sake of distributive justice, social status should be taken into account. The person, who, objectively, contributes more to society should receive more from it.[48] These two strands of thought remain unreconciled.

Value, property, income, and work

An examination of Aquinas on the just price lends little support to a claim like that of the historian R. H. Tawney that 'The true descendant of the doctrines of Aquinas is the labour theory of value. The last of the Schoolmen is Karl Marx.'[49] St Thomas does not ascribe the creation of value to the expenditure of labour. Rather, it is human need which is the operative factor. The just price, which is a return necessary to ensure the maintenance of production, should cover the labour costs involved in that production. But it should also compensate sellers for distribution charges such as transportation and storage fees, and for the assumption of risk of loss in their business undertakings.[50]

One aspect of Aquinas' thought which lends much more weight than does his discussion of price to Tawney's contention, is his treatment of property rights. Support from this quarter is not readily perceived by modern commentators, since St Thomas is a firm advocate of the institution of private ownership on grounds which seem unrelated to expenditure of labour. However, his views on the bases of the right to acquire property introduce the labour element.

[47] S. T. Worland, loc. cit. On the increasing dissociation of commutative from distributive justice in the evolution of St Thomas' thought, see E. Bartell, op. cit., pp. 354–5.
[48] On this point, see J. J. Spengler, 'Hierarchy *v.* Equality: Persisting Conflict', *Kyklos*, Vol. XXI (1968) pp. 217–38. See also Sister M. Jane Frances Ferguson, *The Philosophy of Equality* (Washington, 1943).
[49] R. H. Tawney, *Religion and the Rise of Capitalism*, rev. ed. (N.Y., 1937, reprinted 1952) p. 36.
[50] *Summa theologica*, II–II, qu. 77, art. 4.

The institution of private property is not something which can be established as a basic principle of natural law, according to Aquinas. Rather, because man is a fallen creature, a social system where private ownership prevails can be shown to be a necessary feature of temporal existence.[51] If men were perfect, such a system would be unnecessary, but given imperfection, it makes for the maintenance of the best form of social life attainable by most men. Private property ownership gives the best guarantee of a peaceable and orderly society. Above all, it leads to the achievement of maximum economic efficiency, since the incentive for human industry will be much greater than in any variant of a communal system.[52]

Here, the argument of Democritus and Aristotle concerning the division of resources is employed by Aquinas as a major plank in his stand on the best form of social structure. Through the agency of St Thomas, their advocacy of the economic superiority of private resource ownership becomes a fundamental tenet of scholastic social thought. Further, the scholastics, like Aristotle, temper this position on ownership with the principle of communal use. Making a sharp distinction between ownership of resources and use of the products they yield, St Thomas and his successors propose the widest possible distribution of the fruits of industry throughout the community.

On the use of goods, Aquinas affirms that 'In this respect man ought to possess external things not as his own but as common, so that he is ready to communicate them to others in their need.'[53] Again, Aristotle's observation in the *Politics* (II, 5) that 'it is best to have property private but to make the use of it common,' recurs in St Thomas' writings in a much more emphatic form. 'The temporal goods which God grants us are ours as to the ownership,' Aquinas claims, 'but as to the use of them, they belong not to us alone but also to

[51] Op. cit., I a, qu. 98, art. 1, ad. 3.
[52] Op. cit., II–II, qu. 66, art. 2. St Thomas writes that 'every man is more careful to procure what is for himself alone than that which is common to many or to all: since each one would shirk the labour and leave to another that which concerns the community, as happens where there are a great number of servants.'
[53] Loc. cit.
[54] Op. cit., II–II, qu. 32, art. 5, ad. 2.

such others as we are able to succour out of what we have over and above our needs.'[54]

Private ownership of resources coupled with communal use of surplus produce is Aquinas' programme for the maximisation of total social product and the optimisation of its distribution from the viewpoint of economic welfare. The advocacy of private ownership is based mainly on grounds of superior economic efficiency. The policy of communal use is given by moral imperative. 'Feed him that is perishing of hunger,' he writes, 'if you fail to do so you are guilty of his death.'[55] The possibility that communal use of surplus now might reduce the future growth of social product does not seem to be envisaged. Capital accumulation is given no positive role to play in the programme. While St Thomas cannot be said to be positively opposed to economic growth as was Aristotle, he is as far from adherence to any capitalistic ethos as he is from expounding a doctrine of all-embracing communism.

It is evident then, that in his discussions of private property as an institution and of its use, Aquinas is reasoning in terms of categories which are quite different from those of Marx. In particular, no light is shed one way or the other on the relationship of his thought to the fundamental Marxian doctrine of labour as the source of all value. However, moving from the question of property as an institution to the issue of the acquisition of property, the beginnings of a line of affiliation with Marx become evident. According to St Thomas, the right of acquisition of property is grounded on two fundamental titles, occupancy and labour. He writes:

The natural right or just is that which by its very nature is adjusted to or commensurate with another person. Now this may happen in two ways: first, according as it is considered absolutely ... Secondly, a thing is naturally

[55] Loc. cit. There is strong evidence to suggest that moral imperative was reflected by European practice in the age of St Thomas, at least in certain regions. According to Professor Tierney, the poor were cared for during the thirteenth century to an extent that was not to be repeated until the twentieth. See B. Tierney, *Medieval Poor Law: a Sketch of Canonical Theory and its Application in England* (Berkeley, California, 1959) p. 109.

commensurate with another person, not according as it is considered absolutely but according to something resultant from it, for instance, the possession of property. For if a particular piece of land be considered absolutely, it contains no reason why it should belong to one man more than another, but if it be considered in respect to the opportunity one may have to cultivate it and the unmolested use of the land, it has a certain commensuration to be the property of one and not of another man, . . .[56]

The expenditure of labour in cultivating an area of land, or occupation of it, can give rise to a just claim of ownership. Standing behind St Thomas' position is the Roman law tradition concerning the natural modes of acquisition of property. According to the lawyer Gaius, for example, the natural ways of acquiring titles to property include tradition, occupation, accession, and specification, i.e. the conversion of materials into a new product.[57] The latter implies expenditure of labour.

Aquinas' point is made even more forcefully by an early disciple of his, John of Paris (Jean Quidort) (c. 1250–1306), who was a member of the community of St Jacques in Paris to which St Thomas had also belonged, and who defended Thomistic thought against a variety of critical attacks launched by Franciscan theologians. About 1302, during a controversy between Pope Boniface VIII and Philip the Fair of France, he wrote a treatise, *On Royal and Papal Power*, in support of Philip's position. This was to become a classic work in the continuing debate on Church–State relationships, and in the course of his argument Quidort gave considerable prominence to labour as the source of property rights. He wrote:

. . . lay property is not granted to the community as a whole as is ecclesiastical property, but is acquired by individual people through their own skill, labour and diligence, and individuals, as individuals, have right and power over it and valid lordship; each person may order his

[56] St Thomas, op. cit., II–II, qu. 57, art. 3.
[57] On the Roman tradition, see Richard B. Schlatter, *Private Property, the History of an Idea* (London, Allen and Unwin, 1951) Ch. 2.

own and dispose, administer, hold or alienate it as he
wishes, so long as he causes no injury to anyone else; since
he is lord.[58]

Quidort goes on to state that because of the risk of injury
to individuals or society as a whole in some circumstances,
men have entered into a type of social contract to restrict
their property rights. To cater for conditions in which
property may be misused, '. . . a ruler has been established by
the people to take charge of such situations, a judge between
the just and the unjust, a punisher of injustices, a measurer of
the just proportion owed by each to the common need and
welfare.'[59] The prince can intervene to control the use of
property 'in time of necessity', when the common good
demands it. Otherwise, the 'lordship' of the individual, which
is based on prior expenditure of labour, remains inviolate.

The establishment of a link between labour and property
by John of Paris, and by Aquinas some thirty years before,
ensured that the Roman tradition on acquisition, to which
they were indebted, remained an important element in later
Scholastic thought. Ultimately, this element was taken up in
1690 by the philosopher John Locke whose thought in a
number of respects demonstrates dependence on scholastic
ideas. In Locke's hands the scholastic position concerning
acquisition was given a new, radical dimension. Using
'property' in a very broad sense, he argued that its ownership
based on labour was a right of man in the 'state of nature',
and was prior to any rights of community and government.
Further, he took the crucial step of claiming that labour not
only accounted for property rights, but was the factor,
above all else, which gave property its economic value.

St Thomas and the later scholastics did not make the
transition from a theory of rights to a theory of economic
value as did Locke. However, they form important links in

[58] John of Paris, *On Royal and Papal Power*, trans. J. A. Watt (Toronto, Pontifical
Institute of Medieval Studies, 1971) p. 103.
[59] Op. cit., pp. 103–4. Cf. St Thomas, *Summa theologica*, II–II, qu. 66, art. 8,
ad. 3: 'It is no robbery if princes exact from their subjects that which is due to
them for the safe-guarding of the common good, even if they use violence in so
doing; but if they extort something unduly by means of violence, it is robbery
even as burglary is.'

the intellectual chain with which Locke's reasoning is associated. In the eighteenth century, Adam Smith was to employ Locke's labour theory as a central pillar of classical political economy. Then, by progression through the early part of the nineteenth century, it took on enhanced significance as the metaphysical foundation of the economics of Karl Marx. It is their theory of property acquisition, not their theory of the just price, which provides a basis for an assertion that the scholastics are forerunners of Marx. In this respect, a claim like that of R. H. Tawney's can be vindicated.

It is also important to appreciate that expenditure of labour was not only a title to the acquisition of property for the scholastics, but was also the major ground on which receipt of income could be justified. As J. W. Baldwin observes, 'additions of "labor et expensae" seemed to be at the basis of any permissible economic gain or increment in the discussions of both the canonists and the theologians. The economic factor to which the theologians paid the closest attention was that of labor.'[60] St Thomas, for example, treats fair compensation of labour services as one of the positive acts of justice.[61] Further, he regards gain in mercantile undertakings as a type of payment for labour – *quasi stipendum laboris.*[62] Thus the right to acquire income, as well as the right to acquire capital, i.e. property, can be derived from the same source.

This is not to suggest that expenditure of physical labour is seen as the sole source of income and capital creation by the scholastics. The mystique of materialism in which Karl Marx made his act of faith is diametrically opposed to the rational metaphysics of the schoolmen. Thus in Aquinas' discussion of business partnership the acceptance of the function of risk-bearing in commercial enterprise is seen as a legitimate source of income.[63] Again, scholastic writers distinguished between *labor* and *industria*, the latter referring to the

---

[60] J. W. Baldwin, op. cit., p. 66. See also Gabriel Le Bras, 'Conceptions of Economy and Society', in M. M. Postan and others (eds), *The Cambridge Economic History of Europe*, Vol. III (1963) p. 560.

[61] *Summa theologica*, I–II, qu. 114, art. 1

[62] Op. cit., II–II, qu. 77, art. 4.

[63] Op. cit. II–II, qu. 78:2, obj. 5.

exercise of entrepreneurship, a function whose exercise warranted remuneration.[64] St Thomas cites this function as a basis for profit-taking when he writes: 'Any advantage or gain which comes to the borrower from the money I lend him, beyond the actual amount of the loan, comes from the borrower's own industry in employing the money wisely.'[65]

Risk-taking and entrepreneurship as well as labour are income-generating factors which have a foundation in the economic realities of production and distribution as Aquinas understands them. However, the most widely recognised title was that of labour, and this emphasis may have contributed in some measure to the eventual emergence of a labour theory of value in European thought.

This emergence may also have been lent some impetus by the new status which labour, in the sense of toil or physical exertion, attained in the scholastic theology of work. With the Greek philosophers, particularly Aristotle, there was disdain for many forms of physical effort, especially manual labour for economic gain. The latter was seen by Aristotle as best suited to those who by their very nature were cut out for servitude and slavery. However, for the schoolmen, as for their monastic predecessors and contemporaries, work, including physical work, was not degrading.[66] St Thomas, for example, in *Quodlibeta* (VIII, 7, 17), argues that manual labour is useful as a counter to laziness and as a means of disciplining the body. It is also a dictate of both positive and natural law. Further, it is seen as a participation in a Divine plan of creative action. Concerning Aquinas' view of the matter, Professor Stark has commented: 'As the Saint sees things, the material creation — the world and all it contains — is so much raw material for human labour. Man is called

---

[64] Cf., Bernard W. Dempsey, *Interest and Usury* (Washington, American Council on Public Affairs, 1943) p. 183.

[65] *III. Sent.*, d. XXXVII, art. VI ad. 4.

[66] The impact of monasticism on European economic thought and practice has often been underestimated. Yet, as Bertrand de Jouvenel remarks: 'It is perhaps a fact worthy of notice that the modern use of profit, expansion from retained earnings, arose and was systematised in the monasteries . . . the saintly men . . . are the true original of the non-consuming, ascetic type of capitalist. And Berdyaev has truly observed that Christian asceticism played a capital part in the development of capitalism; it is a condition of reinvestment.' From J. Gilchrist, *The Church and Economic Activity in the Middle Ages* (London, Macmillan, 1969) p. 40.

to break it into shape, and in doing so he is merely proving himself a true image of his Maker, for God, too, is essentially one who moulds material reality and makes it serve his purposes.'[67] With the scholastics, man as the moulder of the physical universe has replaced man as a being who merely adjusts to or harmonises natural forces as in Socratic thought.

When the idea that the expenditure of labour can be a salutary participation in a God-given enterprise is combined with the idea that the same expenditure supports the acquisition of property, then a most fertile ground is prepared for adoption of a labour theory of value. The medieval schoolmen did not reap the potential harvest, but the existence of that potential is illustrated in the writings of some of their nineteenth- and twentieth-century successors. For example, a contemporary professor of ethics argues:

> Appropriation or ownership by itself alone is insufficient; property will not sustain and perfect a man unless something else is added to ownership. For instance, one of our primitive ancestors might have gone to the edge of the forest and appropriated himself a tree . . . He has acquired a piece of property, but it will not serve him in any way, will not do him any good until he does something with it, until he uses it — until [he] cuts it down and saws it up and makes a house or fire of it. Property will not serve man until it is used or worked on. It is there to serve man, but it will not serve him until he does something with it — until he adds on his work to his ownership.'[68]

Only a small step is required to take one from this line of reasoning to the labour value doctrines of Adam Smith. The link with Marxian doctrine, although present, is somewhat more remote. Marx's metaphysic of materialism, and his neglect of the beneficial effect on the development of human personality which is thought to flow from possession of private property, represent significant differences between the Marxian and scholastic traditions.

[67] W. Stark, *The Contained Economy: an interpretation of medieval economic thought* (London, Blackfriars, 1956) p. 8.
[68] Matthew O'Donnell, *Property in Catholic Social Teaching* (Oxford, Catholic Social Guild, 1963) p. 9.

7 Scholastic Monetary Thought: 1300–1600

Aquinas and his near contemporaries had written against a background of unprecedented economic development in Europe. By the thirteenth century, a reorganisation of older feudal economic relationships in terms of new capitalistic principles had spread from its birthplaces, the towns of Northern Italy, to many other regions of the Continent. France, Germany, Flanders, and even England, felt the impact of the new modes of organisation. Populations had expanded steadily from about the year 1000, and a fresh growth of urban centres accompanied the expansion. In Germany alone, during the thirteenth century some 400 new towns were established. Such centres provided fertile grounds for industrial and financial innovation and, as a modern historian observes, 'With the growth of urban industry and trade there emerged the whole complex of a capitalist system, such as partnerships, joint liability, banking, double-entry bookkeeping, bills of exchange and letters of credit.'[1]

The process of expansion was halted and then reversed, during the first half of the fourteenth century. A variety of factors contributed to this reversal. Prominent among them was the sudden decline of population induced by the spread of the Black Death from 1348. Innovation based on technological advance also lost much of the impetus gained during the preceding 200 years.[2] In addition, the entire financial structure of Europe was struck a crippling blow after 1345 by the bankrupting of three of the most powerful

[1] J. Gilchrist, *The Church and Economic Activity in the Middle Ages* (London, Macmillan, 1969) p. 26.
[2] A. C. Crombie, *Augustine to Galileo: (II) Science in the Early Middle Ages and Early Modern Times*, 2nd ed (London, Heinemann, 1961) pp. 109–10.

banking organisations of Florence, which was then at the hub of the international monetary network.[3]

In the era of economic decline, scholastic monetary analysis also languished. The one major new direction in that analysis to emerge during the fourteenth century arose out of the serious problems of public financing experienced in France. As Colin Clark states: 'We now know that the Black Death of 1348, dramatic and terrible though it was, was only the first of a series of devastating epidemics, which checked or even reversed population growth. In France, in particular, these troubles were augmented by civil war and foreign invasion to a fearful degree, . . .'[4] By as early as the mid-fourteenth century, currency arrangements in France had been reduced to a chaotic state through successive money debasements undertaken in the interest of augmenting the public purse: 'Weighed down financially by the Hundred Years War, the kings of France prior to Charles V's assumption of the Regency in 1360 tried to raise money through their right of coinage by constant modification of the coinage. This finally threatened to destroy the monetary system.'[5] The grave situation in the kingdom called forth a response from some of the leading scholastics of the day. Through that response, certain of the leading ideas of St Thomas on money were brought into question.

The challenge of currency debasement
The two most significant contributions on money came from Jean Buridan de Bethune (1300–58) and Nicholas Oresme (1325–82). Together they helped establish a line of thought which was continued in the scholastic tradition, most notably by Gabriel Biel (1430–95).[6] Buridan, who published com-

[3] R. De Roover, 'New Interpretations of the History of Banking', *Journal of World History*, II (1954) p. 44.
[4] C. Clark, 'Medieval Economics, Some Assumptions Re-examined', *The Tablet* (14 May 1960) p. 468.
[5] H. Estrup, 'Oresme and Monetary Theory', *The Scandinavian Economic History Review*, XIV, 2 (1966) p. 97.
[6] A much earlier French writer who might be held to be an important precursor of their thought is Peter Cantor (d. 1197), professor of theology and Chanter of Notre Dame. His *Summa de sacramentis et anime consiliis* includes discussion of currency regulation by rulers, the desirability of maintaining stable money values,

mentaries on Aristotle's *Ethics* and *Politics,* was rector of the University of Paris. His pupil Oresme, who also commented on the Philosopher's works, went on to become a noted mathematician and physicist, and capped a successful clerical career with an appointment as Bishop of Lisieux. Their follower in monetary theory, Biel, exercised a powerful intellectual influence in the next century, as professor of philosophy at the University of Tübingen.

These three men were leading figures in a new intellectual movement within scholasticism the *via moderna* of nominalism, stemming from the thought of the Oxford philosopher William of Ockham (1285–1347.)[7] This movement, which emerged again at Oxford University in the mid-twentieth century, denied the reality of abstract and universal concepts. In opposition to philosophies such as those of Plato or of Aquinas, they argued that general ideas are merely verbal labels which designate a collection of things or a certain number of events. Their verbalism and particularism led them to turn away from speculative theological studies in the manner of St Thomas. Instead, they stressed the importance of empirical investigation, while encouraging a renewed interest in the physical sciences. This stress on empiricism was to assist in the eventual growth of casuistic methods in scholastic reasoning, a growth which was responsible for much of the future progress in the economic analysis of the schoolmen. In the fourteenth century, however, the specific fruit for economics of the new empiricism was a fresh approach to the questions of the nature and functions of money stemming from reflection on contemporary French experience.

The best known among the writings of these three nominalists on the subject of money is Oresme's *Tractatus de*

---

and the difficulties engendered by currency manipulation. See John W. Baldwin, *Masters, Princes and Merchants,* Vol. I (Princeton, Princeton University Press, 1970) pp. 241–4.

[7] Another nominalist of some note who followed Buridan's views on money was Henry of Hesse (Heinrich von Langenstein, 1325–97), a German theologian who taught at both Paris and Vienna. See A. E. Monroe, *Monetary Theory Before Adam Smith* (Cambridge, Harvard University Press, 1923) p. 26.

origine natura jure, et mutationibus monetarum.[8] Written about 1360, this treatise served to influence the monetary reforms undertaken by Charles V of France. Much of the original ground for Oresme's arguments, however, can be ascribed to his teacher's *Quaestiones Super VIII Libros Politicorum Aristotelis* and *Quaestiones in Decem Libros Ethicorum Aristotelis Nicomachum.* Buridan takes up and emphasises the metallist aspect of Aristotle's treatment of money, which, as was suggested in Chapter 3, entered the Philosopher's reasoning only in the context of international transactions. Generalising from Aristotle, Buridan claims that all money should be made of precious material. This generalisation is embraced wholeheartedly as a fundamental principle by Gabriel Biel, who brings together the essentials of Buridan's and Oresme's views in his *Tractatus de Potentate et Utilate Monetarum* in the following century.

In these writings, the tradition which supported St Thomas' treatment of money as a standard of value established by the prince is called into question. The prince's right with respect to setting the standard is seen as severely limited, and the non-metallism associated with the feudal conception is challenged.

It is contended that if a particular currency is to act effectively as a medium of exchange then the nominated values of the units of that currency must be acceptable to the citizens who are the users of the medium. Legal determination must reflect a general consensus concerning currency values if money is to act, as it is intended to act, for the good of the community as a whole. Further, the users of the money are the owners of the money and thus have the right to be consulted by the prince. Biel sums up the argument as follows:

[8] An English translation is *The De Moneta and English Mint Documents* trans. Charles Johnson (Camden, N. J., Nelson, 1956). In the nineteenth and early part of the twentieth centuries, there seems to have been a prevalent view amongst historians that Oresme's ideas represented *the* scholastic statement on monetary theory. These historians might have been more accurate to describe it as *the* nominalist statement. At the same time, the ideas of another nominalist, Henry of Hesse, were often identified as *the* scholastic statement on the subject of just price.

... since money, as we have already assumed, was invented and introduced for the good of the community, it is fitting that money should be coined by the ruler of the community. But such is the prince or one having authority from him.

Although it is the privilege of the prince to coin money and to stamp it with his own image and name, yet for this reason money in circulation among the people is not his, nor is he himself the owner of the money current in his dominion. For money is the medium of exchange for natural riches and the equivalent of them. Therefore money belongs to those that have natural riches. For when a man gives his bread or the labor of his own body for money the money is his own after he has received it, just as the bread and labor were his and at his disposal.

Moreover Nicolas Orem [i.e. Oresme] says that although coining money is the prerogative of the prince, yet authority to fix the value of money or the ratio of one denomination of money to another should not be vested in the prince but in the community to which the money belongs ... This I take to mean that the prince has not the power to fix the value of money according to his own wish but according to the just and natural ratio of gold to silver and of silver to such a 'liga.' Determination in this regard is vested in the community.[9]

Among the interesting features of this argument is its use of the Thomistic principle concerning the dominant end of money to undermine the traditional approach to money as a measure of value. Again, there is the novel rejection of the prince as the owner of the currency.[10] Thirdly, the ownership title of the users of the money seems to reside not so

[9] Gabriel Biel, *Treatise on the Power and Utility of Moneys*, trans. R. B. Burke (Philadelphia, 1930) pp. 31—2. An anticipation of the principle that the prince should consult the community is present in the *Apparatus super libros decretalium* of the canonist Sinabaldus Fliscus who reigned as Pope Innocent IV, 1243—54. However, in this instance the principle was applied in the context of a discussion of the prince's right of seigniorage.

[10] 'The idea that the right of coinage was fundamentally different from other dominial rights and privileges — hunting rights for example — was entirely novel.' H. Estrup, op. cit., p. 116.

much in the fact of their use but in their expenditure of labour or the fruits of labour to obtain it for use. Finally, there is a shifting of the grounds for monetary investigation from the morality of individual exchange contracts to the operation of the system as a whole.[11]

To reinforce their position, the writers on debasement came out against the longstanding tradition of non-metallism. With Buridan especially, as with Biel, there is the insistence that money to function effectively as money must be composed of a material that has a value independent of its role as money. It is of the essence of the medium of exchange to be so constituted. The precious metals are suited naturally for use in this regard because of their portability, divisibility, durability and so on. Buridan catalogues these qualities in his commentary on the *Ethics* of Aristotle (Bk V, Q. 17).

If the precious metals are essential to the idea of money, then money cannot be treated, as it was treated by St Thomas, as a special category of fungible, the just price of which is exempt from determination by the consensus of the market. There is a commodity aspect of the currency which cannot be denied, and Buridan writes: 'The value of money must be measured by human need, for although we do not need gold or silver for our necessities, still the rich need them for their luxurious purposes. And therefore we see that gold and silver in the mass are of the same value, or about the same, as in money.'[12]

'Human need', the traditional basis of ordinary market evaluation, has been introduced by Buridan to rule out a strictly legalistic approach to the price of money and to limit the discretion of the prince. Biel, for example, can envisage a situation in which a recoinage by a prince directly contravenes the basic morality required in market exchanges:

> . . . if a prince should reject valid money, in order that he may buy it up more cheaply and melt it, and then issue

---

[11] Professor Estrup contends, loc cit., that 'The importance of Oresme in monetary theory does not lie in his economic arguments, which are in fact few, but in the weight he attaches to the monetary system and its management as a matter of concern to society as a whole.'

[12] J. Buridan, *Quaestiones in Decem Libros Ethicorum Aristotelis ad Nichomachum*, Lib. V, Q. 17.

another coinage of less value, attaching the value of the former currency to it, he would be guilty of stealing money and is required to make restitution. This is the opinion of Hostiensis and Panormitanus. It is quite obvious, because he sells a cheaper article at a higher price, which is contrary to justice[13]

Here, money is given no special status with respect to price determination but, because it is a commodity, is subject to the general rules governing exchange justice.

Although these writings struck at some of the basic assumptions of St Thomas on money, they do not seem to have had the effect of stimulating a general reassessment of his doctrines within the scholastic tradition.[14] Among the reasons for this failure may be the fact that they allowed that the prince should continue to control the minting process, and that there could be circumstances in which the general welfare of the community was served by the prince's altering the metal content of the coinage. Again, although they were adamant that the value of the currency was not established by the will of the prince acting alone, they were not clear on what they meant by 'the value of money'. Arthur Monroe remarks that in these writings one encounters '. . . stipulations that money should be "proba" or "justa"; but these were vague, and still subordinate to the will of the prince, who was bound by them in conscience alone. Later writers grew more insistent; but progress in setting up standards of "probitas" was slow, and the "valor impositus" was still held to be final.'[15]

The medieval distinction between money as a unit of account and as coin in circulation may also have permitted the schoolmen to hold that money can be treated as a measuring rod of legally fixed value while it is also subject to changing evaluation in terms of human need as is any other commodity. Many coins of different metal content and

---

[13] Gabriel Biel, op. cit., p. 32. Panormitanus, Nicholas de 'Tudeschi (d. 1453?) was archbishop of Palermo and author of a commentary on canon law.

[14] The doctrine of metallism may have been generally accepted, but there was no extensive exploration of its implications. In addition, Aristotle's pseudo-historical account of the origin of money was popularised.

[15] A. E. Monroe, op. cit., p. 27.

source of issue could vary in value over time in any one country, but that portion of the circulation which was directly based on, or constituted, the fundamental accounting system in the country concerned could be altered in value only by legal enactment. Further, in some circumstances, there could be two types of money of account. In the Netherlands, for example, according to Professor Van Der Wee:

> ... there were two catogories of money of account. In *B* category the value of the money of account was in principle dependent on a current real silver coin, which was accepted as basis, as 'link' money of that money of account. This means that the value of the money of account was in fact not stable but fluctuated with changes in the silver content of the link money, or more precisely with the silver content which was attributed to the link money and with the trust or distrust which it inspired ... As well as monies of account of the *B* type, there were in the Netherlands also monies of account of the *A* type. They had mostly originally been real gold or large silver coins, but had gradually disappeared from daily circulation, although maintaining themselves as imaginary money of account and their original content of precious metals intact.[16]

The continuation of a dualistic treatment of money by the medieval scholastics is made even more explicable by the fact that interaction between currencies of different countries was an intermittent and even occult process carried on in a multitude of isolated trading transactions or at intervals determined by the occurrence of fairs. However, the dualism became increasingly difficult to sustain in the fifteenth and sixteenth centuries as fairs gave way to the establishment of permanent international money markets and bills of exchange came to be employed freely. On the impact created by the use of bills, it has been observed in the *Cambridge Economic History of Europe,* (V, p. 387), that 'The funda-

---

[16] Herman Van Der Wee, *The Growth of the Antwerp Market and the European Economy* (Nijhoff, The Hague, 1963) Part I, pp. 107–8.

mental character of this activity was the repeated alignment of moneys of account, representing—then as now—the confrontation through foreign exchanges of different economic and monetary conditions.' In earlier centuries, such confrontation was less frequent, and far less obvious.

The acceptance of *Lucrum Cessans*

During the fifteenth century, large areas of Europe continued in the grip of economic stagnation and failed to return to the levels of activity attained in the twelfth and thirteen centuries. In Italy, however, a number of cities retained considerable significance as commercial and financial centres, and these found counterparts, late in the century, in certain towns in northern Europe. As the historian C. H. Wilson states: 'The two areas which in 1500 represented the richest and most advanced concentrations of trade, industry and wealth were the quadrilateral formed by the Italian cities Milan, Venice, Florence and Genoa; and the strip of the Netherlands that ran from Ypres north-east past Ghent and Bruges up to Antwerp . . .'[17]

It is mainly in the context of the financial practices of the Italian cities that scholastic writers of the times began to work towards new analytical insights relating to money. In particular, they arrived at the concept of money as capital, and found a basis in economic reality for the payment of interest on some loans during the loan period itself. This basis was the title *lucrum cessans*—a gain which ceases or does not result, which title was usually investigated in association with *damnum emergens*—a loss arising because of a loan. The idea involved was that a lender, in some circumstances, had the right to claim the same return on his loan as that which he might have obtained in alternative employments of the money. As Professor de Roover has stated, this 'is the same thing as the modern concept of opportunity cost.'[18] In the case of these titles it was either the failure to gain, or

---

[17] C. H. Wilson, 'Trade, Society and the State', in E. F. Rich and C. H. Wilson eds, *The Cambridge Economic History of Europe*, IV (1967) p. 492.
[18] R. de Roover, *San Bernardino of Siena and Sant' Antonino of Florence* (Boston, Baker Library, 1967) p. 31.

experience of loss, by the lender of money which was the relevant consideration.

Associated with the greater degree of penetration into the phenomenon of interest payment was a more intensive exploration of the significance that could be attached to money in balance. An attempt was made to distinguish between motives for holding money and to categorise the various types of balances which might be held.

Behind these developments in analysis stood the view that involuntary loss of profit by a lender, due to delay in repayment of his loan, or by the victim of theft, constituted a ground for receipt of restitution in addition to the sum borrowed or stolen. As was seen in Chapter 5, St Thomas had argued this case in the thirteenth century. He was supported by a minority of scholastic writers over the next 100 years, and one of these, Peter of Ancharano (1333–1416) employed the phrase *lucrum cessans* to indicate a title to compensation for delay in repayment. This phrase became standard, and was incorporated by Panormitanus in his influential commentary on canon law.[19]

Although there was this perception by some earlier writers, of a cost which may be involved in lending, it did not necessarily involve recognition that payment in the form of interest was due from the outset of a loan. Nor did it involve allowance of anything more than costs which were incurred involuntarily. Further, not all lenders were necessarily in a position to be subject to opportunity costs.

The case that interest can be due from the beginning of a loan is first argued effectively in 1403 by Lorenzo di Antonio Ridolfi (1360–1442), a lay canon lawyer, lecturer at the Athenaeum of Florence and, at one time, ambassador of the Florentine Republic. During the fourteenth century, Florence, like Venice and Genoa, had begun raising public funds by means of forced loans, entitling the lenders to the ownership of public shares and to interest payment on those shares. This payment was attacked as usury by Augustinian

---

[19] A definitive treatment of the emergence of the title *lucrum cessans* may be found in J. T. Noonan, op. cit., Ch. 5. But, see also J. W. Baldwin, op. cit., pp. 282–6.

and Dominican theologians, but was defended by the Franciscans. Lorenzo contends that the Florentine merchants, who are the principal subscribers to these loans, clearly incur *lucrum cessans,* and given the low rate of interest paid, as compared with prevailing rates of profit, their certain losses warrant payment from the beginning of the loan. In such public lending then, interest was not due merely because of delay.[20]

Further important steps in the analysis of *lucrum cessans* were undertaken by the Franciscan missionary St Bernardine of Siena (1380—1444), and by St Antonine of Florence (1389—1459). Among other offices, Antonine held that of Apostolic Commissary for the repression of usury in Tuscany. He was an administrator and a judge, obliged to make decisions on a great variety of commercial practices. This activity is reflected in his writings on economic morals, writings which embody a method of reasoning that was to be paramount in stimulating the analytical achievements of the scholastic economists of the next century. This method was casuistry, the solution of problems of right and wrong in human conduct by the systematic application of ethical or moral principles to concrete cases. St Antonine's *Summa Moralis Theologiae* (1449) is the first outstanding casuistic treatise, and foreshadows the era of the method's predominance, from the Council of Trent (1545—1563) to its decay in the seventeenth century. It was in this era, spurred on by the empirical enquiry which casuistry demanded, that scholastic economics reached full flower.

In their analyses of *lucrum cessans,* both St Antonine and St Bernardine evidence an enhanced awareness of the role of money when compared with the perceptions of earlier schoolmen. St Thomas had recognised that, on occasions, money in the hands of businessmen may have some special significance; now, that significance is more closely defined. When a businessman lends from balances held for commercial purposes, according to St Bernardine, he 'gives not money in its simple character, but he also gives his capital.'[21] Else-

---

[20] J. T. Noonan, op. cit.
[21] St Bernardine, *De Evangelio Aeterno*, Sermo 42:2:2.

where, he writes:

> ... what, in the firm purpose of its owner, is ordained
> to some probable profit, has not only the character of
> mere money or a mere thing, but also beyond this, a
> certain seminal character of something profitable, which
> we commonly call capital. Therefore, not only must its
> simple value be returned, but a super-added value as
> well.[22]

For St Bernardine then, transactions balances are capital.
Their depletion involves a cost in profit forgone, a cost which
is incurred from the outset of a loan. According to St
Antonine, certain forms of speculative balance are also
subject to cost, even where such funds are not held by a
businessman. He states: 'I believe that anyone can claim
compensation, not merely for the harm done him, but also
the gain he might otherwise have obtained, if he be a
merchant accustomed to engage his money in business. The
same holds good even if he be not a merchant but have only
the intention of investing the funds in lawful trade; but not if
he be a man who hoards his wealth in coffers.'[23] Underlying
his view, like that of St Bernardine's, is the belief that
money, in some circumstances, takes on 'the character of
capital'.

It would appear from the above, that the speculative
balances concerned are those held for direct investment, and
do not include those held for the express purpose of lending.
Again, precautionary balances are singled out and excluded
from *lucrum cessans*. By implication, transactions balances
held for personal consumption are excluded also.

Commenting on this monetary analysis, and in particular,
the emergence of the idea of money capital, Werner Stark
states that, 'Such sentiments herald the end of the middle
ages'. Certainly, they seem to indicate the development of a
new frame of reference for economic analysis, although, as
we have seen, the ideas themselves have some affiliation with

---

[22] Op. cit., Sermo 34:2. It is striking that St Bernardine's references to 'capital'
are accompanied by a greater appreciation of the role of entrepreneurship
(*industria*) than is evident in previous scholastic writing.
[23] St Antonine, *Summa*, 2:1:7.

those of Aquinas on the subject of restitution in the case of delay in repayment or of theft. Herbert Johnson has also noted that on capital St Bernardine is adapting an even older line of thought than that stemming from St Thomas. Bernardine's analysis, he suggests, is an application of the Augustinian doctrine of *rationes seminales* to money. On the greater scope given to the operation of *lucrum cessans,* Johnston writes, 'St Thomas, in the thirteenth century, did not consider business investments safe enough for the lender to consider himself sufficiently sure of a profit to stipulate in his agreement for interest on that title. St Bernardine, in the fifteenth, did consider business investments (at least as he knew them in northern Italy) safe enough for that condition to be made.'[24] Regularisation and institutionalisation of commercial and financial practice seem to have been instrumental here in changing scholastic attitudes on interest-taking, just as later, in the sixteenth century, they were to contribute to a new appreciation of banking and currency exchange.

In line with tradition, both St Bernardine and St Antonine hold to the view that there is a real basis for interest payment only where the sacrifice of money in balance has not been a strictly voluntary undertaking. Loans given under the pressure of the dictates of charitable obligation or enforced by the state provide such a basis. Further, interest is due in these cases because of loss of profit. It is not due to sacrifice by the lenders of the subjective satisfaction which may be conferred by a certain level of personal liquidity. There is no recognition that stocks yield a form of benefit, as stocks, to their holders. 'Industry', i.e., entrepreneurship, not liquidity, is the reality which supports legitimate interest-taking. St Bernardine writes (*Sermo* 41:1:3):

> . . . it is to be said that money was truly worth more to its owner than itself because of the industry with which he would have used it . . . And therefore that money has value

[24] On these issues see, H. L. Johnston, 'Some Medieval Doctrines on Extrinsic Titles to Interest', in C. J. O'Neil (ed.) *An Etienne Gilson Tribute* (Marquette University Press, 1959) pp. 96—8, and W. Stark, *The Contained Economy* (London, Blackfriars, 1956) p. 17.

not from itself, but from the owner's industry, and therefore the receiver of the money not only deprives the owner of his money, but also of all the use and fruit of exercising his industry in it and through it.

Recognition of the role of liquidity, together with the view that the sacrifice of money out of any type of balance affords a real basis for interest payment, is implied by Professor Noonan's interpretation of the analysis of Conrad Summenhart of Tübingen (1465–1511). Writing in 1499, Summenhart contends that interest is derived directly from the lender's lack of use of money.[25] Commenting on this view, Noonan observes: 'He (Conrad) is arguing that . . . the voluntary sacrifice of any good has, in itself, a pecuniary estimation, regardless of what use would have been made of it. The lack of a consumptible for a period has a value distinct from the value of the substance of the consumptible.'[26] If lack of use of a stock itself has a price, then the stock itself must have been providing a service to its possessor. This line of reasoning is not pursued in subsequent scholastic treatises from some time. However, it reappears again, in a much more highly developed presentation, in the revolutionary monetary analysis of the Belgian Jesuit, Leonard Lessius, at the start of the seventeenth century.

Summenhart also contributes an important refinement of the Thomistic view that the use and ownership of money are indistinguishable. There was a seeming conflict between this view and certain longstanding medieval traditions concerning the ownership and use of goods in general. A distinction between 'right to own' and 'right to use' was basic in medieval welfare thought. Further, 'right to own' and 'right to use' were employed as distinct categories in interpreting the status of religious bound by vows of poverty with respect to property. Duns Scotus was one influential theologian who had cited this distinction in opposition to St Thomas' treatment of money loans. Summenhart resolves the conflict by his argument that, whereas ownership and right to use of

---

[25] *Tractatus de Contractibus*, Q. 23, ad. 6, 7. Summenhart had been a student under Biel.
[26] J. T. Noonan, op. cit., pp. 341–2.

commodities are separable, in a loan, where ownership is transferred, the value of that ownership is the same as the value of the use of the money concerned. It is the question of identity of value which is relevant to the analysis of loans.[27]

During the first half of the sixteenth century, *lucrum cessans* as a title to interest payment continued to excite controversy and division in the ranks of the schoolmen. At the time, scholastic thought was in the throes of rediscovering the speculative theology of the middle ages and attempting to reconcile it with insights stemming from the nominalism and empiricism of the fourteenth and fifteenth centuries. A leading figure in the Thomistic revival was an Italian Dominican, Thomas de Vio, Cardinal Cajetan (1468—1534), who was elected General of his Order in 1508. He was followed by the Spanish Dominicans who laid the foundations for the intellectual pre-eminence of the University of Salamanca, notably Francisco de Vitoria (1480—1546) and Domingo de Soto (1494—1560).

The treatment of *lucrum cessans* by Cajetan is particularly significant in that this most authoritative commentator gives explicit recognition to aspects of the role of money which were not emphasised by St Thomas. Cajetan points out that, in focusing their attention on money as a medium of exchange, St Thomas and the other medieval theologians, did not pay sufficient attention to the profit potential of money in the hands of businessmen.[28] Given this potential, voluntary loans can be subject to *lucrum cessans* in a manner not perceived by St Thomas. When a businessman lends out of funds intended for the conduct of his business he incurs the cost of loss of profit potential. However, if he had loaned a sum to another businessman, the latter would have increased his profit potential. The sum of money involved in the contract has not lost the value it had in the hands of the lender, and the transfer of this value warrants payment of interest. Because there has been a transfer of an objective

---

[27] On these issues, see B. Tierney, 'The Decretists and the "Deserving Poor"', *Comparative Studies in Society and History*, I (1958–9) pp. 360–73, J. Gilchrist, op. cit., pp. 209–15, and J. T. Noonan, op. cit., pp. 60–1.
[28] *Commentarium in summam theologicam S. Thomas Aquinatis*, II–II, Q. 78, art. 2, IV. Cajetan compares money to a seed or a tool of trade.

value, the subjective question of whether or not the loan was voluntary or involuntary is irrelevant. In this respect, Cajetan goes beyond not only St Thomas, but also St Bernardine and St Antonine. The subjective question remains relevant, however, in the case of loans for consumption purposes. Money obtained by the borrower for use in non-business exchanges does not retain any profit potential relevant to the particular loan contract concerned.[29] In this argument, the distinction between consumption and production loans, and the significance given the status of money in a loan represent important divergences from the tradition of exclusive concentration on the status of the lender of money. Also, the way might appear open for the adoption of a productivity theory of interest which is foreign to both earlier and later scholastic thought. This would be the case if the additional value of the sum of money borrowed, and hence the payment of interest, is derived from the profit earned through its use by the borrower. However, it is doubtful that this is Cajetan's meaning. He may be suggesting that the special value of a sum to a business borrower is derived from the elimination of a cost which he has been experiencing, viz., the cost of not borrowing. This cost is measured by the potential profit he forgoes in not borrowing and is the exact equivalent of the extent of *lucrum cessans* experienced by the lender in lending. The lender is now bearing a burden formerly shouldered by the borrower, and it is the transfer of cost which provided the basis for interest payment.

Another feature of Cajetan's analysis is his awareness of the problems which can be involved in the measurement of *lucrum cessans*. This issue is discussed in the sixth section of his treatise *De Usura*, written in 1500, where he asks: 'in cases where it is lawful to seek recompense for "lucrum cessans," can the entire amount of the loss be sought?' In his reply, Cajetan argues that because the profit forgone is not actual but only potential, interest payment should be less than the profit which *ex-post* judgement suggests would have been earned. The judgement should be based on 'the estimation of prudent men'. Given the rate of profit, there is

[29] Op. cit., Q. 78, art. 2, VI.

a range of possible interest payments depending especially on 'how near the possibility of loss came to being realised'.[30]

Cajetan's more liberal approach to *lucrum cessans* came under attack from the conservative Domingo de Soto. However, supported by thorough exploration of contemporary commercial realities, subsequent Spanish theologians were able to perceive the limited scope of much medieval monetary enquiry. In the hands of the Jesuit doctors of Spain in the latter half of the sixteenth century, *lucrum cessans* is established firmly as a common basis for the receipt of interest.

Key figures at this time were Martin Azplicueta Navarrus (1493—1586) and Luis Molina (1536—1600). Navarrus was sometime professor at Toulouse, Cahors, Salamanca and Coimbra. He acted as counsellor to the King of Portugal, and later to Philip II of Spain. Later still, in Rome, he was adviser to three successive popes. His works on economic matters began in 1544 and continued to appear throughout his long life. Molina studied at the universities of Alcala, Lisbon and Coimbra, and lectured at the University of Evora in Portugal (1570—90). In retirement he produced his massive treatise, *De Justitia et Jura* (1593—7).

For these authors, the forgoing of profit, whether voluntary or involuntary, provides an objective ground accounting for the existence of interest payment.[31] Loss of profit pertains in loans involving the sacrifice of certain types of money balances held by businessmen. As with St Antonine these include transactions and speculative balances intended for direct investment.[32] Explicitly excluded are transactions balances for personal consumption purposes, and funds reserved for lending.[33] In general, there is a variety of

---

[30] In the light of Cajetan's approach to *lucrum cessans*, the following statement of Professor de Roover seems most questionable: 'Lucrum cessans was, therefore, rejected by Thomas Aquinas and most of the theologians. Later, in the sixteenth century, it was permitted by some latitudinarians, but only between merchants." *International Encyclopedia of the Social Sciences*, 4 (1968) p. 7.

[31] Navarrus, *De usuris*, 15, n. 42 and 52; 16, n. 53. See also Molina, *De justitia*, II:315:11.

[32] Navarrus, *De cambius*, 34, 35; *Manuale*, 17, m296, 301; *De usuris*, 19, n.58. See also Molina, op. cit., II:318:3.

[33] Navarrus, *Manuale*, c.17, *De septimo praecepto*, n. 212.

purposes for holding money, and the non-fulfilment of some of these purposes accounts for the existence of just demands for interest.

Underlying this sixteenth century movement away from the hesitant acceptance of *lucrum cessans* in earlier periods is the new-found dynamism of the European economy. In conditions of growth and change, the premium which can be associated with money in hand was more readily appreciated. Command over present resources was more obviously advantageous. A rationale for interest had been much less clearly discernible in earlier circumstances which had frequently approximated those of a stable circular flow.[34]

Among the factors responsible for an increasing tempo of economic activity in many parts of Europe was the increasing monetisation of their economies. Imports of gold and silver from Spanish territories in the New World were diffused throughout the Continent. Inflationary forces were unleashed which, in conditions of less than full employment, stimulated a growth of real output. In the diffusion process, the military campaigns of the Spanish kings were most significant. Public borrowing for the conduct of war by Philip of Spain, as well as by Francis I of France and his son Henry II, served to circulate the treasure of the Americas and, at the same time, encouraged the growth of large-scale international capital markets. This growth, in the sixteenth century, led not only to new scholastic insights on the subject of interest, but also to a much more comprehensive analysis of monetary exchange and banking practices than had been undertaken hitherto. It is to the evolution of scholastic thinking concerning these latter practices that we now turn.

Money as a commodity: *cambium* and *census*
In the tracts on currency debasement discussed above, there was some suggestion that money could be regarded as a

[34] 'In an economy whose normal course flowed year in and year out through familiar, well-worn channels, what grounds can there be for systematic under-valuation of means of production as compared with products? Competition on the one hand and imputation on the other must annihilate any surplus of receipts over outlays, any excess of the value of the product over the value of the services of the land and labor involved in it.' J. A. Schumpeter, *Theory of Economic Development* (Cambridge, Mass., 1936) p. 8.

commodity, the price of which was dependent on 'human need'. It was implied that the value of money like that of other forms of merchandise was subject to the ebb and flow of market forces. Yet this implication does not seem to have led to those writings effecting a reassessment of the medieval view that in contracts dealing with the transfer of money, the money could be thought of as a measure of unvarying value. When the reassessment came, it was prompted mainly by analyses of foreign exchange dealings (*cambium*). Some influence may also have been exerted by analyses of purchases of a *census,* i.e. purchases of an annuity derived from returns on property.

The vast majority of the theologians of the twelfth and thirteenth centuries had entertained the gravest of doubts concerning the morality of exchange dealings. St Thomas, we have seen, diverged from Aristotle in giving guarded approval to the vocation of merchants on the ground that they supplied their fellow citizens with necessary goods which could not always be produced locally. Nevertheless, in his commentary on Aristotle's *Politics,* he appears to follow the Philosopher in the condemnation of the *ars campsoria*, the business of money-changing. This issue concerning the possible existence of a legitimate market in money is not pursued, even though St Thomas allows that money is something that can be bought and sold. This latter is only a secondary feature of money and not one of its essential properties.[35]

During the fourteenth century, one area of Europe which avoided decline into economic stagnation was Lombardy. This region had become notorious for the scope and liberality of its financial practices, and the Piedmontese from the hill towns of Chieri and Asti — like the Tuscans of Siena, Pistoia and Florence — were widely regarded as debased dealers in various forms of usury.[36] It is in this region that one finds the beginnings of an informed approach to currency exchange dealings leading to the acceptance of the legitimacy of markets in money.

[35] *Summa Theologica*, II–II, Q 78, 1.
[36] On the Lombards, see Raymond de Roover, *Money, Banking and Credit in Medieval Bruges* (Cambridge, Harvard University Press, 1948).

The writings of Franciscan theologians, one of whom was St Bernardine of Siena, are most significant in this respect. Perhaps they were less disposed than a good many other schoolmen to regard the views of the Dominican St Thomas as definitive on questions of economic morality. Indicative of the willingness of the Franciscans to innovate in practice as well as in theory was their sponsorship of the *montes pietatis,* public pawnships lending sums to the poor at low rates of interest. These were first introduced at Perugia and Orvieto in 1462, and were attacked by Dominican moralists as institutions dealing in usury. Defended by the Franciscans, notably by the outstanding preacher, Blessed Bernardine of Feltre, the *montes* eventually gained official church approval during the Council of Lateran V (1512—17). This later controversy reflects divergences between Dominican and Franciscan monetary analysis that are apparent as early as the opening years of the fourteenth century.

Alexander Bonini (Lombard), the Franciscan provincal of Lombardy, was in a good position to observe the details of currency exchange practices. This is evident in his *Tractatus de usuris* based on an address given at Genoa in 1307. Particularly significant is his allowance that it may be lawful for an exchange dealer to require repayments over and above the face value of a sum of money which he has transferred to a merchant on credit. This allowance turns on the perception that the demand for money can vary over time, giving rise to variations in the value of money. It also involves the application to money dealings of a principle that had been applied by earlier writers only to the credit sale of commodities, excluding money. This principle, *venditio sub dubio,* recognised that the passage of time may have a real impact on the value of merchandise. A commodity purchased on credit now may be worth more when payment falls due. Hence, a higher price could be asked for a credit sale than for a cash transaction, provided there was genuine doubt concerning the future value of the commodity in question.

Alexander's reasoning was supported by another Franciscan theologian, Astesanus (d. 1330), a native of Piedmont who wrote a *Summa de casibus conscientiae* in eight books. However, almost a century was to elapse before his ideas on money were to be reasserted with some force. Writing in Florence, then the major financial centre of Europe, Lorenzo Ridolfi, in his treatise of 1403 on usury, considered contemporary exchange dealing at some length. Lorenzo, who generally sided with the Franciscans in matters of commercial morality, affirms that there can be real differences in the value of money from one place to another as well as over time. These differences arise from variations in the metallic content of coinage, changes in the price of gold, and fluctuations in the demand for money relative to supply. *Venditio sub dubio* is seen as relevant in considering cases in which exchange dealers receive more than the face value of the money originally transferred.[37] This principle is also employed by St Bernardine of Siena who finds that profit arising out of delay in repayment of a bill of exchange may be justified if there is any doubt as to the future course of the exchange rate.[38]

Some support for the position of these Franciscan writers was forthcoming from at least one Dominican theologian. He was Johannes Nider (c. 1380—1438), a Swabian who occupied a chair in theology at the University of Vienna and was active in the reform of the Dominican order in southern Germany. Nider is by no means a major figure in scholastic thought, but a short treatise of his, *De Contractibus Mercantorum*, was published in Cologne about 1468 and was frequently reprinted in the later years of the fifteenth century. The author is familiar with Franciscan thought, citing Duns Scotus on a number of occasions as an authority, and also referring to Alexander Lombard and Astesanus. Nider's views on commercial morality almost certainly reflect

---

[37] *De usuris,* 3:1. On *venditio sub dubio,* and on its use by Lorenzo and Alexander Lombard, see J. T. Noonan, op. cit., pp. 90—5 and 183—7.

[38] Raymond de Roover, *San Bernardino of Siena and Sant' Antonino of Florence* (Boston, Baker Library, 1967) p. 36. De Roover observes that Bernardine's Dominican contemporary, St Antonine, discusses *cambium* at some length, but is 'more uncompromising than the Sienese friar'. Of Antonine's views on *cambium per litteram,* exchange by bills, de Roover writes that his moral 'advice, if followed, would have abolished banking altogether, a rather strange attitude on the part of the archbishop of the leading banking center in Western Europe.' (p. 37). On the banking system of Florence at this time, see the same author's *The Rise and Decline of the Medici Bank, 1397—1494* (Cambridge, Harvard University Press, 1963).

those of a large segment of the educated opinion of his time.

According to Nider, there is no fundamental moral distinction to be made between the vocation of merchant and that of banker. Both are activities in which profit can be earned in a morally acceptable fashion. He writes of

> ... the conversion, or exchange of moneys or of other things, which is, as it were a kind of selling and buying of one currency for another, and presents, so to speak, the same moral problems as does commerce in goods ... For whatever thing, cause, or activity a merchant can receive gain by reason of his wares, so likewise may a banker receive pecuniary profit, that is, the activities concerned with money have their place and are exercised just as in the case with merchandise.[39]

Currency exchange, he says, is a 'kind of selling and buying', and Nider goes on immediately to suggest that there are markets in money. Its value, of which the criterion for measurement is not specified, will vary in accord with 'common estimation' as will the values of commodities. Exchange bankers, like merchants, sometimes profit legitimately, and sometimes incur losses, because of such variation:

> It is clear that just as wares vary in the estimation of men so also does the value of money, although perhaps not so commonly or in so great a quantity. To repeat, just as one can have care, work, risk, and other hazards in connection with importing goods, so (too) these may exist in connection with money ... In accordance with all this the financier may receive more or less, dependent upon how by common estimation his money has been changed to advantage or disadvantage.[40]

The writer's point of departure in this passage appears to be St Thomas' observation, in commenting on Aristotle, that money, although relatively stable, will vary in value. (See

---

[39] J. Nider, *On the Contracts of Merchants,* trans. Charles H. Reeves, (Norman, Oklahoma, University of Oklahoma Press, 1966) p. 50. See also p. 27.
[40] Loc. cit.

Chapter 6). However, he builds on the observation in a direction not pursued by Aquinas. Nider's remarks do not seem to have led any other scholastics to take the matter further, and his vagueness on the question of the meaning of 'the value of money' must certainly have weakened any impact he might have had in stimulating new monetary analysis.

Outside Nider and the Franciscans, the idea of money as a commodity continued to languish. Nevertheless, a significant development in this direction can be attributed to an author who was earlier shown to have considered the commodity aspect of money in his treatment of currency devaluation, Gabriel Biel. In his commentary on the *Sentences*, Biel justifies a banker's profiting on the purchase of a bill of exchange. When the bank accepts the bill, it is permitting the drawer of the bill to obtain cash in another city. His money has been 'virtually transported' to the city where he draws, and he is relieved of the expenses and possible dangers of undertaking his own transportation. This service warrants a fee.[41] Biel's argument is repeated by Conrad Summenhart and becomes common in the scholastic analyses of banking in the sixteenth century. J. T. Noonan writes: 'The "virtual transportation" argument, developed by the Tübingen school, is standard among the later scholastics of major importance. But more significantly, the concept serves as a construct by which the idea of a market in money becomes acceptable.'[42] Money, like merchandise, requires transportation, and a banking system is designed to facilitate the transfers of this particular type of commodity.

The next attempt to go beyond the narrow medieval conceptions of money and banking was not undertaken by a Norminalist or a Franciscan, but by the orthodox and influential Thomist, Cardinal Cajetan, whose discussion of *lucrum cessans* has been seen as significant. His *De cambüs,* written in 1499, provides a general justification of the business of exchange dealing while extending the analysis of money in directions unexplored by St Thomas.

[41] *Collectorium Super IV libros sententiarum,* 4: 15: 11 MM.
[42] Op. cit., p. 317.

The treatise is relatively short, consisting of eight chapters, the first four of which are devoted to describing different types of exchange practices and the opinions of earlier moralists concerning them. Then, in Chapter 5, he argues that since the vocation of merchant is legitimate, the vocation of exchange dealing which supports the activities of merchants is also justified. St Thomas' departure from Aristotle in approving of merchants is used to counter his apparent adherence to the Philosopher on the question of foreign exchange business. He writes:

> Since experience shows that many necessities would be lacking to many states if there were no merchants, and that merchants cannot conveniently do business without exchange dealing, it is needful and right that it should exist in states ... Thus exchange dealers may not only guard themselves against loss, but they can also make a profit and draw their earnings from their industry, since they apply it to a licit business which is profitable for the State.[43]

In the following chapters, Cajetan proceeds to explore features of the market within which exchange dealers operate. Money, he suggests, has two aspects – the expendable and the non-expendable. Considered as expendable, money has a fixed legal value as the measure and price of other goods, and this value cannot be altered lawfully by individual citizens. As non-expendable, money ceases to be a legal measure and becomes instead a commodity. Money becomes non-expendable '... when it is "absent" from the place where one wants to spend it. Thus, money in another city, sold by the drawer of a bill of exchange, is non-expendable. As non-expendable and thus as a commodity, such money is subject to the laws governing the price of commodities.'[44]

---

[43] *De cambiis,* C.5. The necessity of exchange transactions for the conduct of trade is also argued by another Dominican, Fra Santi (Pandolfo) Rucellai (1437–97). The Saint had been the son of a banker and an exchange dealer himself. See R. de Roover, 'Il tratto di fra Santi Rucellai sul cambio', *Archivio storico italiano* (1953) 111: 3–41.

[44] J. T. Noonan, op. cit., p. 318. Professor Noonan finds it a 'mystery' (p. 322) that Cajetan does not apply this commodity approach to the question of the morality of money loans. A possible answer to the mystery may be found in the

Not only does the value of money depend upon existing demand and supply conditions, but on expectations concerning the future state of the market. Expectations concerning events such as wars and famines, and even the future movements of supplies of money, will affect its current price. Because the value of money varies from place to place, and over time, a legitimate profit can be realised on exchange transactions.

Cajetan is vague concerning the meaning to be attached to the phrase 'the value of money'. This same vagueness had been present both in earlier discussions of exchange and in the writings on currency debasement.[45] It is not altogether clear whether he is referring to the purchasing power of money in general or merely to the exchange ratios of quantities of different metals. Both ideas are to be found, for example, in Cajetan's comments on Aristotle's treatment of money. In Chapter 5, the value of money is reckoned in terms of the goods with which money is exchanged. Cajetan writes: '. . . goods unobtainable in one land would not be available from elsewhere without the equivalent of their value being given . . . consequently men have decided that gold, silver, copper and anything similar which is easily portable and serviceable would be equated with goods to be bought or sold.'[46] However, at the same time the genesis of profit-making in exchange dealing is said to have been associated with the exploitation of divergent ratios of exchange of different types of metal: 'Profit making in the exchange of currency seems first to have come about, according to Aristotle, when, say, a gold coin was put at a higher value in some place, and more copper coin was given for it there than in its place of origin. Human industry then skilfully opened the way to making a profit in this kind of exchange. This is

---

distinction noted above between 'money of account' and 'coin in circulation'. The latter is the material of exchange transactions and is variable in value. Domestic lending, however, is an activity for which the former, a supposedly fixed measure of value, provides the basic point of reference.

[45] 'Although the problem of the value of money received considerable attention during the middle ages, no one, apparently, had taken the trouble to discuss just what was meant by changes in this value or how such changes were to be measured. Few discussions, indeed, are found in the whole period covered by this study [i.e. before Adam Smith].' A. E. Monroe, op. cit., p. 68.

[46] *De cambiis,* loc. cit.

how the art of exchange dealing was devised.'[47] The fact that
Cajetan is careful to use the latter point merely in a generic
and not a definitive sense, suggests that his emphasis is on the
purchasing power of money. Nevertheless, this emphasis is
weakened by the absence of any clear conception of
fluctuation in a money supply as a whole. Such a concept
seems to have eluded earlier writers also, and only the tracts
on currency debasement approached it by directing attention
to problems of a monetary system.

Some of the basic defects inherent in Cajetan's analysis
were eliminated by the Spanish schoolmen writing in the
mid-sixteenth century. By this time, Spain had become the
hub for the thinking of the Counter-Reformation. The
University of Salamanca in particular had assumed an
importance similar to that of the University of Paris in an
earlier phase of the scholastic tradition. Thomism had been
revived there, but not to the exclusion of the newer currents
of empiricism and casuistry.[48]

At the same time, old problems of commercial morality
were taking on new guises in inflationary surroundings. The
inflow of precious metals from America was effecting a price
revolution which in Spain, in the absence of official currency
debasements, could be more easily identified with that
inflow. In addition, new moral issues were posed by the
extension of international credit arrangements within the
framework of an expanding system of exchange banking.

Changing economic conditions and a new spirit of enquiry
combined to produce fresh insights on money and banking.
The most important figure here was Navarrus. In his
Commentarius resoltivus de cambüs, he abandons Cajetan's
distinction between money as expendable and as non-
expendable. Hence, he rejects the view that whereas the
value of money as merchandise can fluctuate, it can be

[47] Ibid.
[48] Cf. Reijo Wilenius, *The Social and Political Theory of Francisco Suarez*
(Helsinki, Societas Philosophica Fennica, 1963) p. 113: 'Renaissance Scholasticism, however, was not a purely Thomistic movement. It was also influenced by
the via moderna, the nominalistic movement which signifies a change from
'constructive' to 'analytical' thinking, from metaphysics to the knowledge of
'individual things'."

treated as a stable measure of value of other goods. Money as a measure may vary.[49] Associated with this departure is the unequivocal understanding that the value of money is to be measured in terms of its purchasing power. Further, this value is inversely related to the quantity available for use. These insights which are implied in the work of Cajetan are made explicit by Navarrus. The latter writes:

> ... other things being equal, in countries where there is a great scarcity of money all other saleable goods, and even the hands and labour of men, are given for less money than where it is abundant. Thus we see by experience that in France, where money is scarcer than in Spain, bread, wine, cloth, and labour are worth much less. And even in Spain, in times when money was scarcer, saleable goods and labour were given for very much less than after the discovery of the Indies, which flooded the country with gold and silver. The reason for this is that money is worth more where and when it is scarce than where and when it is abundant.[50]

Marjorie Grice-Hutchinson has claimed that here one encounters 'the first clear statement' of a quantity theory of money.[51] This is so, provided that one appreciates that in 1556 when Navarrus wrote, it was not an absolute novelty to affirm that the value of money is influenced by supply factors. This idea is present in the work of Ridolfi, to name one much earlier author. The genuine novelty and importance of Navarrus' innovation is in the clear relationship of 'value of money' with 'purchasing power'. As has been seen, Cajetan, like his contemporary Copernicus, who is sometimes said to have made the first statement of the quantity theory, is quite ambiguous on this vital point. Of at least equal importance as an innovation is the prominence given the idea of fluctuation in the value of the money supply as a whole. Whereas earlier writers on banking or on debasement thought in terms of the value relationships of different forms of

[49] *De cambiis,* 20, n.55 and 57.
[50] Quotation from translations of selected texts of Navarrus in M. Grice-Hutchinson, *The School of Salamanca* (Oxford, Clarendon Press, 1952) p. 95.
[51] Op. cit., p. 52.

money, Navarrus' analysis focused attention on the relationship of money as a whole to goods of various kinds. When the
immediate successors of Navarrus employed this way of
thinking they felt obliged to underline the new emphasis.
Luis Molina, for example, explains: 'Not this or that sort of
money . . . but all the money taken together is worth more in
one place than all the money of another place taken together
is worth in this second place, when a comparison is made of an
equal quantity of money of one place with an equal quantity
of the other place, . . .'[52]

Such a fundamental change of viewpoint led directly and
quickly to other developments. As Grice-Hutchinson has
observed, Navarrus' analysis suggested a type of purchasing-
power parity theory of exchange rates. The theory was
adopted by writers as opposed as Domingo de Banez
(1528–1604), the Salamancan theologian who was confessor
to St Theresa of Avila, and Luis Molina (1536–1600), the
critic of Banez at the University of Evora. According to
Banez:

> . . . in places where money is scarce, goods will be cheaper
> than in those where the whole mass of money is bigger,
> and therefore it is lawful to exchange a smaller sum in one
> country for a larger sum in another. Since the primary end
> for which money was ordained is the purchase of goods, it
> follows that wherever money is more highly esteemed for
> this purpose it may be exchanged for a larger sum than
> where it is less so . . . We admit that one party may
> lawfully agree to repay a larger sum to another, corre-
> sponding to the amount required to buy the same parcel of
> goods that the latter might have bought if he had not
> delivered his money in exchange.[53]

[52] Luis Molina, *De justitia et jura,* 410: 1. See also Leonard Lessius, *De justitia et
jure,* II, 24: 34: 'The whole of the money at one time is worth more or less both
with respect to things for sale in the same place, and with respect to money which
is in other places.'
[53] Domingo de Banez, *De Justitia et Jure* (1594) Q 78, *De Cambiis,* art. 4. See
also Luis Molina, *Disputationes de Contractibus* (1601) quoted in M. Grice-
Hutchinson, op. cit., pp. 112–15. Molina's analysis is of special interest in that he
notes that in a regime of fixed exchange rates, the course of commodity trade is
likely to be damaged. He writes that 'To control it [the exchange rate] would do
a great deal of harm to the republic, because such a course would bring about a
shortage of necessary goods.'

Again, Navarrus' admission that money considered as a measure of value can vary, posed a fundamental problem for traditional usury analysis.[54] Navarrus himself did not solve the problem, but its solution was to come as an innovation in this area of scholastic analysis by Leonard Lessius (see Chapter 9).

More important perhaps, than either of these direct consequences was a third concerned with price determination in general. In the work of Navarrus and his immediate successors, supply considerations are given a new prominence. These considerations provide a counterweight to the traditional scholastic emphasis on demand, an emphasis associated with their utility theory of value. This led to a much clearer understanding of the meaning of 'a market', and a more comprehensive analysis of price formation.[55] In this respect, the scholastic probings of the morality of exchange banking yielded most significant dividends for economic analysis.

It was not only through their investigations of the foreign exchanges that the Spanish scholastics reached an appreciation that the value of money varied in terms of goods. They also realised that the same sum of money could at the one time be worth less in terms of present goods than future goods. More money would be exchanged for a quantity of goods now than for the right to the same quantity in the future. As Navarrus writes: '. . . a claim on something is worth less than the thing itself, and . . . it is plain that that which is not usable for a year is less valuable than something of the same quality which is usable at once.'[56]

Explaining this phenomenon some 300 years later, Böhm-Bawerk, in his *Positive Theory of Capital* (1889), put forward a subjective and an objective explanation. The greater money value of a present good is due to individual preference for present as against future enjoyments. Considered objectively, however, it is due to the possibility of

[54] J. T. Noonan, op. cit., p. 324.
[55] For example, see Lessius' summary of price determining factors, *De Justitia et Jure* (1605) II:2:8, or Molina's *De Justitia et Jure* (1593—7) 348:7. In both of these, supply and demand considerations are balanced.
[56] *Consilia, V. De Usuris,* 18. Among earlier writers to recognise the superior value of cash in hand, and to apply this recognition to the problem of pricing was John Nider, op. cit., pp. 29—30.

increasing one's future enjoyments by an enhanced command of resources now within productive processes.[57] The scholastic writers, too, attributed a real divergence of the values of present and future money to this second factor. On the other hand, the majority denied that subjective discounting was relevant to the determination of justice in exchanges of present for future money. Individual preferences of the parties to a contract afforded no firm basis for a just agreeement. For example, a borrower in extreme need may be led to under-value future money heavily, but his need does not establish the legality of the price he may be willing to pay any lender willing to exploit it.

The view of the Spanish doctors is illustrated by Molina's analysis of the contract of personal *census*. In this contract, the seller of the *census* obtained a sum of money, unsecured by the pledge of property, in return for an undertaking to make annual payments to the buyer. The source of the payments was the income derived from the seller's labour. The buyer, Molina acknowledges, is exchanging present for future money, but he is not entitled to repayment of more than the original sum transferred merely on that account. He writes: '. . . although one hundred present gold pieces are worth more to one using them for business purposes than the same number of future gold pieces, in themselves they are not worth more nor in themselves are they productive.'[58]

It is only the objective existence of profit possibilities in a business context which creates a real difference in the values of present and future money.

This line of thought is continued by Leonard Lessius in his treatment of the sale of notes at a discount. He refers frequently to the desirability of present as against future money in a business context. He notes that 'present money furnishes control over many things which these rights [to

---

[57] Eugen von Böhm-Bawerk, *Capital and Interest*, Vol. 2 (South Holland, Ill., 1959). On the subjective factor, he writes (p. 268): 'We systematically undervalue our future wants and also the means which serve to satisfy them.' With reference to the objective element, it is stated (p. 273): 'As a general rule, present goods are for technological reasons preferable means to the satisfaction of wants and for that reason they are a warranty of higher marginal utility than are future goods.'
[58] Molina, op. cit., 385: 2:7.

future money] do not supply.'[59] 'Present money', he observes, provides 'a capacity for gain and other advantages.'[60] To purchase notes at a discount is legitimate if one is likely to lose 'some power which present money gives, which a note of debt does not have.'[61] As is shown in Chapter 9, this emphasis on the power of present money is bound up with the formulation of a new title to interest-taking which is one of Lessius' more important innovations in the scholastic tradition.

[59] Lessius, op. cit., 11:21:8:66.
[60] Op. cit., 11:21:8:67.
[61] Op. cit., 11:21:8:73.

8 Price and Value in Scholastic Thought: 1300–1600

Aquinas' remarks on the just price and his related observations on the question of value determination were made against a background of economic growth and increasing prosperity in many areas of Europe. In general, he found that the just price was the prevailing free-market price and that the value of a commodity was governed by its usefulness as a means of satisfying human need. However, events were soon to lead some of his scholastic successors to begin questioning the adequacy of these findings. The initial problem seems to have been rising food prices. David Herlihy writes:

> By the late thirteenth century, for a variety of reasons, not the least of which was the swollen size of urban populations, the larger towns could no longer rely exclusively on the free market to assure the abundant and cheap supplies of grain their citizens needed. By a variety of measures, ranging from simple embargoes on grain export to the creation of grain-purchasing monopolies with power to fix the price of locally produced grain, the larger towns had assumed responsibility for keeping the price of grain at a level even their poorest citizens could afford.[1]

The vast majority of moralists did not question the right of municipal authorities to take this type of action to interfere with the operation of free market forces, especially when it was confined, as was the case generally, to regulation of the prices of basic necessities. Such action was an example of

[1] David Herlihy, report of comments on a paper given by Raymond de Roover, in *Journal of Economic History,* Vol. 18 (Dec 1958) pp. 437–8.

lawful authority exercised to preserve the common good in the society concerned. In principle, it was quite in accord with the doctrines of St Thomas and earlier theologians. There could be particular instances, however, in which the municipal authorities might be said to be acting imprudently by establishing unrealistic or unjust prices. This latter possibility brought to the fore the question of developing criteria for price fixation with a degree of urgency that had not been associated with the issue in Aquinas' day.

This urgency increased with the onset of economic decline in the fourteenth century and was maintained amidst the widespread poverty of the fifteenth. Over these two centuries, as Professor Gilchrist states:

> Price fluctuations became more frequent and extreme than in the previous 200 years. In a good year (1287) in England wheat sold at 20d. a quarter, barley at 26d., and oats at 24d. In the famine years 1315–27 prices were multiplied by more than ten; wheat reached 24s., barley 16s., and oats 20s. A century later, Landucci's diary for the period 1450–1516 in Florence shows a rapid price movement within a short period of time, e.g., wheat on 6 May 1497 was 3 lire a bushel, 31 May 5 lire, 24 June 3 lire, which affected the purchasing power of the wage earner. Peasants committed suicide on failing to buy bread at the price fixed by the commune.
>
> Speculators and powerful economic interests did not have to suffer. Thus the two centuries present a picture of an ever-widening gap between rich and poor. . . . This view may appear at variance with that sometimes held of the Renaissance period as one of unprecedented expenditure on art, building, literature, courtly magnificence and self-indulgence by the upper classes.[2]

In such circumstances, the schoolmen found the strongest grounds for support of the establishment of maximum prices for food, drink, and farm products by local government agencies. At the same time, and also in the interest of the

---

[2] J. Gilchrist, *The Church and Economic Activity in the Middle Ages* (London, Macmillan, 1969) p. 87.

common good, they opposed the attempts by the town guilds of manufacturers and tradesmen to establish minimum prices for their products. The guilds frequently endeavoured to serve the interests of their members through monopolistic pricing practices, and these were condemned by the moralists. Also condemned were 'engrossing', the accumulation of stocks of commodities in an attempt to corner the market; 'forestalling', the purchase of supplies of goods before they reached the market for which they were intended by their producers; and 'regrating', speculative buying in a given market with the intention of selling the same commodities in the same market at a higher price.

The general tenor of scholastic pricing policy then, was for the establishment of just terms of trade between town and country, and the achievement of a free flow of goods uninhibited by private monopolies and by speculative activity of a type which was designed to bring about the very circumstances which the speculator intended to exploit for his own gain. Concern with terms of trade involved some support of price regulation. Opposition to monopoly often resulted in affirmation of the virtues of free-market pricing. These two themes are intertwined in scholastic discussions of the just price, and different authors emphasise one or the other. Associated with this difference of emphasis on price are certain conflicting approaches to the issue of the nature of economic value.

Broadly speaking, there are two lines of scholastic thinking on the just price, extending from near the end of the thirteenth century to the Spanish doctors of the sixteenth. One of these, the major line, emphasises that the just price is established by market consensus (or 'common estimation'). The other line tends to favour direct regulation of prices as the best means of ensuring justice in the exchange of goods and services. Over the same period, in their thinking on value, while most scholastics seem to adopt a utility-based theory, there are also some who can be interpreted as adhering to a cost-of-production theory with stress on the element of labour-cost.

Demarcations between the differing schools and streams of scholastic opinion on price and value are difficult to establish with any precision, although one historian has suggested that it is possible to distinguish three groups: the followers of St Albert and St Thomas; the followers of Duns Scotus; and the Nominalist philosophers. Yet, such a classification breaks down at a number of crucial points, because the analyses of certain writers employ features of the work of all three groups, and otherwise reasonably firm philosophical or theological boundaries are sometimes crossed on the subject of price and value.[3] There may be a case for dealing in terms of contrasting Dominican, Franciscan, Nominalist, and later, Spanish Jesuit traditions in this area of economic analysis. However, in the face of very real diversity of opinion, it seems best to adhere to a chronological treatment of the evolution of this aspect of scholastic thought.

Late thirteenth and the fourteenth century

Among the near-contemporaries of St Albert the Great and St Thomas there were other prominent theologians who were ready to follow the main line of Aristotle's reasoning which put major emphasis on the role of human estimation in the determination of value. These theologians included Henry of Ghent (1217—93), and the British Franciscan, Richard of Middleton (c.1249—1306), who was associated with the University of Paris.[4] However, a more important contribution was made by a relatively obscure Franciscan from Provence, Pierre de Jean Olivi (1248—98).

Olivi's treatise, *Quaestiones de permutatione rerum, de emptionibus et venditionibus,* may have not circulated widely

---

[3] The classification is Raymond de Roover's. See *International Encyclopedia of the Social Sciences,* Vol. 4 (1968) p. 433. One scholastic writer who exemplifies the drawbacks of de Roover's classification is John Nider. He is categorised by de Roover as a follower of St Thomas, yet his work is influenced strongly by that of Duns Scotus and is allied in some respects to that of the nominalists. Another example is John Buridan, a leading nominalist, who, quite correctly, is depicted in another paper by de Roover (*Quarterly Journal of Economics,* Vol. 69 (May 1955) p. 164) as working in the same frame of reference as Aquinas on the subject of price determination.

[4] Some aspects of the economic thought of Richard of Middleton together with that of the earlier British scholastic, the 'Doctor Irrefragibilis', Alexander of Hales (d.1245), are examined in, Max Beer, *Early British Economics* (London, Allen and Unwin, 1938) pp. 26—44.

in the fourteenth century, yet it came to exercise considerable influence on scholastic thought concerning value. A
copy of it came into the hands of a later Franciscan, St
Bernardine of Siena (1380–1444), and he used Olivi's ideas
in his own treatment of the morality of buying and selling.
Through this exposition by a major figure in scholastic
economics, Olivi's thought eventually found a wide audience.[5]

According to Olivi, value is the outcome of the operation
of three factors: usefulness, scarcity, and the ability to please
the will of the buyer (*complacibilitas*). The factor of scarcity
(*raritas*) here has much the same significance as it had in
Aristotle's analysis. A rare article is likely to be valued more
highly because of its very rarity. The distinction between
usefulness and ability to please points up objective and
subjective aspects in the idea of utility. Any one of a certain
class of commodities may possess objectively the capability
of serving an individual's need, but because of subjective
preference he may value a particular item in that class more
highly than the others.

Recognition of the role of *complacibilitas* serves to
emphasise the subjective element in the formation of price.
Exchange ratios between goods cannot be established in an
objective fashion simply by reference to the inherent qualities
of the objects in question. It follows that establishment of a
single, just price for a class of commodities must take
account of individual differences in estimation by potential
purchasers of their capacity to satisfy. The market place is
the venue in which those differences interact to give rise to a
consensus from which a just price can emerge.

This reasoning clarified the idea of value based on 'human

[5] Olivi's work has been brought to light only recently by the painstaking research
of the late Professor Raymond de Roover. The obscurity of the treatise is due to a
period of strife within the Franciscan Order over interpretation of the rule of life
recommended by its founder. In the course of the conflict, destruction of Olivi's
writings was ordered by a rival faction, and an attempt was made to brand his
works as heretical. St Bernardine did not acknowledge his debt to Olivi because of
the latter's still doubtful reputation as a purveyor of unorthodoxy. The remarks
on Olivi's theory of value which follow are based on Professor de Roover's *San
Bernardino of Siena and Sant' Antonino of Florence* (Boston, Baker Library,
1967) esp. pp. 18–19.

need' as expressed by Aquinas and Aristotle. Here, 'the eye of the beholder', as well as any inherent qualities of satisfying want which commodities could be said to possess, is given an unequivocal role in the determination of value. Also, it is suggested, the formation of the just price is dependent on consumer assessment.

A somewhat different note is struck on the question of just price in the writings of another Franciscan, John Duns Scotus (1265—1308). This British scholastic, who occupied academic posts at both the University of Oxford and that of Paris, was the chief, early critic of St Thomas' theology. His influential commentary on Peter Lombard's *Sentences* includes observations on value and pricing, and in it he is prepared to give a much more explicit place to consideration of the merchant's costs of supplying a market than is Aquinas. Scotus contends that price should cover the expense incurred by a merchant in buying, transporting and storing goods plus compensation for the industry, labour and risk involved in bringing the commodities to market. He adds that a just price is one which enables a merchant to support his family adequately.[6]

Some commentators have taken this contention to indicate a definite adherence to a type of labour theory of value on Scotus' part, but this interpretation is doubtful. He does not argue that the initial cost of the commodities to the merchant is determined by their labour cost of production and, in fact, he defines value in the same fashion as St Thomas. Any divergence between their views cannot be classified as fundamental. However, their difference of emphasis helped touch off a controversy amongst schoolmen that was never fully resolved within the framework of later analyses.

The next significant contribution came from John Buridan, the French philosopher-scientist who, it has been claimed, was also responsible for 'the most interesting dynamical theorising before Galileo'[7] In his *Quaestiones in decem Libros Ethicorum Aristotelis ad Nicomachum,*

---

[6] Duns Scotus, *In IV libros sententiarum*, IV:15:2.
[7] A. C. Crombie, *Augustine to Galileo (II): Science in the Later Middle Ages and Early Modern Times* (London, Heinemann, 1961) pp. 45—6, 66 et seq., 152 et seq.

Buridan subjects the Greek master's theory of value to the
most thorough scrutiny it had received (in published form at
least) to that date. The relevant discussion is undertaken in
questions 15–17 of his commentary, where Buridan progresses from a general consideration of the measurement problems associated with exchange justice, to the specific issues of
'Whether human need is the measure of exchangeable things'
and 'Whether coins are necessary for measuring exchangeable
things.'

In question 15, Buridan concludes that Aristotle's basic
position on value is tenable.

> Although those things which are rightly exchangeable
> are not of the same genus, they are altogether of like value
> according to their properties and their absolute order
> [*rationes*]. However, according as they come into human
> use, they belong in the same order [*ratio*] because they are
> useful or because they fulfil a human need.

In arguing to this conclusion, however, Buridan suggests that
differences in durations of periods of production account for
differences in value among commodities. He states:

> No one by way of exchange necessary to sustain human
> nature, without an act of liberality, will give one beautiful
> house in exchange for a pair of good shoes or one garment.
> For if this had to be done no builder could live, since he
> spends a year constructing one house; if for it he got only
> one garment, where would he get his food? Therefore, he
> will not be giving his house for so many things on the
> grounds that they are equal in value to his house.

The reasoning here does not suggest that differences in
value are due directly to differences in the expenditure of
labour-time in the production of particular items of exchange. Rather, it implies that the relevant consideration is:
degree of sacrifice by specialist producers of opportunities to
use their time to satisfy their needs for the range of goods
'necessary to sustain human nature' through their own
productive effort. The sacrifice of the alternative, in terms of
food, involved in building a house is much greater than the

sacrifice required to make a pair of shoes or an item of clothing.

With this analysis, value theory in the Aristotelian tradition is brought closer to a unified treatment of supply and cost, as well as demand, in terms of 'utility'. Unification was not to be established clearly until the nineteenth century and the work of W. S. Jevons and the Austrian, von Wieser.[8] Nevertheless, Buridan's recognition of the relevance of forgone opportunity to satisfy the need for food was a most promising initiative.

Another noteworthy initiative in the general discussion of exchange (question 15) is Buridan's perception that mutual agreement to trade or exchange depends upon mutuality of gain. Trading is not a type of warfare in which gain by one party must be accompanied by loss for the other. the realisation that exchange ratios will be determined in terms of mutual gain in a two-party, two-commodity case, arises in the course of a discussion of goods which it is immoral or unlawful to exchange. Buridan poses the question: 'Because Socrates gave his wife willingly and with her consent to Plato to commit adultery in exchange for ten books, which one of them suffered a loss and which one gained?' He replies that: 'both suffered injury as far as their soul was concerned . . . [but] with regard to the external good, each gained since he has more than he needs, . . .' He continues: '. . . it may be said that the loss to one person can sometimes be equalled by the loss to another and the gain to one by the gain to another. As [happens] if each of them receives the wife of the other, all circumstances being equal, or if each kills the other or each cuts off the arm of the other. But a gain cannot be equalled with a loss even in voluntary exchange . . .'

When Buridan moves on to consider 'human need' as the measure of exchangeable things (question 15), his analysis displays a more explicit grasp of the principle of diminishing utility than is evident with Aristotle. Further, he is clear that price is determined by effective demand, and he also seems

[8] On this point, consult J. A. Schumpeter, *History of Economic Analysis* (N.Y., Oxford University Press, 1959) p. 922.

acquainted with the existence of consumer surplus, a fact
first brought to the attention of modern economists by
another Frenchman, the engineer Jules Dupuit, writing in the
mid-nineteenth century.[9] Some of Buridan's remarks, too,
point to the existence of producer surplus. In addition, he is
at one with W. S. Jevons that alterations in supplies of goods
relative to demand for them will affect prices through
changes in the degree of utility that consumers bestow on
units of the goods concerned.

Buridan expresses these novel insights, as follows:

> Therefore the filling of human need is the true measure
> of exchangeable things. But the filling is of greater value
> insofar as it fills a greater need, e.g., the greater the
> capacity and the emptiness of a jar, so much the more
> wine is needed to fill it ... Likewise, it is proved by this
> fact that we see that at the time when there is a deficiency
> of wine, since we need it more it becomes dearer.
> Similarly, wine is dearer where it does not grow than
> where it grows because there is a greater need for it
> there ...

Noting that there is a contrast in degree of need between rich
and poor, Buridan goes on to grant some logic to the
contention that 'a poor man would have to buy flour at a
greater price than a rich man.' Yet, this is not the case, in
reality, since price determination is a social process. In fact,
any surplus that might be ascribed to a poor man buying at
market price is matched by the greater cost, measured in
terms of physical labour expended, of any item he purchases.
Buridan argues:

> ... the need of one man or another does not measure the
> value of exchangeable goods but the common need of
> those people who can make exchanges among themselves.
> Actually, it must be said that a poor man, with regard to
> those things of which he has a surplus, buys what he needs
> at a greater price than does the rich man because he gives
> more of his bodily labour for one measure of wheat than a

[9] Cf., Emil Kauder, *A History of Marginal Utility Theory* (Princeton, Princeton
University Press, 1965) pp. 18–19.

rich man does for twenty; but, he does not give more money because he needs that thing, e.g., wheat, for he needs all exterior goods.

It would appear that Buridan is prepared to employ labour commanded as a measure of the subjective supply-price of a commodity. However, neither labour commanded nor labour embodied figure in his analysis of the determination of objective, market prices.

In question 17, Buridan applies his general theory of value to money, considered as the measure of exchangeable things. Arguing against Aristotle's position that money is merely a creature of the law, and against the feudal inference from this that the prince can set the value of money at will, Buridan contends that 'the value of money must be measured by human need.'

> When the value of the money is measured according to its relationship to human need, all exchangeable goods can be valued proportionately to money; according as they [exchangeable goods] are proportionate to human need, so they will be proportionate to money, itself proportionate to human need.

For Buridan, the common measure of commodity-value is itself a commodity.[10]

Another nominalist, Henry of Hesse (Henrich von Langenstein) (1325—97), was influenced considerably by Buridan's treatment of exchange value. Langenstein, who taught at both Paris and Vienna, argues that a just price is one which establishes 'a near equality of goods in proportion to the measure of their market or usual or customary value. This measure, however, which is to be roughly considered, is a value as great as the quantity of human need.'[11] The just

---

[10] Buridan's revolutionary monetary analysis is discussed above in Chapter 7. There, it is pointed out that he is the key figure promoting the doctrine of monetary metallism and launching the catalogue of the desirable qualities of money (portability, durability, etc.) that was to be repeated by countless writers on money in later centuries. The vast majority of these failed to improve on Buridan's 'Question Seventeen'.

[11] Langenstein, *Tractatus de contractibus*, Part I, C.5, in J. Gerson, *Opera omnia*, IV (Cologne, 1484—5), fol. 187.

price then, put simply, is the outcome of internal calculations by individuals concerning their wants. Those calculations will be affected by the relative abundance and scarcity of the goods concerned, and market prices will also tend to reflect the abundance or scarcity of potential buyers.

For the purpose of achieving exchange justice in practice, however, Langenstein advocates establishment of the terms of trade by local authorities. Further, he argues, that in cases where those authorities have not exercised their jurisdiction with regard to a price, the supplier of the relevant commodity may only demand that price which permits him to maintain his customary social position or status in the community. If the supplier demands more by way of net income from any transaction out of a desire to enhance his wealth and status, he is guilty of sin.[12]

This attempt by Langenstein to relate just price to net income can be recognised as an attempt to fill a definite gap in the structure of scholastic economics, a gap that was to continue to inhibit their penetration of economic issues. As we saw in Chapter 6, St Thomas had distinguished between distributive and commutative justice, and had associated economic analysis almost entirely with the latter. The theory of pricing was not linked to a theory of distribution, a procedure on which, centuries later, Adam Smith's delineation of economics as a supposedly 'independent' discipline was to depend. However, Langenstein endeavours to bridge the existing gap with the contention that the structure of prices should reflect the existing pattern of income distribution in the community.

Langenstein seems truer to Aristotle than is Aquinas. By his adoption of a static social ideal and emphasis on the relevance of social status to price determination, the nominalist may be regarded as the more faithful disciple of the message of the Greek philosopher. Nevertheless, in his reasoning concerning the sinfulness of certain social aspirations, he is at one with St Thomas. According to Aquinas the sin of covetousness was involved in seeking to accumulate wealth with a view to improving one's status in the community, and on this point, the theologian was later

[12] Op. cit., Part I, C.12, fol. 191.

roundly criticised by his leading, orthodox expositor, Cardinal Cajetan.[13] What later was seen as an aberration in Aquinas' thought by his own followers was used by a nominalist to bring the scholastic treatment of pricing and distribution together. Critics of the attempts at co-ordinated income and price policies in the mid and later twentieth century can draw support from the mainstream Thomistic tradition. Advocates of such measures can look to the nominalists and to some extent, to Aristotle.

The fifteenth century

Langenstein's view that maintenance of status in a society, statically conceived, was relevant to price determination, received considerable attention from commentators in the late nineteenth and early twentieth centuries. There was a widespread impression that his was *the* scholastic view. Such an interpretation was convenient for historians who followed Max Weber in claiming there was an intimate link between the rise of the capitalist dynamic in Europe and Protestantism. It also suited Catholic social theorists in their reaction against the effects on urban proletariats of a regime of *laissez faire* applied simultaneously to commodity and labour markets. In England, where medievalism had undergone a revival at the hands of John Ruskin and William Morris (and the virtues of the guild form of organisation by a variety of leading thinkers, including G. K. Chesterton, Hilaire Belloc and G. D. H. Cole), the ideas of Langenstein seemed most compatible with the idealised version of supposedly pre-capitalist Europe that was believed to have existed. Yet in the fifteenth century, let alone in the thirteenth and fourteenth, it is doubtful if those ideas were dominant in scholastic thought.[14]

---

[13] Cajetan, *Commentarium in summam theologicam S. Thomae Aquinatis*, II—II, qu. 118, art. 1.

[14] The most consistent and convincing opponent of the proposition that Langenstein's is *the* Scholastic view on the just price has been Raymond de Roover. He writes: 'Contrary to a widespread belief they [the schoolmen] certainly did not rely on the price system to maintain the social hierarchy. As a matter of fact, small masters operating under conditions of competition were not likely to accumulate great wealth. Social status in the Middle Ages depended chiefly on inequality in the distribution of property, mainly land, and the levying of dues (feudal payments or tithes) for the benefit of the ruling classes. There was one exception: in Italy the merchants and bankers outrivalled the feudal nobility.' R. de Roover, 'The Concept of the Just Price: Theory and Economic Policy', *Journal of Economic History*, Vol. 18 (Dec 1958) p. 434.

Among those who adopted approaches similar to that of Langenstein were Matthew of Cracow (c.1335–1410), professor of theology at Prague, and later rector at Heidelberg and archbishop of Worms, and Jean de Gerson (1363–1429), the French mystic who was chancellor of the University of Paris. According to Gerson, for example, it is usually immoral for a merchant to earn a substantial profit over and above a return which compensates him for the labour, expenses, and risks involved in supplying a market.[15] Again, since the legal authorities are in a better position to make a judgement on prices than is any private individual, it is desirable, Gerson claims, to bring all goods within the framework of a system of price fixation.[16]

Some influence stemming from the nominalists is discernible in the treatise on the contracts of merchants by the German Dominican, John Nider (1380–1438). This is combined with views that are attributable to St Thomas, and with a strong element of the reasoning of Duns Scotus.[17] Nider does not manage to bring these disparate strands together into a convincing synthesis; such an achievement would have placed him in the front rank of economists of any age. Nevertheless, his is an interesting failure, indicative of the general strengths and weaknesses of the scholastic analysis at that stage.

Nider begins by justifying profit-taking by merchants, in principle. Major emphasis is placed on the fact that the business of commodity exchange requires market knowledge, and the merchant must exercise 'industry, diligence, or providence' in obtaining the relevant information.[18] But then, Nider warns that 'a merchant ought to receive with caution a profit reasonably proportioned to the nobility,

[15] J. Gerson, *Regulae morales*, n.79.

[16] J. Gerson, *De contractibus*, consid. 19.

[17] One point at which the influence of Scotus seems most marked is in the fifth chapter of *On the Contracts of Merchants*, where Nider considers 'the cause and origin of all transfers of ownership in temporal matters'. Emerging here is a social contract theory of political authority, based on Scotus, and similar to that of John of Paris, as noted in Chapter 6 above. One thinker who made influential use of Scotus' argument in later centuries was John Locke in his essays on government against Sir Robert Filmer.

[18] J. Nider, *On the Contracts of Merchants*, trans. C. H. Reeves (Norman, Oklahoma, University of Oklahoma Press, 1966) p. 17.

seriousness, and usefulness of the care, exertions, industry, and costs which he undertakes, as well as with thought to the size, number, and value of the services which he performs for men.'[19] He goes on: 'I say "in proportion to the nobility," because granted that the exertion of a businessman bringing his wares to market is as great as that of a soldier defending his country, nevertheless, the work of the soldier, other things being equal, is nobler than that of the businessman because it is directed toward a nobler end.'[20]

Here then, it is suggested that where two types of service are equally useful, that which has the 'nobler end' should receive the greater financial return. It is the social status of the work done rather than the social status of the person doing the work, which Nider is putting forward as a determinant. However, provided one is reasoning in terms that identify the person by his type of work, his position is similar to that of Langenstein.

From the relevance of social status, Nider moves on to the impact of objective usefulness (St Thomas Aquinas) and then cost of production (Duns Scotus), on the achievement of justice in exchange. He concludes his opening chapter with an attack on those who wish to enjoy a level of consumption which is beyond that warranted by their expenditures of labour and capital in the service of the community at large. 'If everyone would be willing to live in accordance with his status and take profit according to his merit,' he claims, 'everything would be so much the better.'[21]

When Nider turns from discussion of the general conditions for the establishment of exchange justice in his first chapter, to the specific conditions for the determination of just price in Chapter 2, he places maximum emphasis on the role of subjective utility. Social status disappears altogether, and cost of production is only a subsidiary consideration. He

---

[19] Op. cit., p. 19.
[20] Loc. cit.
[21] Op. cit., p. 20. Presumably, those of lower status but greater merit will be obliged to refrain from using their profits to achieve a level of consumption expenditure that is too grand for them. Saving and alms-giving, appropriate responses to the problem, are not mentioned by Nider. Neither does he link the above dictum concerning consumption expenditure and profit income explicitly to the question of market price levels.

distinguishes between objective utility, i.e. the inherent properties of a good for use by men, and subjective utility, i.e. the status of a good 'in the estimation of men'. It is the latter which is decisive in determining just market price. Like William Stanley Jevons some 450 years later, Nider suggests that a variation in the supply of a commodity in relation to demand will change its exchange value by altering the degree of utility ascribed to a unit of it. This may mean that at times, goods are sold below the value commensurate with the skill that has been exercised in their production. Nider adds that he assumes the absense of fraud in the market or extreme need on the part of buyers. His position is stated, as follows:

> Moreover, by as much as a greater number of men have need of a commodity and desire to possess it, whereas the available supply of it is less, by so much is it more likely to be estimated and sold at a higher price.
>
> Now to sell a thing according to the common estimation by men is a necessary and safe procedure. One necessary in fact, and goods should be thus sold, even if by their nature or the skill of artificers the goods are known to be worth more ... Because of this, the laws say that a thing is worth as much as it can be sold for, that is, according to how purchasers can be got to buy when at liberty and by free choice, and assuming that the purchasers are not fools, pinched, or deceived.[22]

Later, Nider observes that the just price can be affected by the manner of sale of goods. A higher price is warranted for credit as against cash sales, and he cites Astesanus and Alexander Lombard in support of this contention.[23]

For the most part, then, Nider's discussion of price is in the subjective utility tradition. 'The proper value of a thing', he sums up, 'depends upon the ways buyers or sellers may think about prices.' Yet, where there is no price established by common estimation, a seller may adopt a value-added approach in arriving at the right price to ask. He can consider his costs plus 'how far in good faith the product can be

[22] Op. cit., pp. 25—6.
[23] Op. cit., pp. 29—30.

improved, and whether the improvement is actual or esti-
mated, . . .'[24]

There is very little to suggest any labour theory of value in
Nider's discussion of price determination. However, as in the
case of St Thomas and his disciple John of Paris which was
considered in Chapter 6, there are broad hints of its future
development when one examines Nider's statements on
property together with his views on entitlement to income.
As to property, it is claimed that all transfers of it now are
sanctioned by 'public authority or by the private authority of
the owner himself who is in immediate possession.'[25] Apart
from titles stemming from original occupation, the bases of
that private authority are not directly explored by Nider, but
earlier in the treatise he makes in quite clear that one type of
title arises out of the expenditure of labour (using the term in
its broader, non-materialistic sense).

At the outset of the treatise, we have seen, Nider justifies
merchant's profits on the grounds of the exertions he must
make to acquire the knowledge which is necessary for orderly
marketing. Subsequently, business incomes, including those
of bankers, are seen as justified, 'because of the expenses,
exertions, cares, qualities of industry, risks, and other
reasonable engagements or burdens which they undergo in
bringing together things useful to men or in preserving or
setting out necessary things in the common market place, and
because they remain [there] in order that anyone in need
may promptly have such goods.'[26] From this, Nider proceeds
to quote St Paul the Apostle to the effect that 'each will
receive his reward according to his own work,' and to justify

[24] Op. cit., p. 37. It is also stated (p. 33) that where a price has been fixed by
statute, this must take precedence over any private contractual arrangement.
[25] Op. cit., pp. 71—2.
[26] Op. cit., pp. 30—1. Nider's list of the functions accounting for entrepreneurial
income is very similar to that supplied by Alfred Marshall in his explanation of
what he calls 'the earnings of undertaking or management'. Marshall includes
risks, the bringing together of things, the study of market forces, and the need to
exercise judgement. See, e.g., A. Marshall, *Elements of Economics of Industry*
(Macmillan, London, 1919) pp. 162—4. Also, it should be remarked that Nider's
suggestion that merchants should be rewarded 'because they remain' in the
market implies he perceived that there was an opportunity-cost involved in so
doing. Explicit recognition of opportunity-cost as the basis for normal profit was
to come later in the analysis of Cardinal Lugo (see Chapter 9).

wage income on the ground of work-effort.[27] Finally he
states that where a man 'honestly and usefully serves the
commonwealth . . . it is fitting that he live by his labor. Not
only this, but all individuals whosoever, are entitled justly to
sell their industry and care.'[28] Sentiments such as these
concerning income and the possession of its fruits provided a
fertile ground for the continuance of a tradition from which
a labour theory of value could emerge.

Nider's more prominent Italian contemporary St Bernardine of Siena (1380–1438) adopts a position on value and
price which is very similar to that of the German Dominican.
Building on the value analysis of Pierre Olivi, with its
emphasis on the role of subjective utility (*complacibilitas*),
Bernardine states that the just price is 'the one which
happens to prevail at a given time according to the estimation
of the market, that is, what the commodities for sale are then
commonly worth in a certain place.'[29] Elsewhere, he writes
that 'the price of goods and services is set for the common
good with due consideration to the common valuation or
estimation made collectively by the community of citizens.'[30] Like Nider, he allows that where there is no price
established by the market for a particular commodity, a seller
may look to his costs of supplying the market in arriving at a
just price for it. Again, where there is a market price, this
must be charged, even if selling at that figure involves the
merchant in loss.[31]

Citing Duns Scotus, Bernardine observes that the just
price, in any particular instance, cannot be distinguished as a
unique magnitude but rather, is represented by a range of
possibilities. This range will be influenced by the relative
scarcity or abundance of the goods concerned.[32] Cost of

[27] J. Nider, op. cit., p. 31.
[28] Op. cit., p. 32.
[29] *De Evangelio aerterno*, Sermo 33, art. 2, cap. 7.
[30] Op. cit., Sermo 35, art. 2, cap. 2.
[31] Raymond de Roover notes that Bernardine refers to the earlier writers,
St Raymund of Pennaforte (1180–1275) and Hostiensis of Susa (d. 1271), in
support of this position. Both of these authorities were distinguished canonists.
See R. de Roover, *San Bernardino of Siena and Sant' Antonino of Florence*
(Boston, Baker Library, 1967) p. 22.
[32] St Bernardine, op. cit., *Sermo* 35, art. 1, cap. 1.

production, including allowances for returns to skill employed and risk incurred, will have an impact on market price through its effect on supply. Commodities transported over long distances, for example, are likely to be more expensive to purchase than locally produced goods.[33] Unlike Nider, St Bernardine does not suggest directly that variations in supply relative to demand cause changes in price because of the resultant alterations 'in the estimation of men' concerning the goods in question.

St Bernardine's treatment of price and value was incorporated by St Antonine of Florence in his own authoritative writings on economic morality. Both of these authors then, put the greatest stress on the free interplay of market forces, in the absence of private monopoly, as the foundation for justice in exchange. The vast majority of lesser schoolmen of the period may have subscribed to this general position, although there seems to have been a few who dissented. For example, there was John Consobrinus (d. 1486). A Portuguese scholar, he taught for a time at Oxford, and in 1494 a short work of his on commutative justice was published in Paris. In the manner of Duns Scotus, he put greater emphasis on cost of production as the determinant of just price than was allowed by the majority position. Indicative of Consobrinus' general stance is his broad statement that 'every lucrative contract which does not depend on a man's industry or diligence or on his own property is illicit.'[34] On this view, the kind of windfall gains and losses which free market arrangements permit could not be tolerated by the moralist, unless the terms 'industry or diligence' were stretched to include the ability to anticipate windfalls. Justice in exchange can be achieved only where relative prices bear a direct relationship to relative effort and employment of 'property' in supplying a market.

The sixteenth century
The idea that the just price was the outcome of the operation of competitive market forces received further authoritative

---

[33] Op. cit., Sermo 35, art. 2, cap. 2.
[34] J. Consobrinus, *De justitia commutativa*, Part II, Ch. 6. The immediate context evoking this generalisation is a discussion of the morality of insurance.

support in the economic analyses of Thomas de Vio, Cardinal Cajetan (1465–1524). As was seen in Chapter 7, the idea was extended by him to embrace the buying and selling of foreign currencies, and even expectations concerning the future movements of exchange rates were given a definite role in determining the legitimate current price. It is not surprising then, that in his comments on St Thomas, he claims his predecessor's view to be that a just price is 'one, which at a given time, can be obtained from the buyers, assuming common knowledge and in the absence of all fraud and coercion.'[35] That price will fluctuate in accord with changing conditions of demand and supply.

Cajetan's comments are also significant for their attempt to remove an element in Aquinas' reasoning which appeared to lend weight to Langenstein's contention that a seller could only demand that price for his wares which ensured maintenance of his customary social status. St Thomas is criticised for holding that any attempt to accumulate wealth with a view to better one's status, involves the sin of covetousness. According to Cajetan, it is quite legitimate for persons of outstanding ability who have achieved much, to move up to a level in society which matches their attainments.[36] The evident ease with which Cajetan contemplates the phenomenon of social mobility is indicative of the presence of a new climate in scholastic social thought. In particular, it is a harbinger of the more extensive economic liberalism that was to manifest itself especially in the writings of a number of leading Spanish scholastics.

Before that liberalism could emerge in full force, however, a champion of economic conservatism arose in the ranks of the Dominicans, in the shape of Dominic de Soto (1494–1560). A most distinguished Spanish academic, de Soto studied at Alcalá de Henares and in Paris before his appointment as a professor of theology at the University of Salamanca. His career affords an outstanding example of one of the then current avenues of social mobility, since he rose from a lowly status by birth to become the representative of

---

[35] Cajetan, Op. cit., II–II, qu. 77, art. 1.
[36] Op. cit., II–II, qu. 118, art. 1.

Charles V at the Council of Trent and later confessor to the
Emperor. Nevertheless, he turned the force of his considerable intellect to a rebuttal of his fellow Dominican, Cajetan,
on many aspects of the latter's theories concerning money,
interest, and banking. He was also an advocate of price
determination by statute.

On the question of the just price, de Soto states that in
determining its correct level, attention must be paid to the
state of demand and supply, 'the labour, trouble and risk'
involved in the transaction, and whether or not 'the exchange
is for better or worse, to the advantage or disadvantage of the
vendor.' He then goes on:

> The just price of an article is two-fold: the legal and the
> natural price. The legal price is always indivisible; but the
> natural or discretionary price is, broadly speaking, divis-
> ible. The just legal price is that which is fixed by the
> prince. The discretionary or natural price is that which is
> current when prices are not legally controlled ... To
> understand this Conclusion and to judge its validity, and to
> see why it is necessary for prices to be controlled, we must
> realize that the matter is a primary concern of the republic
> and its governors, who, in spite of the arguments repeated
> above, ought really to fix the price of every article.[37]

De Soto realises that it is not practicable, however much
desirable, to establish a regime in which every price is
centrally determined. Yet he is not prepared to leave the
fixation of natural price, in which there is some latitude, i.e.
divisibility, to merchants working on a cost-plus basis. De
Soto is no friend of any doctrine of 'enlightened self-
interest'. Rather, natural price is to be set 'by the opinion of
prudent and fair-minded men', in the light of prevailing
market conditions in a given area. Such men will be those
whose 'own interests are not concerned' in the transactions
to take place. He adds, but does not expand on, the
interesting observation that 'a vendor is not dealing only with
his own property, but with something which belongs jointly

---

[37] Dominic de Soto, *De Justitia et jure*, Book VI, qu. 2, art. 3.

to himself and the purchaser. And of this he is not a legitimate judge.'[38]

In the course of the above discussion of price determination, de Soto observes that 'the price of goods is not determined by their nature but by the measure in which they serve the needs of mankind . . . If no one needed the goods or labour of his fellows, men would cease to exchange their products. We have to admit, then, that want is the basis of price.'[39] This observation would seem to commit the writer to a utility theory of value in the orthodox Aristotelian–Thomistic tradition. However, when one turns to de Soto's writings on usury and on *lucrum cessans* as a basis for interest payment, he appears to adopt a labour theory.[40] He is most conservative in allowing *lucrum cessans* only in circumstances where the lender of money has been physically prevented from exercising his labour, i.e., in cases of delay in repayment, theft, or forced lending, where some force external to the person concerned has deprived him from working with his money.

For de Soto, money by itself can never be a title to gain, and it is only labour which can justify profit on an investment. This, as Professor Noonan states, is 'a severe theory, which perhaps should have been held by the medieval authors and best explains some of their argumentation on the usury prohibition, but which, in fact, had never been consistently supported by them.'[41] Noonan's analysis of de Soto's position and its historical roots is most valuable in that it points to a fundamental dichotomy persisting in the economics of the medieval scholastics. Utility was the determinant of price, yet personal effort was the title to income or gain. At the policy level, there was the problem that a structure of prices based on relative utilities would not yield an income structure compatible with relative degrees of effort.

The dichotomy was heightened by the practice of allowing that utility was a subjective property arising out of an

[38] Loc. cit.
[39] Loc. cit.
[40] Cf., J. T. Noonan, op. cit., p. 260.
[41] Op. cit., p. 256.

internal, preferential calculus. Work-effort, on the other hand, tended to be treated as an objective property. On the question of interest payment, for example, disutility experienced by an individual because of loss of liquidity in lending, or through worry concerning risk of loss when his funds were transferred into other hands, was not seen as relevant to issues of economic justice. The issues here concerned income, and only the frustration of the opportunity to work, objectively demonstrated, gave a basis for compensatory payment. On the question of commodity pricing however, subjective experience as expressed through market consensus, was relevant. Only when it began to be realised that money might be treated as a commodity and that there were markets in money, could the dichotomy between interest and price theory begin to be resolved. The more general problem of incompatibility between price and income structures, given certain welfare criteria, is still with us today.

In Chapter 7, it was shown how the Spanish schoolmen, after de Soto, made considerable progress in the analysis of money, interest and banking. They also contributed to the theory of commodity pricing. Prominent among the contributors was the contemporary critic of de Soto, Martin de Azpilcueta Navarro (Navarrus) (1493—1586).

Navarrus was an opponent of a system of statutory price fixation, arguing that when goods were abundant it was quite unnecessary, and that when they were scarce the system might do the welfare of the community more harm than good. His most important analytical work was a clear statement of the quantity theory of money which, it was suggested in the previous chapter, opened up the possibility of a more comprehensive theory of price formation. A new emphasis was lent to the operation of supply determinants, and the idea of 'a market' was brought into sharper focus.

The statements of Navarrus and his successors are firmly in the subjective utility tradition. For example, Diego De Covarrubias Y Levia (1512—77), a pupil of Navarrus who later became President of the Council of Castile, writes: 'The value of an article does not depend on its essential nature but on the estimation of men, even if that estimation be foolish. Thus, in the Indies wheat is dearer than in Spain because men esteem it more highly, though the nature of the wheat is the same in both places.'⁴²

Covarrubias continues that cost of production is not to be adopted as the criterion for assessment of a just price.

After Navarrus, the most significant figure to emerge in the Spanish school of scholastic economists was Luis Molina (1536–1600). A Jesuit theologian from Castile, he published a massive work, *De Justitia et Jure*, of which the second section on the subject of commutative justice contains very extensive discussions of economic issues. These discussions published in 1597 are the most important immediate precursors of those of Leonard Lessius which appeared some eight years later.

In Molina's writings the current of economic liberalism runs high. 'The price of goods', he writes, 'is not to be gauged by .the gains of merchants or their losses but from the common appraisal of them in the place where they are sold in view of all the current circumstances. And this is true whether through ill-luck or lack of skilful dealing they gain little or even suffer loss or with good luck and energetic trading they make a great gain.'⁴³ Among 'the current circumstances', Molina includes a wide range of supply and demand determinants that extend even to the manner in which goods are sold. If, for example, goods are supplied at retail in small quantities they will command a higher unit price than in bulk.⁴⁴

Duns Scotus and another British theologian John Major (1478–1548) who followed Scotus, are criticised for their suggestion that the just price of merchandise is set with reference to cost of production.⁴⁵ However, Molina subse-

---

⁴² Covarrubias, *Variarum ex pontifico, regio et casesareo jure resolutionum*, IV, vol. 2, book 2, ch. 3. Comparable passages from the works of less prominent Spanish authors at this time are also given in Marjorie Grice-Hutchinson, *The School of Salamanca* (Oxford, Clarendon Press, 1952). Of particular interest are texts from Saravia De La Calle (pub. 1544) and Francisco Garcia (pub. 1583).

⁴³ Molina, *De justitia et jure*, Vol. II, disp. 348, para. 8. It is significant that in this same disputation, paragraph 4, Molina uses the term 'competition' (*concurrentium*) to refer to market forces influencing price. This is possibly the first instance of the term's use in this way by a Scholastic writer.

⁴⁴ Op. cit., disp. 348, para. 7. Selling for credit as against cash will also influence the just price. See disp. 357, paras 3 and 4.

⁴⁵ Op. cit., disp. 348, para. 8.

quently allows that where it is necessary for the public authorities to set up a monopoly outlet for sales of a particular commodity, there should be recourse to costs as one of the means of gauging the appropriate price to be asked. But Molina is not favourably disposed to interference with market mechanisms. For example, in an attack on a policy of fixed exchange rates, he writes:

> When, therefore, the republic fixes the value of larger coins in terms of those of smaller denominations, this is only to facilitate the changing of money in one and the same place, the purchase of goods, and the payment of their price. But the republic never intended to fix this second kind of value when money is exchanged for money in another place. This value is inconstant, and yet it is just, even though the tale of the money is fixed by law. To control it would do a great deal of harm to the republic, because such a course would bring about a shortage of necessary goods. The practice has always been, and rightly, for the value of money in exchange to be left to vary freely; . . . [46]

Harm is also caused by instances of injudicious domestic pricing regulations, particularly in the establishment of ceiling prices for agricultural commodities. Molina complains that: 'Very many of those who own grain are farmers to whom it sometimes happens in a year of bad crops, that when account is taken of all the outlays they have made and the labour and industry they have applied, a measure of grain stands at a far greater price than that at which it is directed to be sold. Equity in no way allows this.'[47]

It can be noted that here, despite his criticism of Scotus and Major, Molina employs cost of production as a criterion for judging equity.

That the relevance of cost as a point of reference for the judgement of economic values had not been completely submerged by the emphasis of the Spanish doctors on utility, is strikingly portrayed in a discourse published not long after

[46] *Disputationes de Contractibus* (Venice, 1601) quoted in M. Grice-Hutchinson, op. cit., p. 115.
[47] *De justitia et jure*, Vol. II, disp. 364, para. 3.

Molina's treatise had appeared. The work is *Discurso sobre el precio del trigo* (1605) by a little-known theologian, Pedro de Valencia.[48] The writer advocates the establishment by the government of a fixed price for corn, and considers the problem of the level at which it is to be set.

Pedro argues that to set a price in monetary terms is useless: 'The value and estimation of money and of the metals from which it is made is diverse and variable in different provinces, occasions, and times, so that by considering the price of money we cannot set upon corn a price that will be universally just and appropriate to all times and places.'[49] It is equally useless to employ another commodity as the measure of price: 'Moreover, to compare the value of other common articles with that of corn (such as saying that a "fanega" of corn ought to be worth a certain quantity of wine or oil) will prove equally useless for our purpose, because we should simply be measuring one unknown thing by another, and the value and quality of such articles varies from year to year and from place to place.'[50] In the face of these difficulties, Pedro has recourse to the relationship of labour expenditure to food requirement per unit of time. He writes:

> God and all reason require that men shall earn their bread by their toil, that this may be sufficient to support them in life, and that those who will not work, neither shall they eat. Setting all else aside, we should consider only how many working days ought in justice to be given for a measure of corn, so that the labourer may support himself, however poorly and roughly, and may eat, drink, and

---

[48] The work was reprinted in *Pedro de Valencia, Escritas sociales* (Biblioteca de clasicos sociales espanoles, Madrid, 1945), and an extract is given in English translation by M. Grice-Hutchinson, op. cit., pp. 116—19.

[49] Op. cit., p. 117.

[50] Loc. cit. In the course of this argument the writer touches on the existence of the 'Paradox of Value': 'If we measure the price of bread by the benefit and utility it brings, and by its own intrinsic value, we shall find that a loaf is worth more than all the gold and diamonds in the world. Yet in this respect air, water, and light are still more valuable, and God willed that these three things should cost us nothing . . .' When Galileo, John Law, and then Adam Smith contrasted water and diamonds in their writings, they were referring to a dichotomy that was quite familiar to schoolmen.

clothe himself, keep a roof over his head, marry and beget children and support them while they are little, and not have to work every day, because sometimes there will be no work for him, and because there are days of tempest, and of sickness, and of rejoicing. It seems that even if he must go to the workhouse or beg in his old age, a man cannot live unless he can earn a 'fanega' of corn in not more than five or six working days, which at present in this province are worth 14 or 15 'reales'.[51]

This line of reasoning was to become increasingly significant in the economic thought of later decades. For example, over sixty years later the Jesuit-educated Englishman Sir William Petty (1628-87) was to make use of it in his celebrated discussion of value. He attributed the source of value to the exploitation of land by the expenditure of labour, putting the greater emphasis on the effect of the latter. When he came to the problem of the best measure of value, he employed the concept of a day's food. The value of a day's labour is the quantity of food which can be produced when labour is expended in co-operation with the resources of the soil. The difficulty that prices are expressed in money terms is met with the contention that the quantity of precious metal which represents one day's food is as much as can be produced by the same amount of labour as produced the day's food.[52]

Not only Petty, but a number of other significant economists of the era of Mercantilism show marked traces in their work of ideas already current in later scholastic debate. Detailing of the channels of influence linking one set of writers with the other is an area of research in which much work remains to be done.

[51] Op. cit., p. 118.
[52] On Petty's theory of value consult, Hannah R. Sewall, *The Theory of Value Before Adam Smith* (N.Y., American Economic Association, 1901) pp. 70—3.

9 Venerable Leonard Lessius

The high point of the development of Scholastic economic analysis was reached at about the turn of the sixteenth century. During the next 100 years, much of the impetus it had accumulated in the hands of Italian theologians in the fifteenth and Spanish moralists in the following century, was lost. Before the onset of the era of decline, however, scholastic economics was brought to a new pitch in the writings of the Belgian Jesuit, Leonard Lessius (de Leys) (1554—1623). Later contributors of some note were Juan de Lugo (1583—1660) and Giambattista de Luca (1613—83). The seventh and eighth volumes of Cardinal Lugo's *Disputationes scholasticae et morales* (Lyons 1642, repub. Paris 1893), for example, contain comprehensive treatments of analytical issues of traditional concern for the schoolmen. Cardinal Luca's scholarly *Theatrum veritatis et justitiae* (Rome, 1669—81) and his shorter *Il dottor volgare* (Rome 1673) are also wide-ranging in their examination of economic questions.

The latter writers were concerned mainly with orderly and systematic presentation of the thought of their forebears. Lessius too displays an encyclopaedic command of earlier economic thought, but in addition he is an innovator of the first rank. For example, of one particular aspect of his work, his treatment of usury doctrine, Professor Noonan states: 'He is the theologian whose views on usury most decidedly mark the arrival of a new era. More than any predecessor he would probably have felt completely at ease in the modern financial world. Careful, perceptive, boldly logical, modest, and sure of himself, Lessius is a master of scholastic economic analysis.'[1]

---

[1] J. T. Noonan, *The Scholastic Analysis of Usury* (Cambridge, Mass., Harvard University Press, 1957) p. 222. For a similar assessment by another modern scholar see B. W. Dempsey, *Interest and Usury* (Washington, American Council on Public Affairs, 1943) pp. 122—4. These assessments may be contrasted with that of Raymond de Roover who asserts that Lessius 'made two minor contributions' to scholastic economic thought. See *International Encyclopedia of the Social Sciences*, Vol. 4 (1968) p. 435.

Lessius was born at Brecht near Antwerp. His parents originally planned a mercantile career for him, but after graduating from the University of Louvain at the age of seventeen, he entered the Jesuit order in 1572. From 1575 to 1581 he taught philosophy at the English college at Douai of which Cajetan had been the Cardinal Protector.[2] Then he left for two years study in Rome with Francisco Suarez (1548–1617), who is generally regarded as the most important thinker of the Jesuit Order.[3] Returning from Rome, Lessius took a chair at the University of Louvain in 1585 and quickly established a reputation for outstanding intellectual ability. 'Prince of Philosophers' and 'Oracle of the Low Countries' were two among the titles bestowed on him by admirers who included the eminent classicist Justus Lipsius.[4] At the age of forty-six, having suffered very poor health for most of his adult life, Lessius retired from teaching and spent his remaining years in research.

Lessius is best known among modern theologians for his work on such topics as grace, free will, and predestination. He also entered the political arena with an attack on the divine right theory of kingship as sponsored by James I of England.[5] His most important book was *Justitia et Jure* (1605), which was published throughout Europe in some forty separate editions. This work was notable especially for its analysis of contemporary commercial practice, and Lessius' opinions on the morality of various business arrangements exercised a substantial influence on the thinking of statesmen and church leaders. Some indication of the extent of that influence is provided by an early biographer. He writes: 'Albert the Pious, surely the wisest among sovereigns of Belgium of his time, along with his sword, always kept

---

[2] Navarrus' *Manuale sive Enchiridion* was used as the basis for staff-student seminar work at Douai. See Thomas F. Knox (ed.), *The First and Second Diaries of the English College, Douay* (London, Nutt, 1878) p. xlii.
[3] According to Reijo Wilenius, *The Social and Political Theory of Francisco Suarez* (Helsinki, Societas Philosophica Fennica, 1963), p. 70, Suarez's *Conselhos e Pareceres*, I, II, 1–2 (Coimbra, Acta Universitatis Conimbriginsis, 1948–52) embraces a wide range of topics of economic interest.
[4] See T. J. Campbell, introduction to Leonard Lessius, *The Names of God and Meditative Summaries of the Divine Perfections* (N.Y., The America Press, 1912) p. xii.
[5] His former teacher Suarez's own treatise on the subject, *Defenso Fidei* (1613), was publicly burnt in London on the King's orders.

Lessius' book on justice on the table before him as his most trusted counsellor when he held hearings, to show that his decisions were buttressed by the arms of Austria and the wisdom of Lessius.'[6]

According to a more recent commentator: 'Lessius' judgement on most serious scientific matters was sought by the most learned men of his age, Suarez, Vasquez, Molina and others. Paul V, Sixtus V, ... St Francis de Sales, ... St Charles Borromeo ... held him in highest regard.'[7]

Combining a full command of earlier scholastic authorities with a hitherto unprecedented grasp of market phenomena, Lessius provided fresh insights that challenged traditional economic doctrine in authoritative fashion. Lessius is, certainly, the foremost continuator of the Spanish school of economic thought. Further, he has claims for consideration as a major original contributor to the development of economic analysis. These claims are based mainly on the innovations contained in chapters 20 to 28 of the second book of *De Justitia et Jure*. Of these, the patrologist Joseph de Ghellinck wrote, 'The chapters on interest and other commercial subjects are epoch making in the treatment of those difficult questions.'[8] The framework of his discussion is given by the traditional forms of business contract, but these contracts are dealt with as they apply in contemporary circumstances. Particularly, the sophisticated financial centre of Antwerp is a constant reference point.

As Joseph Schumpeter has pointed out, the economic world which Lessius and his contemporaries analysed was one which 'so far as the fundamental categories of the capitalist economy are concerned, did not differ so very greatly from ours. There were money markets and speculators. There was the negotiable paper, big business, high finance. If those Schoolmen rose from the dead today, they would readily understand our world ...'[9] At the heart of contemporary

[6] Leonard Schoofs, *De Vita et Moribus R. P. Leonardi Lessii* (Paris, 1644) pp. 38–9.
[7] J. B. Ferreres, *Compendium Theologiae Moralis,* Vol. I (Barcelona, 1932) p. xxviii.
[8] Charles G. Herbermann and others (eds), *The Catholic Encyclopedia,* Vol. 9 (N.Y., Encyclopedia Press, 1910) p. 192.
[9] Introduction to B. W. Dempsey, op. cit., p. viii.

commercial activity stood Antwerp. During the sixteenth century, 'in the course of four decades Antwerp developed into a trading centre such as the world has never seen before or since; for never since has there been a market which concentrated to such a degree the trade of all the important commercial nations of the world.'[10] Money, bullion, and bills were traded with freedom in the markets of Antwerp, and its Bourse became the focal point for international speculators. Permanent agencies were established there by the kings of England, Portugal, Spain and the Netherlands to raise loans and arrange trading agreements. Large-scale lending took place by means of Ricorsa bills and bourse deposits, and the prices of bills together with the bourse rate of interest were determined as market prices subject to international speculative forces.[11] Commodity prices too were influenced by speculative dealing.

Writing against such a background, it is understandable that an analyst of Lessius' power, although steeped in the economic doctrines of St Thomas and his medieval successors, would arrive at insights which the latter could not attain. He adopts an analytical technique similar to that of his immediate Spanish predecessors, while avoiding their penchant for long-winded presentation. The conclusions of writers like Navarrus and Molina are used as points of departure for further extensions of their work, and for new directions of his own.

[10] Richard Ehrenberg, *Capital and Finance in the Age of the Renaissance* (London, 1928) p. 234. For details, see the outstanding study by Herman Van Der Wee, *The Growth of the Antwerp Market and the European Economy* (The Hague, Nijhoff, 1963).

[11] By this time a number of other centres throughout Europe were also linked in a network of speculative activity. Raymond de Roover states that 'One of the major developments of the sixteenth century was the rise of the fairs of Castile, Lyons, Frankfort-on-the-Main, and above all, Besançon, as international clearing centers. From 1579 on, the Besançon fairs, while keeping their name, were actually held in Piacenza, on the initiative of the Genoese bankers who monopolised the financial business of the Spanish crown.' The same writer notes that 'cambio con la ricorsa' was 'a device which involved drafts and redrafts going back and forth between Genoa or another banking place and the fairs of Besançon.' This device, comprising exchange and re-exchange at a rate of exchange set in advance, posed new analytical problems for the scholastic moralists. See, R. de Roover, 'Scholastic Economics: Survival and Lasting Influence from the Sixteenth Century to Adam Smith', *Quarterly Journal of Economics*, Vol. LXIX (May 1955) pp. 170–1, and J. T. Noonan, op. cit., pp. 331–2.

Among Lessius' contributions is an extension of the scope of *lucrum cessans*, involving further clarification of the distinctions to be drawn between various types of money balances. Further, there is recognition that the holders of balances derive a certain utility from possession of the money held. The emphasis is transferred from interest as a compensation for profit forgone to interest as a compensation for the sacrifice of liquidity. More important still is the new, unified treatment of money in its commodity, capital, and numeraire aspects. Underlying these innovations is a definite break with the medieval view of transfers of money for money as isolated exchanges between individuals. Such transfers occur in the context of a market where any buyer or seller can lawfully exchange at the just price established by concensus of the members of the market. Lessius specifies the range of determinants at work in that consensus and identifies the conditions necessary for a just price to emerge.

Lucrum cessans

In Chapter 20 of the second book of his *De Justitia et Jure*, Lessius takes up the question of the nature of usury and of *damnum emergens* (loss which occurs) as a title to monetary compensation. He then considers *lucrum cessans*. 'Loss which emerges and gain which ceases', he observes, 'are commonly called interest [*interesse*]'[12] Basic to the analysis is the idea that money in the hands of an individual businessman has a special, additional value for that person. He writes: 'Such money . . . in so far as it is subject to your industry in order to gain by it, is worth more to you than it is considered in itself; for it is, as it were, the fruitful seed of gain by industry [*semen fecundum lucri per industriam*] in which the gain itself is contained virtually as in a seed; and therefore, more may be asked for it than it is worth by and in itself.'[13]

Here, Lessius is referring to a scholastic tradition concerning money in balance which stretches back at least as far as Aquinas' writings on the subjects of compensation for delay

[12] *De Justitia et Jure,* II:20:10:68.
[13] Op. cit., II:20:11:80.

in repayment of a loan and restitution after theft. However, in the new financial circumstances of Lessius' day, his application of the idea involved is far more wide-ranging than that of St Thomas.

Lessius goes on, like the Spanish theologians, to allow that loans from certain of the balances held by businessmen can warrant application of *lucrum cessans.* He distinguishes between transactions, speculative, and precautionary balances, and cites Navarrus in support of the view that interest may be due on loans out of the first two of these even if the lender holds a precautionary reserve. Whether or not there are solid, objective grounds for the lender's retaining such a reserve is an irrelevant issue. It may be only *inani timore* (i.e. empty fear) which accounts for the retention, but still interest may be charged on funds forgone.[14] The lender's conception of his position is the relevant consideration.

The type of subjectivist approach which Lessius adopts here is quite consistent with his attitude to the determination of price in general in later chapters of his book. It should also be remarked that in this opening chapter on economic questions, he makes it clear that his analyses are based on the assumption that the persons of whom he writes are acting in accord with an internal calculus concerning commercial loss and gain. He is writing, he indicates, of the *negotiator diligens,* the careful businessman who is anxious to make the best of favourable opportunities.[15] Similarly, some years later, Cardinal Lugo affirms that his reasoning applies to the same diligent businessman who 'in his mind and intention' aims at 'gaining by every just title which he can'.[16] The actors in the economic world of Lessius and Lugo are at some remove from those of the medieval schoolmen, and a very long way from the ideal citizens of a *polis* according to Plato and Aristotle. Their actors are much closer to that abstraction 'economic man', whose egoistic calculations concerning maximisation were later to figure prominently in the reason-

[14] Op. cit., II:20:11:86, 87.
[15] Op. cit., II:20:12:103.
[16] J. de Lugo, *De Justitia et Jure,* disp. 25, para. 181.

ing of some economists.[17] This evident shift of emphasis
might be traced, in large measure, to changing concepts of
personality involved in the intellectual currents of the
Renaissance.

By adhering to the logic of his subjectivist reasoning on
loan contracts, Lessius goes beyond his Spanish predecessors
in finding scope for *lucrum cessans*. He allows that loans out
of speculative balances held not only for direct investment
but also for the purpose of lending, might command interest.
Profit is forgone in this latter case if the funds concerned
were previously employed in business or were intended for
such employment if there were no demand for loans.[18] By
taking this step, Lessius implies that, where there is an active
market for loanable funds, only money held against personal
consumption requirements or against incalculable contin-
gencies is not likely to be subject to the cost of forgone
profit when loaned.

Carentia pecuniae

Although some balances may not involve the sacrifice of
potential profit when depleted by lending, all loans, according to Lessius, involve the lender in the sacrifice of a degree
of liquidity. Within certain institutional frameworks for
financial and trading operations, loss of liquidity provides a
new title to interest, *carentia pecuniae* (i.e. lack of money).

---

[17] This is not to suggest that the Renaissance scholastics would have subscribed to
the concept of 'economic man' if they had encountered it in its naked form.
Rather, it is likely that their reaction would have been similar to that of Alfred
Marshall's. They would be at one with his sentiment, if not his Victorian
phraseology, when he writes: 'In all this economists deal with man as he is: not
with an abstract or "economic" man; but a man of flesh and blood; one who
shapes his business life to a great extent with reference to egoistic motives; but
also one who is not above the frailties of vanity or recklessness, and not below the
delight of doing his work well for its own sake; who is not below the delight of
sacrificing himself for the good of his family, his neighbours or his country, nor
below the love of a virtuous life for its own sake.' A. Marshall, *Elements of
Economics of Industry* (London, Macmillan, 1919) p. 26.
[18] L. Lessius, op. cit., II:20:11:89 et seq. Here, J. T. Noonan, (op cit., p. 263)
points out 'how far Lessius' general argument goes to justify all professional
lenders. No major authority before had ever allowed "lucrum cessans" to any but
businessmen or investors actively planning to use their money in commerce or
agriculture. Here, for the first time, the title is granted to men whose main
business would be moneylending. It is a momentous, if logical, step.'

In a business community such as Antwerp, to be liquid is to possess a certain advantage, and businessmen in particular are prepared to pay to have this advantage. Money in hand provides a service, a 'facility and convenience' which is absent otherwise. Loss of this service through a loan warrants compensation for the lender by way of receipt of interest. For Lessius, as for John Maynard Keynes 300 years later, interest can be viewed as a phenomenon related to the desire to hold cash balances. Underlying that desire are three types of motive: transactions, precautionary, and speculative. An important segment, the most important segment in the estimate of some historians, of the so-called 'Keynesian revolution' may not have been nearly so revolutionary in its day if the ideas of Lessius had taken a firm hold on the course of economic thought and monetary policy during the intervening years.

The significance of the presence of a preference for liquidity is a recurring theme in Lessius' analysis of commercial dealings. For example, in his discussion of the purchase of notes, i.e. rights to future money, at a discount, he writes: 'Such rights, as long as they are proposed as saleable objects in the commercial sense, are held to be of less value in the general estimation of men than actual money in the hand. This is a matter of common experience in that money provides the means to a multitude of things which those rights do not provide. Therefore they may be bought at a lower price.'[19]

Again, at the end of the same discussion, in reply to objections to such purchases he affirms that 'anyone who pays cash deprives himself of some power or advantage which he does not possess when he has rights to future money.'[20] Later, in examining the contracts known as *census*, he contrasts 'money in hand' with which 'fruitful goods can be bought or business executed with great profit' and rights to money which are 'almost always' subject to risk.[21] The same

[19] L. Lessius, op. cit., II:21:8:66. Support for this position, Lessius claims, may be found in the works of much earlier writers including 'Innocent', i.e. Sinibaldo de Fieschi (Pope Innocent IV, d. 1254), and 'Panormitanus', i.e. Nicholas de Tudeschi (1386–1453).

[20] Ibid, n. 73.

[21] Op. cit., II:22:4:31.

emphasis is found in the next chapter in the discussion of foreign exchange dealings.[22]

In the case of money loans then, it is understandable that Lessius puts forward the view that interest charges can be considered as a compensation for loss of the liquidity—service of cash in balance. Further, the magnitude of these charges may vary with the length of time for which the loss is sustained and the degree of risk of its becoming permanent through default by the borrower. He reasons:

> Since money is their instrument of doing business, and to deprive oneself of the instrument of one's art is estimable in money, why cannot the merchants set some price for the lack of money by common consent, especially if the common good demands it? That the common good demands it, however, is proved, because, since many need present money and there is not easily found anyone who wishes to lend freely – partly on account of the risk of capital or the difficulty in recovering it, partly lest one deprive oneself of the advantage of doing business in various ways, especially through exchanges, which flourish at this time – reason demands that the merchants by common consent constitute fixed prices for the lack of money, after having weighed all those circumstances from which that lack can be estimated at more or less, at a particular time.[23]

Later, he states that those who are deprived of their money, '. . . value more the lack of their money for five months than the lack of it for four, and the lack of it for four more than three, and this is partly because they lack the opportunity of gaining with that money, partly because their principle is longer in danger . . .'[24]

The introduction of the element of risk of loss as a factor determining the magnitude of the interest payment that could be requested has few precedents in scholastic thought. Yet, some aspects of the significance of risk-taking had long been recognised. For example, it was a traditional ground on

[22] Op. cit., II:23:1 and 4.
[23] Op. cit., II:20:14:123.
[24] Op cit. II: 23:6:56.

which part of the profits of merchants were justified. Again, St Thomas used this element to distinguish genuine participation by a financier in a business partnership. However, its application to capital transferred by a lender was first undertaken by John Medina (1419–1516), a Spanish theologian who taught at Alcala. Luis Molina was the next to consider it relevant, and after Lessius, Juan de Lugo supported the case for its inclusion.[25] This break with medieval precedent, perhaps even more than the greatly enlarged scope for *lucrum cessans* found by some of the writers of the sixteenth century, indicates their new subjective approach to economic behaviour. The idea that a lender may charge for the mental discomfort he as an individual may experience due to worry while his funds were in the possession of another seems to have been quite foreign to most medieval minds. Legally, and hence objectively, as St Thomas taught, ownership of money was transferred in a *mutuum*. That objective reality was decisive.

Lessius' sponsorship of *carentia pecuniae* as a probable ground on which interest-taking can be justified is considered critically by Juan de Lugo. As Lugo understands it, Lessius is claiming that, 'Just as, by reason of cessant gain, something beyond the capital may be asked, so also can something be asked by reason of the obligation to be without the capacity for making gain. Not only is the cessant gain assessable at a price but also the very capacity to make gain is assessable, even though one was not as a matter of fact going to use that capacity and was not going to make any gain.'[26] Having recast Lessius' liquidity preference argument in these more traditional, objective terms, Lugo objects that the reasoning

[25] On the analysis of risk by Medina and de Lugo, see J. T. Noonan, op. cit., pp. 283–9. Among the earlier authorities to oppose risk as a title to interest payments on money loans were St Antonine and St Bernardine. The latter argues: 'if someone lending 100 ducats wishes to have thence something beyond the principle because they are not so secure to him as if he had them in a chest, because, indeed, by lending he exposes himself to many chances of losing them, he is not excused because of such risk from usury. In truth, the risk of this case is nothing different from the character and act of lending, or at any rate it is inseparably connected with it, because it has no more vendible a character than a loan qua loan. Therefore to profit from this risk is to profit from the act of lending alone.' *De Evangelio aeterno*, Sermo 39, art. 1, cap. 3.
[26] J. de Lugo, op. cit., disp. 25, para. 18.

reduces to a mere statement that a loan has been made. Loss of capacity to make gain must always be associated with any *mutuum*, since the loan must extend over some interval of time. He adds that when the loan is repaid, the lender will get back the equivalent of what he gave. The capacity for trading and gaining which may have been given up initially is fully restored.

These objections of a traditional nature serve to point up, once again, the novelty of the dimension of subjective, internal calculus which Lessius has introduced into the scholastic analysis of loan contracts. Further, they indicate the new institutional focus for the treatment of transfers of money. As Bernard Dempsey observes, in this particular instance Lugo is reverting to the practice of his medieval predecessors in considering 'a case where there is no question of an organized market and a true common price, where the bare loan stripped of all conditioning factors is considered between two isolated individuals.'[27] Lessius, on the other hand, is dealing with an active and highly organised market. The external reality of a communally created market price for loans is the objective counterweight to Lessius' emphasis on the relevance of private calculation in determining economic morality concerning them. The former is a vital element conditioning private calculation concerning legitimate gain, even though it is the outcome of the conjunction of many such calculations. This reciprocal relationship of objective and subjective had been recognised in the case of commodities for some centuries.

Loans and exchanges

Through the conception of interest as the compensation for loss of liquidity, a much broader ground for interest than *lucrum cessans*, Lessius is able to make good some of the more persistent deficiencies in scholastic monetary thought. Particularly, he is able to eliminate the dichotomy between the treatment of money as an object of trade in foreign exchanges and money as the subject of loans. To appreciate Lessius' achievement here it is useful to refer to the work of

[17] B.W. Dempsey, op. cit., p. 169.

Leon Walras in his *Elements of Pure Economics* (1874—77).

With the interest title, *lucrum cessans*, the schoolmen approximated an important relationship in the Walrasian system. According to Walras, the money rate of interest is the monetary expression of the rate of net return on physical capital. In equilibrium, the money rate of interest is the equivalent of the rate of net income, i.e. the unit price of the hire of numeraire capital. Again, in equilibrium, the ratio of the net value of the annual services of each capital good to its selling price is the same for all capital goods, and the rate of net income (rate of interest) expresses this ratio. Thus,

$$i = \frac{p - (\mu + \nu)P}{P}$$

where, i is the rate of interest; p is the gross value of the annual services of a capital good; $(\mu + \nu)P$ is the allowance for depreciation and insurance; and P is the capital value (selling price) of the capital good.

For the scholastics also, the existence of a positive rate of interest was explained by the presence of a positive return on physical capital. Further, the magnitude of the just rate of interest was given by the usual rate of return on physical capital (in Walrasian terms, the rate of net income).[28]

After Navarrus, the scholastics also achieved a close approximation of another Walrasian relationship. In Lesson 30 of the *Elements of Pure Economics*, Walras observes that the price of money considered as a commodity varies directly with its utility and inversely with its quantity. This observation can be expressed as,

$$p_u = \frac{H_\alpha}{Q_u} \, ,$$

where, p_u is the price of money in terms of the commodity chosen as numeraire; H_α is the aggregate value (in terms of

---

[28] The money rate of interest was not determined by the rate of profit. Rather, for justice sake, it ought to be established as the equivalent of the capital return element in the prevailing rate of profit. On this point, see B. W. Dempsey, *Interest and Usury* (Washington, 1943) pp. 219—20.

the numeraire) of desired cash balances; and Q_u is the quantity of money.[29]

Walras then goes on to formulate another relationship, one that escaped the Spanish writers but not Lessius. The variable commodity price of money is linked to the rate of net income, as follows:

$$p_u = \frac{p_{u'}}{i},$$

where, p_u is the price of money; i is the rate of net income, and $p_u{}'$ is the price of the service of availability provided by money held in balances, i.e. as a stock.[30]

This concept of the price of money's service of availability is Walras' equivalent of Lessius' price of loss of liquidity. Armed with this concept Lessius was able to link the analysis of the market in foreign exchange, in which p_u was seen as variable, with the market for loans in which i was considered. The money rate of interest for Lessius, the price of money's service of availability for Walras, is established as a market price subject to two types of influences. These are the influences on the demand for money balances relative to the supply of money, and the broad spectrum of forces bearing on the return to capital investment. In Walrasian terminology,

$$p_{u'} = \frac{H_\alpha i}{Q_u},$$

where $H_q i$ is the aggregate value of the services of desired cash balances.[31]

Lessius summarises this new insight by reference to 'the

---

[29] Leon Walras, *Elements of Pure Economics*, trans. W. Jaffe (Allen and Unwin, London, 1954) p. 327. According to Lessius, the price of money apart from changes in metal content and legal face value, will vary with the quantity available, the demand for bills of exchange relative to their supply, and the need for cash (*necessitate pecuniae*). Op. cit., II:23:4:35.

[30] Op. cit., p. 329.

[31] 'The "rareté" or value of the service of money is directly proportional to its utility and inversely proportional to its quantity,' op. cit., pp. 328–9.

practice of the Bourse or Peristyle of Antwerp where the merchants gather every day and take account of the abundance or shortage of money, of the number of exchanges, of the amount of merchandise and all other sources of gain in which there is need of present money. Then either by themselves or their agents [they] establish the price for the privation of money. Merchants who lend may demand this price for the reason that they are deprived of their money for such and such a time and may not call it back before the time agreed. This price is sometimes 6% per year and sometimes 7%, 8%, 9%, 10%, 11%, or 12%; more than 12% they are forbidden to demand by the Constitution of Charles V, given at Brussels on the 4th October, 1540, page 767.'[3][2]

With this analysis, Lessius breaks free of the implicit assumption of St Thomas Aquinas that in considering the morality of money loans, the price of money was to be taken as unity. For St Thomas, any inequality between the quantity of money available and the cash balances desired was either non-existent or irrelevant. In this he was followed by the later scholastics, even the Spanish writers, when they considered money loans. With the expression $p_u = H_\alpha/Q_u$ always taken as unity, then i was the only element to be reckoned with in establishing the just price of most loans made by businessmen.

Another crucial element in the new approach by Lessius is a recognition of the existence of a market in money loans. St Thomas, for example, had considered markets for goods and services, but this analysis was not extended to embrace money. Cajetan had made good this defect with respect to money traded internationally. Lessius by observing the intimate connection that existed in a centre like Antwerp between international exchange transactions and the granting of credit generally, further augmented the restricted medieval view.

Where a loan market exists, the morality of interest-taking is altered radically. In particular, the incidence of loss to an individual lender, which is relevant in a loan considered as an isolated exchange, is immaterial. What is material is the presence in the community of an objectively stated and just price for loss of liquidity. Lessius expresses the new thought, as follows:

> Moreover, any merchant seems able to demand this price in that same place even though there is no gain of his that stops because of his loan. This is the just price for the privation of money among merchants; for the just price of an article or obligation in any community is that which is put upon it by that community in good faith for the sake of the common good in view of all the circumstances ... Therefore, even if through the privation of money for a year there is no gain of mine that stops and no risk of capital, because such a price for just causes has been put upon this privation, I may demand it just as the rest do.[33]

Prices and markets

After dealing with the problem of interest, Lessius moves on, in Chapter 21, to a discussion of the determination of price in general. 'The just price', he writes, 'is held to be that price which is determined by the public authority for the common good, or the price determined by peoples' general estimation.'[34] The first of these is the legitimate or legal price. The second is the popular or natural price. In both cases, he observes, 'Prices of things work as a communal matter, not out of the feelings or advantage of individuals, i.e. this is how they are created. The reason is that private judgement is fallible and easily swayed by desire for gain. Common judgement is less liable to error.'[35] The significant difference between legal and natural price is that the former 'consists in

---

[33] Op. cit., II:20:14:125. On the failure of the medieval theologians to consider a market in loans, T. F. Divine writes: 'As we have previously noted, in the whole discussion of usury the assumption seems to be that of isolated exchange between borrower and lender ... Nowhere is any mention made of the presence of a market for inter-temporal exchanges. This assumption would correspond to the economic conditions of the times ... the institution of the capital market was only present in the middle ages in a very rudimentary form ... In isolated exchange there is no external objective standard controlling the ratio of exchange, either in the economic sense of the market price or in the ethical sense of the just price.' *Interest* (Milwaukee, 1959) p. 217.

[34] Lessius, op. cit., II:21:2:7.

[35] Ibid, n. 9.

an absolute amount; the natural price does not do so, and allows a certain range (as Scotus and others hold).'[36]

As in traditional scholastic analysis, Lessius affirms that the legal price must take precedence over the natural price if they begin to diverge for any one commodity. However, he introduces two qualifications of this general principle which greatly restrict any idea of absolute reliance on public authority in economic affairs. The first of these is where the legal price is above the natural price. In this circumstance, market consensus should be decisive. Lessius' economic liberalism is even more tellingly demonstrated when he states that the natural price can be allowed precedence over the legal in some instances where the natural price is the higher. These instances are those in which 'in change of circumstances of increasing or diminishing supply and similar factors, the authorities were notably negligent in changing the legal price, . . .'[37] Even a 'private individual', acting as an individual, can request a price above the legal maximum when the authorities are 'ill informed about the commercial circumstances, or have fixed the price out of enmity towards the buyers or sellers.'[38] With Lessius, it is clear, the logic of the marketplace has a powerful bearing on the just ordering of social relationships.

Not only variations in supply conditions, but a wide range of other forces, quite properly, influence the making of price. Among the factors he lists as relevant are the following: '. . . the goods themselves, and their abundance or scarcity; the need for them and their usefulness; the sellers, and their labour, expenses, risks suffered in obtaining the goods, in transporting and storing them; the manner of their sale, whether offered freely, or on demand; the consumers, and whether there are few or many, and whether money is plentiful or scarce.'[39]

For these factors to interact to produce the emergence of a just price for any one commodity, the market context must be one of perfect competition. Lessius specifies precisely the

---

[36] Ibid., n. 10.
[37] Ibid., n.14. John Medina is cited in support of this proposition.
[38] Ibid.
[39] Ibid., n. 8.

two basic conditions that later in the development of economic thought came to be widely recognised as defining that context. For example, near the close of the nineteenth century Alfred Marshall wrote: 'In our typical (perfect) market then we assume that the forces of demand and supply have free play; that there is no combination among dealers on either side ... But though everyone acts for himself, his knowledge of what others are doing is supposed to be generally sufficient to prevent him from taking a lower or paying a higher price than others are doing.'[40] Lessius too reasons in terms of a market which excludes '... every machination and effort of merchants by which they bring it about that they alone either have the sale of something or sell it at a certain price.'[41] Further, there must be perfect knowledge unhampered by time and location differences. He writes that when a just price has been arrived at, the value of the articles will be the same as that '... at which they would be valued at a public valuation if they were openly displayed in the market place with the whole town coming together at the voice of the town crier.'[42]

In these circumstances, the just price will approximate the normal costs of production of those usually supplying the market. This price can be charged by a particular seller even if his costs are below normal or even zero. Only where there is no established market are the costs of an individual supplier of immediate relevance to the calculation of prices. He writes:

> One may charge a higher price by reason of labour and expense which one has undergone in getting, transporting,

---

[40] A. Marshall, op. cit., p. 196.
[41] Lessius, op. cit., II:21:21:144.
[42] Op. cit., II:21:9:76. Some years before this statement by Lessius, one Tommaso Buoninisegni, O. P. (d. 1609), in his *Trattato de' traffichi giusti et ordinari* (Venice, 1588) had observed that where market knowledge is very good, as in wholesaling activity, a unique market price is likely to emerge. This was a departure from the usual scholastic view that the just market price at any one time was represented by a narrow spectrum. Most schoolmen assumed that even in the absence of monopoly, markets were rarely perfect. Some lack of knowledge must almost always be present and could be tolerated by the moralist. On Buoninisegni, see R. de Roover, 'The Concept of the Just Price', *Journal of Economic History*, Vol. 18 (Dec 1958) p. 424.

and storing goods; that is, if goods have not a price set for
them. If they have, then the merchant can take account of
extraordinary expenses in the setting of the price at the
time when it is first fixed . . . The case is different if goods
already have their own price at which they are generally
sold; then the merchant is bound to sell at the price or to
keep the goods . . . But in arriving at a price of this kind
account has already been taken of the expenses which are
ordinarily and usually incurred. But if the merchant's
expenses have been greater, that is his hard luck, and the
common price may not be increased for that reason, just as
it need not be decreased even if he had no expenses at all.
This is the merchant's situation; just as he can make a
profit if he has small expenses, so he can lose if his
expenses are very large or extraordinary.[43]

Lessius' analysis lacks Marshall's helpful distinction between the long and short run, but it is clear that the
theologian's natural price hovers around an equilibrium point
established by the normal costs of production.

Although they are implied, it does not seem to be clear in
Lessius' account that these normal costs include an allowance
for normal profits in the sense of returns necessary to
compensate an entrepreneur for not moving into other lines of
business activity. However, this deficiency was soon remedied
by de Lugo who introduced the element of opportunity cost
in a merchant's not pursuing alternative commercial undertakings. This cost is a rationale for the receipts of net income
by an entrepreneur. Lugo states:

When a person sells as a regular business ('ex officio'), as
merchants commonly do, he may for this reason sell at a
higher price to make money for his own maintenance
because the fact that they attend to the assembling,
storing, and distributing the goods and the fact that they
give up other occupations and sources of gain can be
appraised at a price . . . But strictly speaking this is not
selling above the true value, for in evaluating the common
price of goods, attention is paid to these costs and profits

[43] Op. cit., II:21:4:29.

of merchants and the common and natural price arises for all of these . . .[44]

Another significant feature of Lessius' economic thought which should be emphasised at this point is its fundamental unity. His analysis of pricing in general in Chapter 21 is a direct reflection of what he writes in the previous chapter concerning interest and the Antwerp Bourse. The Bourse is a competitive market in which all parties can be simultaneously aware of prevailing commercial circumstances. The price of lack of money is objectively established, and can be taken even by an individual who incurs no cost by lending. Outside this context, the lender's actual costs in giving any particular loan are decisive.

For Lessius then, the one theory of exchange justice applies to organised markets in money loans and in commodities. The same theory applies to organised foreign exchange markets. Further, in his discussions of the forces at work in each of these markets, he reveals a well developed appreciation of the fact that the three types are interdependent in any one economy. Lessius' work marks an important stage in the movement towards seeing an economy as composed of a number of related markets which, despite special features in each, operate according to the same basic set of principles.

Wage determination

Another type of market to which the unified theory of price determination is applied is that for labour. The problems of justice in the pricing of the services of labour had received relatively little attention in earlier scholastic thought. St Thomas had remarked that a wage payment is a natural reward for labour 'almost as if it were the price of the same'.[45] Wage payments are governed by the same canons of

[44] J. de Lugo, op. cit., disp. 26, para. 88. Lugo might also be claimed to have improved on Lessius' treatment of the cost to price relationship when, in discussing fixation of prices, he writes: 'First of all, in order that the rate be just, account must be taken of the costs and expenses and a moderate profit which is a sort of wage of one who serves the commonwealth. Therefore, when in a whole province, the costs incurred by a seller are greater than the price set, the price is unjust.' See disp. 26, para. 53.

[45] St Thomas Aquinas, *Summa theologica,* I–II, qu. 114, art. 1 resp.

justice that relate to payments for commodities. Without
very much reflection on the issues involved, the vast majority
of schoolmen seem to have been content to follow this
line.[46]

Lessius, too, treats wage determination as a particular case
of his general theory of pricing, but his analysis is sufficiently
extensive to yield specific insights concerning the forces at
work in labour markets. In Chapter 24 (Dubitatio IV) he
poses the question, 'What may be judged the fair remuneration of workers, servants and people performing some
office?' His immediate answer is that it is the rate 'custo-
marily paid in a given place over a given period'. He then
takes up the issue of how the minimum justifiable wage
payment for any particular occupation can be established if
there is doubt concerning the customary minimum.

We have seen that in the matter of commodity prices, the
seller could have recourse to his cost of production when
doubt existed as to fair market price. However, Lessius does
not directly invoke the idea of the cost of producing labour
services to aid in establishing the appropriate wage rate.
Rather, he looks to supply response by workers to the wage
in question. He writes: 'It can be established that it [the wage
payment] is not below the minimum from the fact that there
are others who are willing to perform such work or office or
service for the remuneration in question. That is a clear
indication that such a remuneration, all circumstances considered, is not below the right value for that occupation, . . .'[47]

The absolute minimum just wage in any form of employment is a subsistence wage. This ought to be paid when the
work-value or productivity of the particular employee is at or
very near zero; 'when the employer does not need the labour

[46] One notable scholastic who gave considerable attention to wage payment
practices was St Antonine who wrote of conditions in the manufacturing
industries of Florence. However, he does not appear to have developed a theory
of wage rates. See R. de Roover, *San Bernardino of Siena and Sant' Antonio of
Florence* (Boston, Baker Library, 1967) pp. 24–7.
[47] Lessius, op. cit., II:24:4:24. That Lessius should use supply response and cost
of production as criteria to solve the same problem in two areas of pricing policy
suggests that he perceived that states of supply were closely linked to cost
conditions in the production of goods and services.

of another person and employs him at his insistence solely
out of compassion. In this case it is sufficient to provide him
with what sustains life [*alimenta*] .'[48] Where the productivity
of a worker yields a positive surplus to his employer over and
above the amount necessary to cover the employee's subsistence requirements, the wage payment should be at least
the minimum customary for that occupation in the local
market. Lessius argues: 'If however his work brings an
advantage to the employer far outweighing the value to him
of the employee's sustenance he would be bound to
compensation, at least at the level of the minimum just wage
. . . when the work is of notably more value to the employer
than what it costs him to provide sustenance for life, he must
pay something more for it.'[49]

Lessius adds that a just wage structure will not only be
influenced by productivity differentials, but also by the
relative net advantages of various occupations. In his opinion,
'if the work brings with it social status and emoluments, the
pay can be low because status and associated advantages are,
so to say, a part of the salary.'[50]

In this section of his work then, Lessius emerges as the
sponsor of an approach to wage determination in competitive
labour markets which only began to make its appearance in
non-scholastic economic thought towards the end of the
nineteenth century. The two criteria of net productivity and
net advantage interact in conditions of a free labour market
to produce a wage structure appropriate to a given social and
economic milieu.

The theologian is at one with the marginalist W. S. Jevons,
who, reacting against the views of the more prominent British

---

[48] Ibid., n. 25. *Alimenta* in legal Latin means more than just 'food'. However,
there is no suggestion that the minimum just wage is a 'family wage'.

[49] Ibid. In his discussion he assumes that the minimum market rate for any
occupation in which a worker's net product is positive will always be an
above-subsistence rate.

[50] Ibid., n. 24. Cf. Alfred Marshall, op. cit., 51: '. . . every occupation involves
other disadvantages besides the fatigue of the work required in it, and every
occupation offers other advantages besides the receipt of money wages. The true
reward which an occupation offers to labour has to be calculated by deducting
the money value of all its disadvantages from that of all its advantages; and we
may describe this true reward as the Net Advantages of the occupation.'

economists of the early nineteenth century, argued that the value of a productive service is derived from that of its product. The value of labour, for example, must be determined by the value of the produce, not the value of the produce by that of the labour. Underlying this affinity between Lessius and Jevons is their common belief that economic magnitudes are ultimately the result of individual feelings and states of mind.

Lessius' consistent subjectivism is brought to the fore in his treatment of wage payments when he poses the question, 'Can someone who hires out his work as an undivided activity to several persons receive the several remunerations in full?' Against those who would reply to this query with an universal negative, Lessius argues as follows:

> If someone undertakes to do a service for several people as an undivided activity and it is just as advantageous for each of them as it would be if done for one of them alone, as much can be charged to each of them as would be charged were the service done for one of them alone ... Because I can do a thing by one and the same piece of work with equal advantage for several persons or for one this does not diminish valuation of the work with regard to each one of them. My work is not less valuable to you because someone else profits by it while it is also being done for you. So if the work done for you alone is worth two gold francs it will not be worth less to you because I can accommodate another person by it at the same time.[51]

Consumer evaluation then is paramount in determining the reward for labour services. Even if an additional service is performed at zero marginal cost to the employee, the fact that it is worth something to the recipient warrants a return.

To explain the higher rewards attained by some individuals despite the apparent expenditure of the same amount of work-effort by them as by the general run of their fellows, Lessius introduces the factor of entrepreneurship or 'industry' which certain persons possess. At this point, his

[51] Lessius, op. cit., II:24:5:28.

reasoning is similar, once again, to that of Alfred Marshall who contended that certain above-normal returns could be regarded as 'the rent of exceptional ability', a type of quasi-rent.[52] Where a man goes on a journey to execute business for several persons in a distant city, for example, it may be said that the agent is charging each of those who employ him for his making the one journey. But, says Lessius, the return he receives is actually a reward for the degree of industry he has displayed in combining several jobs, not the journey. He concludes that 'To be able to combine several people's business expeditiously depends on human industry, because cases are rare when it can be done with ease. It is not surprising if an industrious agent does make a good income in a short time.'[53] That income is a mark of his exceptional ability.

Monopoly

Appreciation of the role of entrepreneurship (*industria*) in economic life also figures prominently in Lessius' treatment of monopolistic practices. This treatment departs in a number of important respects from those of medieval writers and most of their successors. Further, in the course of his discussion, the Belgian doctor indicates his awareness of the need for economic analysis to be set in a wider frame of reference than that established for it by St Thomas. There is need, he suggests, to move beyond issues of commutative justice which concerns the relationships of individuals as individuals. Economic analysis, as Adam Smith was to demonstrate, is also bound up with investigation of the broad sphere of general (in modern terms, 'social') justice.

Lessius, like the earlier schoolmen, expresses general opposition to monopoly pricing. 'Prices of things', he writes, 'do not depend on the whim of the merchants. But they depend on price regulation by authority or by common consent, made in good faith with no conspiracy or deceit, in the light of the supply or scarcity of the goods, the number of sellers and buyers and other circumstances. Consequently,

---

[52] The relevant discussion is in A. Marshall, *Principles of Economics,* 6, viii.
[53] Lessius, op. cit., II:24:5:29.

a person who by his counsel or consent is the cause of another paying more than this price, is the unjust cause of loss to him and so is obliged to make restitution.'[54] Four types of price control arrangement are distinguished, and two of these are condemned as being against the principle of justice in commutation.

The first instance in which price fixing is condemned is where price is maintained above that dictated by common estimation 'by a conspiracy among sellers'. The conspirators sin against justice and are bound to restitution of their ill-gotten gains. Lessius also condemns monopsony on the same ground: 'Buyers sin against justice when they conspire or request others not to take the just price for a thing but below it; the reason is that the sellers have a right to the higher price, . . .'[55]

The second case of unjust monopoly practice is 'where by force or fraud, import of goods from another source is prevented in order to maintain a higher price in the state.' Both the state and the merchants who have lost probable profit because of the practice must receive compensation from the monopolist. However, Lessius goes on immediately to state that where the monopolist has achieved his position without the use of fraud or force, no compensation is due. Presumably, an import monopoly obtained by chance or by recognition of a business opportunity which others have neglected, and maintained without deliberate obstruction of the entry of competitors by deceit or by violence, is quite legitimate.[56]

In contrast with the two instances of unjust monopoly is

[54] Op. cit., II:21:21:146.
[55] Ibid, n. 147. Commenting on the treatment of monopoly as 'conspirant', Raymond de Roover states: 'To my mind there is no doubt that the conspiracy idea of the anti-trust laws goes back to scholastic precedents and is rooted in the medieval concept of the just price.' R. de Roover, 'The Concept of the Just Price', *Journal of Economic History*, Vol. 18 (Dec 1958) p. 427. See also the same author's 'Monopoly Theory Prior to Adam Smith: a Revision', *Quarterly Journal of Economics*, Vol. 65 (1951) pp. 492–524. To this comment, it can be added that the schoolmen were inclined to apply their monopoly doctrine to the case of labour unions. These too were conspiracies aimed at raising wages above their just level. There is scholastic precedent then for the nineteenth-century view of unions as combinations of workers acting in restraint of trade.
[56] Lessius, op. cit., II:21:21:153.

one in which a monopoly right has been granted by the prince
for a just reason, and goods (especially staples) are sold at a
price fixed by the ruler or by 'the judgement of prudent
men'. Two examples of 'just reason' are offered. The prince
can give a concession to a particular trader or group of
traders if by sale of the privilege he obtains funds required
for 'the public good'. Again, there is just reason 'if otherwise
no one would want to transport such wares in sufficient
quantity because of expenses which could not easily be
recovered unless a privilege was granted for some time.'[57] In
this second example, Lessius does not specify whether the
expenses he has in mind are capital outlays with a long
gestation period or whether he is referring to trade in goods
which yield only a small margin of profit per unit on prime
cost. Nevertheless, here there is a clear recognition that
coverage of long-run cost sets a minimum condition for
supply of a market.[58]

By far the most important aspect of Lessius' treatment of
monopoly is encountered in his discussion of yet another
case, the case in which 'several persons buy up all the goods
of a certain kind [e.g. corn at harvest-time, before or after it]
in order afterwards to sell it as they judge.'[59] Lessius
observes that 'authors regularly give the verdict that these
people sin against justice and are obliged to restitution.' But
turning away from established scholastic tradition, he argues:
'However, the contrary view has never seemed to me to be
improbable, i.e., that such people are not obliged in rigorous
justice to make restitution and have not sinned against
iustitiam particularem [particular, or partial, justice], but
only against ... *iustitiam legalem seu publicam utilitatem*

---

[57] Ibid., n. 148.

[58] About this time, a contemporary of Lessius, the Italian Giovanni Botero
(1544—1617) also considered the grounds on which publicly sanctioned
monopolies could be established. Botero had studied and taught under the
auspices of the Jesuit order and became secretary to the Vatican Secretary of
State, St Charles Borromeo, and to the Duke of Savoy. In his *Reason of State*
(1589) he argues (Book 8, Ch. 14) that the prince himself can monopolise a
department of commercial activity in any of three circumstances: where the
means of private citizens are insufficient to maintain the trade; where the trade is
so significant that a private citizen would acquire excessive wealth by it; and
where the activity is vital to the well-being of the state.

[59] Lessius, op. cit., II:21:21:150.

[legal justice or public utility]. Luis Molina thinks so also.'[60]

With this argument Lessius takes the analysis of market behaviour out of the realm in which consideration of the relationships between particular individuals is paramount, into the region where the welfare of the economy as a whole is decisive.

In Chapter 3, it was seen how Aristotle divided justice into general and particular. The latter included both distributive and corrective justice, and exchange transactions were dealt with as phenomena combining these two. Explicit consideration of general or legal justice was excluded, and this was the case also with Aquinas' treatment of market exchanges as a matter of commutation. Lessius, however, opens up the possibility of a major shift of emphasis in the Aristotelian and Thomistic tradition concerning the analysis of the morality of pricing.

Lessius sets out to show that his monopolists (who are engaged in 'forestalling' and/or 'engrossing') do not contravene the canons of particular justice. He reasons:

> They have not sinned against justice by buying, for I suppose they bought at the prevailing price. Nor is it relevant that high prices have been brought about in this way, because a large number of buyers also cause prices to rise. Hence, they do not sin against justice in buying because the action giving rise to the price increase is not against justice. Nor do they do this by holding up supplies, i.e., by not selling, because justice did not oblige them to sell at the time, they having in no way obliged themselves to do so. They could have held back the goods for another occasion or taken them off to another place or even destroyed them without inflicting injustice on anybody, because they had absolute proprietorship of their goods. The members of the state also had no title in justice to buy the goods if the sellers had not wanted to sell them. Otherwise you would have to say that they would have been going to sin against justice if they had thrown their wares into the river.[61]

---

[60] Ibid., n. 151. The reference is to Molina, *De justitia et jure*, disputatio 345.
[61] Op. cit., II:21:21:144.

The relevance of canons of particular justice destroyed, one can only have recourse to the criterion of general welfare or public utility to assess the morality of the monopolists' actions. In order to carry out such an assessment, economic analysis would have to move out into problems of income distribution and economic growth ignored by earlier writers. Lessius contemplates a vista for economics which his predecessors did not perceive.

Lessius' argument above turns on the dictum that the just price is the prevailing market price set by common estimation. His monopolists here have at all times bought and sold at a price determined by common estimation. Unlike his 'conspirators' in the first case of monopoly pricing considered, they have not attempted to sell above the just (market) price. They have given and taken what, objectively, the market would bear. They, themselves, however, have been a force in determining the level of market price. They have been part of that consensus termed 'common estimation'.

This logic brings the scholastic analysis of the morality of price formation hard up against the problem of how to deal with the morality of speculation. Should all speculation be outlawed? Obviously, Lessius does not think so. Entrepreneurship and speculation are interwoven, and the former had long been recognised as a factor to be rewarded in economic practice. Lessius underlines the problem by describing his monopolists as persons who 'by their industry [entrepreneurship]' succeed in 'buying up all goods and holding them until the price rises'.[6 2] On the conceptual level the reasoning raises the issue of how time and expectations are to be incorporated into explanations of economic processes. What was a moral problem for the schoolmen is seen as a policy problem by the modern economist. The conceptual issue is the same for both.

Precisely the same set of challenges is posed by Lessius' analysis of money and interest which was discussed above. There we saw that Lessius recognised two types of speculative demand for cash balances. Speculators held balances awaiting a rise in profit rates. They also held money in

[6 2] Op. cit., II:21:21:144.

expectation of a rise in interest rates. If potential lenders hold back funds, create a money shortage, and thereby can command more by way of interest, they can be said to have gained a higher margin on a later loan by forgoing interest on an earlier loan. Yet, for the schoolmen, forgone earnings on an earlier loan opportunity were not admissible as a ground for compensation on the later loan. The modern policy problem, in terms made familiar by Lord Keynes, is the impact of speculators on the rate of interest and hence the level of investment and employment in the economy. In general, it would seem that in these respects, Lessius brought scholastic economic analysis to the brink of engagement in issues that have a contemporary, or at least, near-contemporary relevance for economists.

Later contrasts

One general feature of Lessius' economics which should be remarked on in conclusion, is the contrast between it and much of the non-scholastic analysis that was to follow in the seventeenth, eighteenth, and early part of the nineteenth century. Such parallels as have been drawn between concepts employed in his writings and those of later economists have involved late nineteenth and early twentieth century figures like Jevons, Walras, Marshall, and Keynes rather than representatives from the Physiocratic school or from the eras of Mercantilism or Classical Economics. This contrast is due in part to the regressive aspects of Physiocracy and Mercantilism when compared with economic enquiry as conducted by the later schoolmen.

The projectors and pamphleteers whom Adam Smith called Mercantilists regressed to the ancient form of economic enquiry practised by the Sophists. They were concerned with the economics of nation-state building and aimed at achieving the concrete, practical result. In their hands, economics reverted again to a technology. Most of them cared little for analysis in the abstract and were frankly derisory concerning the careful distinctions and often tedious legalistic logic of the moralists. In the process some valuable analytical initiatives of the latter were neglected.

The Physiocrats, as critics of the projectors, did not regress to the same historical length as their opponents. Instead, they returned to a form of medieval blueprint for a just and prosperous society. St Thomas may have found some of their leading ideas quite acceptable, but they would have appeared most reactionary to Lessius and some of his predecessors. Lessius in Antwerp, and even St Bernardine in Northern Italy over 150 years before, seem to have envisaged the possibility of order and justice in a post-medieval commercial world, and they set about analysing the features of such a world. The Physiocrats, for their part, turned their backs on the task of understanding many of those features in favour of sponsoring a once-over change to a static society modelled on medieval conditions.

Index

DATE DUE